Some Topics:

- "God," Paganism, Buddhism, Zen
- How to Prepare for Death!?
- Sex, Relationships, Plastic Surgery
- Fame & Its Drawbacks
- "The Process" & Why I Hate It!
- Censorship, Now and Then
- Decadence, Decline, & Civilization
- "Radical Eco-Politics?" *Si!*
- "Beat"? "Hippie"? "Punk"? "Gay"?
- Travel Advice, Virtual Travel Advice
- *Collectible CDs?*
- Bootlegs, Live Videos
- Yes to NAPSTER & its Successors!
- Computer Hackers: *Anarchists?*
- BUKOWSKI, KEROUAC
- GINSBERG, CORSO
- Alan Watts & "The Answer"
- Krishnamurti & Meat-Eating
- W.S. BURROUGHS, J.G. Ballard
- Live Nude Models, mostly women
- Disneylandification
- SUVs = Yuppie Tanks
- Dot-coms-and-Not-Gone, Dude!
- Abolish the Stock Market!
- Maximum Wage: six figures!
- The New Corporate Feudalism
- John Lennon Dead
- Government Flu, Govt. Agents
- BECOME THE MEDIA!
- No WTO! No IMF! No W.E.F.!
- Overpopulation? Socialism?
- Coping with Information Overload
- Sillyclone Valley Must Die!
- *The Independent Media Movement*
- San Francisco Brain Drain
- Privatization, Globalization
- Ralph Nader & The Green Party
- Support Global Exchange!
- Columbia = El Salvador, but worse!
- Rightwing "Hipsters": Media Stars?!
- The Electoral College Scam
- Everyone: Try Painting!
- What I'm Reading ...
- LISTS, LISTS, LISTS, LISTS!

www.researchpubs.com

Real conversations no. 1

HENRY ROLLINS

BILLY CHILDISH

JELLO BIAFRA

LAWRENCE FERLINGHETTI

INTERVIEWS BY V. VALE

Real conversations no. 1
ROLLINS, CHILDISH, BIAFRA, FERLINGHETTI

RE/Search Publications
20 Romolo #B
San Francisco, CA 94133
TEL (415) 362-1465
FAX (415) 362-0742
email: info@researchpubs.com   website: www.researchpubs.com

Publisher/Editors: V. Vale & Marian Wallace
Layout design: Seth Robson
Design consultants: Andrea Reider, Judy Sitz, Joachim, Nix
Special Thanks: Nancy Peters, Amy Callahan, David S. Kahn,
    Dennis & Carol Hamby
Copy Editors: Jen Bestpitch, James De Lorenzi, Bret Cohen,
    Carine Chehab, Mindaugis Bagdon, Donovan Bauer,
    Rick Stinson, Kathryn Johnson, Catherine Wallace
Technical consultants: Phil Glatz, James McNamara, City Lights,
    Mason Jones, R.S. Klatchko, Gary Chong, Christopher Trela
Front cover: Henry Rollins; photo by Sue Brisk
Back cover: Billy Childish with Traci; photo by E. Doyen
Cover Design: Marian Wallace

USA Book: SCB Distributors
  15608 S. New Century Drive
  Gardena, CA 90248
  TEL: (310) 532-9400
  FAX: (310) 532-7001
  email: scb@scbdistributors.com

UK & Europe: Airlift
  8 The Arena, Mollison Avenue
  Enfield, Middlesex, EN3 7NJ
  TEL: 011-44-208-804-0400
  FAX: 011-44-208-804-0044

USA Non-Book Last Gasp
  777 Florida
  San Francisco, CA 94110
  TEL: (415) 824-6636
  FAX: (415) 824-1836
  www.lastgasp.com

Australia: Tower Books
  Unit 8/9 Rodborough Rd
  Frenchs Forest NSW 2086
  TEL: 61-2-9975-5566
  FAX: 61-2-9975-5599

©2001 RE/Search Publications. ISBN:1-889307-09-2

Library of Congress card catalog number 2001-132116

781.66
Real

10   9   8   7   6   5   4   3   2   1

Real conversations no. 1

HENRY ROLLINS
BILLY CHILDISH
JELLO BIAFRA
LAWRENCE FERLINGHETTI

INTERVIEWS BY V. VALE

INTRODUCTION

Welcome to *Real conversations #1*.

The *RE/Search* series and my earlier *Search & Destroy* serials utilized the interview format as an accessible, "fun" way to communicate ideas, inspiration and provocation. This new "RE/Search Mini" series maintains the original philosophy —only the format has become smaller and more portable.

The book addresses questions such as: What are the secrets of staying true to countercultural ideals, decade upon decade? What are the ways in which we are controlled? How can we keep our bearings as we navigate through today's overwhelming information overload? Which history truly matters? And, how is technology impacting our lives, creativity, and freedom?

After more than twenty years of speaking out, punk pioneers Jello Biafra, Henry Rollins, and Billy Childish tell how they've "kept their edge" while continuing to grow, create and provoke. Beat godfather Lawrence Ferlinghetti gives a longer perspective on the eternal necessity of fighting fascism, brainwashing, and censorship in its "kindler, gentler" manifestations. Their bitter medicinals are sweetened by generous infusions of acidic humor. Please read!

—*V. Vale*

Swear words have been deleted to be able to reach a wider audience— many libraries, library services and high schools do not order books with four-letter words due to "policy."

TABLE OF CONTENTS

HENRY ROLLINS

Henry Rollins is the former lead singer for early punk group Black Flag. He's also a poet, journalist, book publisher, music producer, punk culture archivist, actor, spoken-word artist, comedian, television show host, record collector and vocalist fronting his own Rollins band.

Born 2.13.61 (also the name of his publishing house), Rollins grew up in Washington, D.C. At age twelve he attended the Bullis School for Boys. During his early teens he befriended Ian MacKaye (who would later form Teen Idles, Minor Threat, and Fugazi); the two were pioneering skateboard activists. In 1980 he joined State of Alert (SOA) as lead vocalist, and in 1981 joined Black Flag and moved to Los Angeles. The rest is history . . .

Two.13.61.com is the official site for Henry Rollins's creative output: to date, at least 10 books, 15 CDs, and a video, as well as his work with Black Flag. Also available from the site are books and/or CDs from artists such as Exene (X), Alan Vega (Suicide), Michael Gira (Swans), and Hubert Selby, Jr.

Henry Rollins at ALA Hall, Austin, Texas, 1981. PhotoBill

Henry Rollins and his band tour regularly out of their home base in Los Angeles, California.

♦ **HENRY ROLLINS:** I'm runnin' too fast, doin' too much stuff with too little time—as always. Just been in the studio for ten hours working on my band's record.

♦ *VALE: And on a Sunday, too—*

♦ **HR:** Yeah, it was the only day we could do it. I've got a voice-over job at 9 AM tomorrow morning. Then I go back to the studio and do the next shift—bright and early the morning after I go to New York for shows. We're just trying to get it all done.

"alternative"?

♦ *V: I have this theory that "underground" or "alternative" has somehow become associated with the kind of violent, pseudo-push-the-envelope content that appears on* Hard Copy. *And this is siphoning off a lot of once-rebellious curiosity and energy that a few years ago used to go toward, say, finding books like you and I publish—*

♦ **HR:** Yeah. I think there are a lot more players and a lot more pretenders to the throne now. **And that's where all this "new access to communication" kind of kicks you in the teeth: because even the mediocre can make their thing look really good.** I see a lot of independent books and I open them up and they're *really bad.* It would make you not want to pay attention to the "underground book world" when you see some of these books—they suck! And why did that book come out? Because anyone can lay out and design a book at home now, take a Zip disk, send it to a printer and get a book back.

I remember the first time I did a book by sending someone a disk—I think it was with your old girlfriend. Before that, me and Laura used to *hand-layout* galleys. Ohmigod, that was excruciating! It was all "busy work" and you couldn't make a mistake—it was like *prison.* Especially if it was a big book: "Oh god, there goes my weekend and four days of next week, my eyesight and my *sanity:* making it line up on that little blue grid with my hot wax roller." Man, you'd come to the end of the book and think you'd been through Dante's Inferno . . . getting to the other side. Whereas now, you kind of blithely modem something to someone in Hong Kong, and then a book comes back in a crate three months later: "Wow!" So there are a lot more people in the pool now.

I just think there are a lot of mediocre books—on the Simon & Schuster level, and on the Manic D level . . . on the big and on the small there's a lot of "*Eh*" material. I think a lot of "Eh" people are picking up pens and guitars these days—I really do.

It also happened with indie music, too. We had all kinds of really cool bands. Then all of a sudden there were a *ton* of bands, and you had to start weeding through them. Then what happens is, you have an indie record store with more records than it's ever had, but only 30% of them are good. And people lose interest after a while when they have too many choices and get stuck with too many mediocre things they dragged home for a big chunk of their paycheck . . . whereas Marlboro *always* delivers! Budweiser *always* delivers . . . and the pot dealer on the bike— he delivers too! (Y'know what I'm sayin'?) And Jack Daniels will always give you the same result.

Just like big music labels like Warner Bros. have always done, **I think a lot of indie record labels started going for the cash. Like, SubPop had a little period where they thought they were gonna be able to sell people *anything* because they had Nirvana for a second** . . . A lot of indie labels, when they got hooked up to a major label for their distributor, are all of a sudden having to go to these meetings at long tables and get filled with b.s. that two years ago they would swear drunkenly they never would have stood for. They're now working happily with people they swore they would never *speak* to . . . going into buildings they vowed to *torch,* in angry poetry in years gone by. And you know, I might be one of those. But I was never the one to say, "F... major labels!" Personally, I've never been burned by a major label—they pay on time. It's the *indie* labels I've had to go after, and yank my stuff away from.

I've never had a problem with Publishers Group West (PGW; independent book distributor), or a Tower Records account, ever. But in the old days, back in the SST world, with Pickwick, Greenworld, Enigma—all those companies . . . we'd be on the phone: "Please pay us! Please pay us! We're starving." "Well, don't worry—we'll get back to you." "But it's supposedly due in 90 days, and now it's been 140 days. Please! Do what you say you were gonna do!" I've never had that happen with Sony when I worked with them; I did Ozzy Osborne's video press kit for his last record, and the last Black Sabbath record. They paid me on time, they did everything they said they were going to do. *Sony,* who could have my legs broken any hour of the day—Pink Dot would do it for them. They can call in an air strike if they want! But they dealt with me fairly, every single time. It doesn't make me like them any more, but y'know, it's hard for me to put them down.

♦ **V:** *Well, the Sex Pistols were always on major labels: EMI, Virgin—*
♦ **HR:** And they took the money and got kicked off. **They got paid and they were paid to leave. Well, good for them! And also they got a cool song out of it ("EMI").** But when I was on Imago, people went, "F... you—you sold out!" I asked, "Do you like the Clash?" and they go, "Yeah!" "Well, they were on CBS"—which is Epic, Sony, from the get-go. So, *whatever.* It's not the label you're on, it's where *you're* at.

I've grown to want to be trustful of labels, because I was aware of the integrity of, like, Dischord, or SST—I worked at SST, kind of; we all did, because we were living on the floor there. These are high-fiber people who wouldn't sign something just "to sell"—they sign something they think is good. Ian MacKaye at Dischord doesn't put out anything unless he thinks it's good—he doesn't care if it's gonna sell ten, or ten thousand. If it's good, it's going on the label. Luckily he sells a jillion Fugazi records, so he can finance his smaller bands.

But I think that **even on the indie level, there are people who go, "Okay. I think this will sell." And all of a sudden they're putting out cutesy stuff** that just *sucks*. It's offensive, cloying, and at its worst it's mediocre. If it were *catastrophic,* it might be kinda cool, like the Vanilla Ice "live" album—that's kinda cool because it's *so* bad. But with his last effort, he tried to do a rock album; it is mediocre and it's a bore . . . because it's a mediocre guy trying to "fly right" and he doesn't *have* it. But when he was at his grossest, he was kind of amazing!

I do see some indie books that I think are really interesting, though. I love that book on Death Metal. It's a book I would want to put out because it's a book I went out and bought. And the topic—that whole world of those people—is really fascinating to me. It's very telling of where this country's at: that kids are so bummed out they're going to that extreme to vent it. So there are good books coming out.

I would trust a label like RE/Search because I *know* you. Even as a consumer, looking at the track record, it's a label where I would put a bunch of money down and say, "Look, here's a hundred bucks, just send me stuff as it comes out until a hundred bucks runs out." Because I know you're not going to put out anything that you didn't put a ton of energy into and don't absolutely love. I wish people had more faith like that, but it's hard for people to have faith in label integrity when so many labels belch out a lot of stuff where you go, "Nope . . . nope . . . nope . . . nope."

There are a lot of bootleg labels now, like Sea of Tunes that always puts out Beach Boys bootlegs. They find the most amazing stuff, like entire session outtakes from the master reels—someone has broken into the vaults. And I buy everything with that logo on it, because I know what it's going to sound like. And if you want Beatles bootlegs, you go to Vigatone. They don't put out anything that doesn't sound great—**you can hear Paul**

McCartney's hair growing, it's so clear. And even though it's a bootleg label, the level of integrity and quality is just outstanding. I mean, if they were a legit label, they'd be the critics' wet dream! Because everything is just top of the line.

So, I'm loyal to labels on account of I want people to be loyal to mine. I know that when we put out a Rollins book, we're gonna do fine. I mean, it sells 10,000 *immediately* and it just keeps on going. The whole company's afloat from my back catalog; print run after print run just goes. It doesn't *fly* out the door, but it's steady enough to keep the lights on, the rent paid, and the employees salaried—and that's not bad . . . the fact that after all these years, those books still sell.

The merchandise, the T-shirts, still go steadily; every three days there's a Glad bag full of orders for UPS to drag out to the truck. And I know a lot of people who, when I had my little record label going, just said, "Look, I don't know who Alan Vega is, but if *you* put him out, he must be good. So I went and bought the record and—man, that dude's cool!" I managed to generate some kind of interest for a minute there, where people said, "I'll take a chance, because I want to be taken somewhere."

I think the challenge you and I face is to find these people. I refuse to think they're not there anymore. I just think that in America they're probably harder to find. There are probably less of them than there were, just because these people have less of an opportunity to let their proverbial "freak flag fly" [quoting Jimi Hendrix]; they're too busy. **The real world encroaches upon our thing more steadily every day, like a rainforest getting eaten away by high-rises.** It's hard to take a book like yours home and read it when you're 21 and balancing a kid on one arm, you can't make car payments, and you've got this really hellish job.

Americans get a lot of gear thrown at them these days—more than when I was a high school graduate. I got out of high school in '79 (Wow, I've been out of high school for *twenty years;* that's a nice, round number!), and man, has it changed. On the level of violence, pollution, consumership, sex—it's all changed. Sex can now kill you. It used to be: at the worst, your girlfriend would get pregnant. And that was like a *catastrophe.* Now, it's like: I could die. And the stakes are higher. If you had a minimum wage job you used to be able to split a crummy apartment with your friend. Now, that's trickier; now there are *three* people in that one-bedroom.

staying *independent*

♦ *V: Let's talk about the state of independent publishing today. I don't know about you, but I'm doing terribly—*

♦ **HR:** Yeah, me too. *Good.* I was kinda worrying about this today: "Boy, how am I gonna be all like, 'It's just GREAT, Vale!' " Tell me where you want to go.

♦ *V: Okay. 1) How do you think independent publishing got this way? 2) What can we do about it?*

♦ **HR:** I can answer Part One better. I know you've traveled America and have been here and there, as have I. There used to be a great network of Mom 'n' Pop bookstores, independent record stores, and comic book stores that had cool book sections that would really cater to a label like yours or mine. We weren't Scribners or Harcourt-Brace ... you go to Amoeba [Bay Area used record store], and the Butthole Surfers are Ricky Martin, you know what I mean? Something left-of-center is the priority there.

The combination of these independent stores going under, being unable to compete with Barnes & Noble and Borders . . . the bad kick-in-the-teeth of that is the fact you're effectively being censored by these huge companies. They wiped out the little guys who support you, and then they don't carry you, so you're being burned at both ends. The Mom 'n' Pops couldn't stay alive because the chains would sell everything at 30 % off, and then, to add insult to injury, those chains never really had an interest in the RE/Searches and the 2.13.61s of the world because they're not turning over as fast as Regan Books [corporate publisher].

In the last four years there's been a new Borders and Barnes & Noble springing up in every suburban shopping mall as quickly as you see a Starbucks. And all of a sudden, pundits declare [sarcastic], "America is going toward reading" . . . but they're going toward Danielle Steel mega-books and not anything that's really gonna challenge them—like something you and I would put out. So we're effectively being shut down.

I've watched over-the-counter sales really decrease; in the past 3 years it's been catastrophic. And we have kick-ass distribution. You can't fault PGW; the problem is really in the stores. They only have so much shelf space, and if you're not selling tonnage, they'll give your titles one shot before you get them in a packing crate drop-shipped back to you, all banged up and really unsalable, except at book fairs for $5 or less.

We went for higher ground. We got our Web site really together and have been trying to reach people with an Internet newsletter and online ordering, knowing that if the people who seek us out can get to a modem, then they can get to us. Because if they're in Kansas, they're potentially not going to be able to find us any other way. Three years ago they could have. There was that really cool indie store that was there from '82 to '92, and then *something happened.* And that's been happening all over America.

All these cool little stores, like in Salt Lake City—that store's gone. And in Minneapolis, those two cool stores are gone. The local people lose out, and it's a real shame. Thank god for Tower Records! Their book department seems to be somewhat adventurous—the L.A., S.F. and New York ones seem to at least have an ear to the ground. That's what I've seen, traveling around.

A pioneer of skate-punk culture before it became a national fad, Henry had a local reputation as an aggressive free-style skater. Early on, he and Ian MacKaye rejected commercial sponsorship.

My own titles sell okay, but our second- and third-tier writers . . . I wouldn't put them out if *I* weren't a fan of them—and we're just getting *no sales* out there. **There are less cool places to do that store-by-store, Johnny Appleseed-style, almost *manual* distribution of books. I mean, I used to do it on the phone myself—literally, with a steno pad, store by store.** And every time, you'd sell twelve books, ten books. Or you'd sling them in your backpack and take them to gigs and sell them right after the show—that's how I got a lot of my books out there.

Corporate CENSORSHIP

What's the solution? The hope is the Internet, and perhaps getting to the Barnes & Nobles and Borders of the world to see if they can pull their heads out of their . . . It's kind of a corny concept to be an American book chain and omit so many titles from your "place" . . . and this is the place where you're not supposed to be censored and shut down. **A book place is supposed to be a place of freedom. If you want to put pictures of naked Nazis in a book, you should be able to sell it and somebody should be able to have access to that.** And when these stores can effectively censor so many labels and therefore so many *artists,* it's the new "Big Brother"! This is a way-more-real censorship than any Tipper Gore sticker on a CD, or a bunch of politicians coming down on rappers when they want to get elected . . . this is way more insidious, longer-lasting, and ultimately more destructive.

On the upshot, this is going to make underground labels blossom. I'm seeing it already: there's a really interesting surge in the underground. One of the most mainstream examples of that is the *Blair Witch Project,* a movie that cracked millions by selling itself over the Internet. I know people who had that movie on video weeks before it came out; and they had a different edit of it, too—

just because it was way lower to the ground. If *that* starts happening, if bands start putting their entire record on the Internet so some kid can download it onto his hard drive, then we'll watch Sony and all these companies start freaking out and begin trying to somehow control the Internet and come down on it, because they see a fraction of their potential money slipping away. **I think you're going to see some for-real cyberpunks and some for-real cyber-chaos, and more of a vibrancy in the underground, because it's gonna be back to "US against THEM."**

The beautiful examples of that were in the Bay Area when you were doing *Search & Destroy,* and when people like Mark Pauline [Survival Research Labs billboard-modifier] and Dirk Dirksen [Mabuhay Gardens' impresario] were really making a statement and it really *was* an "us against them" thing and you had to be *wily* to survive. A guy like Dirk was up against the cops, trying to keep his live music going, and also running all-ages shows. I think we're heading back towards that—which is dismaying *in a way,* yet it puts a real grin on my face in another way! Because **you're going to get some really excellent individuals out there who are outsmarting people and coming up with some really canny ideas.** There's potential to blow some s… wide open!

But as far as trying to run an independent book company . . . I get a lot of mail from young aspiring writers or people wanting to put out their poetry books, asking, "Hey, what's your advice?" And I hate to tell them, but my advice is, "Don't print up 1000 books that are gonna take 3 months of your salary. Because I'll be damned if you're gonna get them all sold."

Believe me, I don't do any short amount of thinking about that because I walk into my office, whenever I'm home, and go, "How are we doing?" And Carol goes, "Uh . . . well, thank god for those tour T-shirts that you brought home!" or "Thank goodness for those 2.13.61 coffee mugs we made." I go, "Well, how's the Jeffrey Lee Pierce lyric book doing?" (*Go Tell the Mountain,*

At age twelve, Henry (left) was enrolled at the private, all-boys Bullis School, a military prep school in Potomac, Maryland, 30 minutes from Washington, D.C. The uniform: blue blazer, gray slacks, and a blue-and-gold tie. Henry's hobbies included snakes, skateboarding and weight-lifting; he graduated in the summer of 1979.

After attending a semester at American University, Henry worked at the Georgetown Häagen-Dazs ice cream shop, and then became manager. His motto at the time was, "Skate mean, live clean." Soon he was to join State of Alert (S.O.A.) as their lead vocalist.

which we put a butt-load of work into). She goes, "Uh . . . no one cares." And I'm sure you've done a number of books which were an excruciating amount of work—detailed—and you put a lot of real time into the project, figuring, "Boy, this is interesting! And interesting people want interesting stuff." And then it doesn't go. You wonder: **"What happened to intelligent people who want cool stuff? Have they been exiled to some foreign country? What happened to them? They can't all be Danielle Steel fans all of a sudden.** *How come we can't get to them?*"

The dilemma of any independent company has always been *distribution*. It's been a struggle since I was in Black Flag. We were always trying to figure out how to get ourselves to people, confident that people would want our stuff *if* they could get it. And I think it's still true that distribution is a constant pain in the ass.

At this point my hat goes off to any independent, like Incommunicado [small press] whose lights are still on—which at this point is kinda *looking good*. If the phone is still being answered, that must mean things are going great! At this point, just *sheer existence* is kinda cool. [bitter laugh]

I never thought I was gonna get rich with a book company, but I never thought I'd be *scrambling* just to put out art, y'know. So . . . it's been kinda depressing.

♦ *V: Nowadays the chains regularly return hundreds of books; and I have to sell them at garage sales at a big loss. There are other factors, too, like the little-known, independent, regional book wholesalers who have all gone belly-up in the past few years, unnoticed—*

♦ **HR:** They've all gone away, right? But do you think it's primarily the Barnes & Nobles of the world kinda shutting people like these down, or do you think there's been a shift—at least in young people—away from checking out "alternative media"?

♦ *V: In general, book sales are down and people are on the Internet more. Actually, they're reading as much as they ever did, but now it's little Net stories averaging two screens' worth. There's also the video game factor—*

♦ **HR:** And there's also the video factor as well. I think that 5 years ago you wouldn't have been able to put a Britney Spears record across to a bunch of people—they would have just gone, "F... You." Now, corporations put out the lamest stuff—not even something that's for little kids, like Britney Spears, but stuff that's supposed to be "rock"—I listen to it and go, "Man, you gotta be kidding me—a *teenager* would go for this?" If *my* hormones were raging, this would not put the fire out for me!

NEW SOCIAL PRESSURES

I think America's youth in the last few years have really turned very passive. I think they probably watch more TV. Music for them has become a *visual* medium instead of an aural medium—they "watch" a song instead of, like, buying an album. But when they *do* get albums, they get albums that don't rock all the way through.

I remember growing up, when you were loyal to the bands you liked: when Van Halen (or whoever) put out another album, you were there from Day One. You wore your Black Sabbath T-shirt every day because that's who you were about. These days, bands are big for a second (Hootie and the Blowfish, 14 million; next record 2 million; record after that goes gold; the record after that—the one they're touring on now—a few hundred thousand). It shows you that people are just really going for what's glittering *at the moment*. They're very fickle—into consumption more than content.

But on the other hand, they're getting more sugar than substance anyway. So you're getting people on a sugar rush metabolism: their attention spans become lower because news and television in general have become soundbites: 4 minutes/commercial, 4 minutes/commercial. If news is being generated for ratings instead of content, then there's something ghastly wrong there.

I also think that social pressures and economic pressures change things; I don't know if there's the *time* to read anymore. And I think that the increase in computer book sales is like *survival:* people trying to keep their damn jobs. I mean, take someone like my mother, who retired a few years ago from a career in the government working for Health, Education, and Welfare trying to figure out "Why Johnny Can't Read in America." Her whole career was about literacy. And here's this woman in her sixties getting ready to retire and all of a sudden they lay a computer on her. This woman who has been with a typewriter of one kind or another all her life—all of a sudden my mom is talking about "gigabytes"! So a lot of people are scrambling. Her generation is probably a group of horses that are pretty hard to lead to that water. "Online"—*what?!* That kind of terminology blows people away.

Hence, a whole wall of yellow books at Borders: *Whatever . . . For Dummies. This* For Dummies; *That* For Dummies. Which is such an insult! Look at all those people buying those books. Of course, it's tongue-in-cheek, but these "dummies" are people just trying to keep their jobs. Just looking at the FedEx guy now with his bar-code reader . . . *everything* has gone from manual to high-tech. And I don't know if there's really time to contemplate a Penguin edition of the *Dialogues and Letters of Seneca* when you are already doing five things at once. I mean, I would hate to have three kids in America today. That'd be science-fiction trying to keep all that together. Kids and a job, *these* days?! Whoa!

♦ *V: Whatever happened to the 40-hour work week? Even "counter-culture" people seem to be working 80 hours a week to keep their jobs: going in on weekends, staying 'til 10 PM . . . that seems crazy!*

♦ **HR:** Yeah. It's *Tokyo* . . . where you see people coming out of office buildings at 11 PM, going to the train station. It's like, "I can't believe it—they've still got their ties on!" And they're working a six-day week. I think it's because **push is coming to**

shove. I think it's harder to carve out a dollar. That was my theory to account for the Columbine massacre: how come the parents didn't know their kid was building friggin' pipe bombs? Well, maybe they were out trying to feed that kid, and it takes a lot more hours than it used to. You don't see Dad propped up in the easy chair anymore with a pipe and the paper—he read it on the train. He doesn't smoke anymore, and he's eating yogurt and rice cakes to keep his blood pressure down.

I mean, things have changed pretty rapidly in the last 5 years—even the weather is changing. It's turning into J.G. Ballard's *The Drought* . . . that book you gave me many years ago. You know: the earth's getting hotter, people are getting a little bit more frenzied, and the people who provide consumer goods are putting out a shinier carrot for those who can make it to the upper-middle-class boys' club. People are scrambling for that BMW 3-series, a cool laptop, that lifestyle, and it makes everyone a little frantic. Yet the lower-middle class and the minorities— their world has not changed much. It was f...ed for their parents, and now it's f...ed for them. It's still eight to a room. For the people who would be in a position to change things, and in the same position to buy books (getting back to the original topic) I think it's a combination of shortened attention span, and a harried "Man, I gotta go out and get it done!" mind-set.

♦ *V: Life is much more stressful now. For smart computer workers, the average job tenure is now nine months—and seeking employment is stressful. There are other factors; corporate marketing techniques are much more effective at ramping up people's levels of consumption. The average person now recognizes 3,000 brand names. All that is clogging up our memory banks—*

♦ **HR:** That's something I think about fairly often. I wonder how much useless information I know. Sometimes at spoken word gigs I torture audiences by singing snatches of twenty bad songs. I say, "You all know the rest, and before you go to sleep tonight you *will* be singing 'Hungry Like the Wolf,' " and everyone's going,

"No! Stop! Stop!" and I'll go into some Boy George, some Duran Duran, and it's endless—there's all kinds of useless crap you now know because you've been pummeled by the bus-stop sign.

There used to be micro-marketing, but now there is, like, *hyper*-micro-marketing . . . it's like a smart bomb! It's a virus: they *will* get your kid. And if they're not gonna sell them Coke, they own four other brands—in fact, they'll even advertise them against each other so you think you're on the winning side—but you're still paying the same guy!

And in years to come, Coca-Cola will own McDonald's, Universal, Sony, and Marlboro. As the world gets smaller, you'll visit one Web site for your entertainment, your nutrition, and your concept of freedom! And soon you'll just be answering to HAL [computer from the movie *2001*], and you won't be able to turn him off: [softly] "I'm sorry, Vale, I can't do that." "*F...!* [gargled scream] I just wanna go outside!" "I'm sorry. I can't allow that."

It's probably not that bad, but things are not as wide open as they used to be. If you read that great article by Gore Vidal in *Vanity Fair [November 1998],* he said that **the upsurge in American surveillance in general is just obscene.** It's a tremendous article—well worth tracking down. He's just a great mind. And he just said, "Look at how many people know what you're up to." Like in the workplace, how many times have you called tech support or whatever and heard that tape saying, "This call may be monitored for customer quality"? How'd you like to work in a place where you're being monitored? I know nothing about that. I never had a job like that when I was working straight jobs, and now I'm in a position where I *own* my building . . . but I wonder what it must feel like.

♦ **V:** *But people who work in situations like that are used to it. "It's for your own good," they say.*

♦ **HR:** Yeah, well that's a whole other Orwellian nightmare: "We're protecting you for your own good." There's a movie there: "The militia will come into your house, beat the s... out of you for your own good—you don't want to go outside, so we'll just chain you to your bed. *It's for your own good.* As we're raping your sister—well, now she understands: it's for her own good."

And I think sometimes if you're innovative and alternative (like your label and my label are), yet you don't have an "in" with Sony or MTV or radio, or you're not tied into Miramax, then you really are back to the days when Systematic Record Distribution was still getting it together [early '80s, Berkeley, California]. We're like, "Okay, now we really ARE indie." You're kinda like Rommel in the desert: you ran outta gas, and you're just out there in the middle of nowhere trying to get through to find your people. And maybe this will make for some really cool alliances.

♦ *V: That's about the only hope I can think of: "strategic alliances."*

♦ **HR:** Yeah—people getting back together. It might come to a situation where "I'll take 500 of yours, and you take 500 of mine," and "I'll take your books to my show," and "You take my books to your show or your storefront," or "I'll hyperlink to your Web site," so if they like what I do, I'll tell everyone to check out what you do . . . that might be something you will see more of. And that might give birth to a whole new independent network.

I do my best to support small business. I live on the road a lot, and I'm always looking for a half-decent cup of coffee in the afternoon—that, like, makes my day! I see the Starbucks and the Seven-Elevens . . . they're everywhere, but I will walk an extra few city blocks looking for that cool indie place. I'd rather give them the business.

FEAR TV

But in general, I just wonder if the intellectual interest in this country is waning. And that happens when you get this vast majority of mediocre people who are easily filled with fear. I watch TV as kind of an *experiment*. I watch it in hotels—I don't have a TV at home. (Oh, I do, but it's just for the VCR.) And **when I'm in hotels I watch stuff like *Hard Copy* and realize that millions watch this program which basically just reinforces stereotypes.** They show you the crime, the overhead camera of the man getting shot in the liquor store (they show you that *four* times), and it's *FEAR TV.* They're teaching you *how to be afraid.* And the more fear . . . **my saying is, "When the going gets rough, the average get conservative."** [laughs]

This is how you "de-horrify" a guy like Mark Fuhrman [cop who wrote about the O.J. Simpson trial]: you make people so damn scared of stereotypes that all of a sudden this Nazi is not so bad because at least he hates those black guys who might rape my little girl. And he may have said "nigger" but, "Well, by god, he's somehow on my side, and we won't say it, but secretly I think he's okay." And when you can *fill people with mediocrity*—Bruce Willis movies, anything with Tom Cruise—it is just a *nightmare for the brain.* And all these TV shows! I mean, Calista Flockhart—that woman! I've watched that Ally McBeal show twice now because it wins awards; I wanna watch what millions of people give the big "thumbs up" to. And it is *diabolical.* It's so depressing. I don't laugh at all. And I'm not sitting there trying *not* to laugh—I'm like, "Okay . . . So change my mind!" And it doesn't. I see the ratings that stuff gets and think, "Man, we're really in trouble . . . We're really *in* for it."

I gotta wonder: in ten years, when you have young people whose first gig was 'N Sync or the Backstreet Boys, whose first reading experience out of school was *HTML For Dummies,* and whose first trip abroad was some summer thing where they smoked pot, puked all over everyone, and beat up a waiter in Holland—I mean, I just think, "What is this?" They're never gonna know who Mark Twain was; you're never gonna be able to explain to them Duke Ellington, Martin Luther King, Malcolm

X, or *anything*—they're gonna just be too busy scrambling for a BMW. You wanna say to 'em, "Read!" But they say, "I read *manuals* because I kick ass; I don't take any s..., and I'm a *mover!*"

♦ **V:** *These people often claim that "All the information you need is on the Web"—which is definitely not true.*

♦ **HR:** There's *nothing* like holding a book in your hand. There's nothing like a read. I mean, I like typing, but there's nothing like writing by hand. If I have the time, I'll write handwritten letters; I'd rather handwrite in my journal. I'd rather read a book, I'd rather not read on the Internet (although I dig that; I read what's happening in East Timor—that's cool) but . . .

I think there's just been a general shift away from *real living.* Whichever futuristic film Woody Allen made [*Sleeper*] where they had the Orgasmatron and they both get in it, and he goes, "No, no, no—*manual!* Let's do it manual!" And she's like, "No, you put this on," and he goes, "No, let me grab you!" I have never forgotten that. Because now, it's so much like: "I know this girl on the Internet; we write each other." I think, "Well, okay. That's cool, but **I really like the old-fashioned way where, you know, my jeans are on her floor. I remember *that;* that was really cool." And pointing-and-clicking is not going to do it for me!**

I think we're moving away from that, and I also think we're moving away from human-scaled performance situations . . . I watched it in the '80s when I saw a lot of the medium-size concert halls in America dry up . . . all the great 800-seaters where you go in and, like, blow the roof off! Black Flag's meat-and-potatoes were the 800-to-1,100-seaters. And they *all* went away. Places like the Farm or the On Broadway in San Francisco: good-looking venues that hold around 800—you could be a medium band and you could pack it. Everyone has a good time, it's small enough, you could be kind of a band living in a van and still eke out a living. Whereas **now, either you play the *dump,* or you play the Warfield [capacity 2500].** Fortunately, in S.F. you've got Slim's. But you know what? There's no Slim's in L.A. Either it's the Palladium (3000 people; sound is bad) or it's every dump where the men's room doesn't work—it sounds great and it'll hold 300 of your friends.

♦ **V:** *Yes, and that doesn't really pay for the trip—*

♦ **HR:** No. A local band may break even, even if they have to rent a van and stuff. A touring band is a different story, unless you're gonna sleep at someone's house—and even then! Someone just sent me Mike Watt's tour itinerary. I always count how many days a band is doing in a row—he's doing 38 shows in 38 days! And I looked at the venues—he's playing places the size of my living room. But that's Mike—he'll play 80 nights straight if you let him; he just loves to play. And that's how a band that's living in a van is going to come home with enough money to pay the rent and phone bills while they were gone, and be able to survive for three months before the next tour.

♦ **V:** *And they need to write some new material, or recuperate, or something—*

♦ **HR:** Yeah! Otherwise, you'd better write it on the road. Which means that within a year and a half you're burned out, under-weight, and everyone's sick of your ass anyway, because you've played their town like four times in ten months! And they love you dearly, but they'd rather hear from you "every once in a while." *Meanwhile,* you can go see some Courtney Love show in front of 18,000 people for like $45! It's kind of dismaying in a way; it's disheartening and demoralizing and destabilizing. On the other hand, if you can get in the right mood, it's kind of gal-vanizing. Although, if you're having *garage sales* to try and sell $150 worth of books, then it's hard to get on the horn—[military sergeant's tone] "Come on, men! Here we go!"—it's hard to raise the flag for that, you know.

What we've done—my company—is, we have totally wimped out. We no longer make new books by unknowns. We just sell *my* stuff. And now, without the cost of generating new titles by people who don't sell, and by increasing our Web profile—people's awareness of us on the Web—we're putting out a newsletter once a month, handwritten by me, banged out on the Internet. Online ordering, new T-shirts, limited edition stuff—we did our first "Internet Only" CD and it's selling 2–5 an hour. We take tour posters—we get an extra hundred or so from the tour and bring them home, I sign them, we put them on the Net and in five days they're all gone. And we are making money. So, by stopping being a book company and just doing mail order, we have been turning a profit for like two quarters now.

I think our last book was Jeffrey Lee Pierce's book, and financially it was a $7,000 hole I jumped into. And I loved that book. To me Jeffrey Lee Pierce [Gun Club] was one of the great American songwriters of the '80s and '90s. His book was made with so much love, intent, and work—Jeffrey died in the middle of making it. All the band members came out of the woodwork and helped, supplying photos and missing lyrics; his mother helped, and so did his sister. I mean I had different members of the Gun Club—everyone from Keith Morris to Jeffrey Lee Pierce to his mother—at my house working on that book at different times. And we put it out like, "*Damn you,* buy this book just out of respect." And no one cared!

I think, "Didn't that guy make enough good records for you people? How dare you not buy this book!" And I don't even want profit; I wanna break even and I want people to read these words. Any book company wants you to read the damn book, you know. And we just stopped. I said, "Carol, I can't be the National Endowment for the Arts anymore." I mean, I was *paying* to put out books for years. And luckily, on my own, I pulled down money. Me, by myself, I make plenty—you know, for me. I don't spend much. I would take some of the money and go, "Okay, let's put out *this* book . . . *this* CD. I love this guy's work; let's put it out."

♦ *V: You told me nobody bought Coyle & Sharpe's CD—*

♦ **HR:** Oh yeah . . . and how good does a record have to be? That thing's brilliant. Those guys are amazing. Mal Sharpe—he's still around, he's working on the next one [*Audio Visionaries: Street Pranks & Put-Ons*]. He's going to put it out with Thirsty Ear. And hopefully he'll be getting back his old Warner Brothers material. And there again, Mal struggled. You hear a Coyle & Sharpe record and that's *godhead!* Those guys are just brilliant, then and now. And people buy *what?* I guess they're buying Chris Rock.

I'm not into saying, "Don't buy *this* record, buy *that* record." I'm more into the idea of "You wanna buy the Offspring? Go ahead. You wanna buy Korn? Fine. But leave room for jello— you know, leave room for dessert. Leave room for Duke Ellington. Leave room for my artists. Leave room in your brain. You've accessed nine porn sites today; you've looked at a bunch of implanted breasts—good. Now read a book that we make. You've got an hour before you go to sleep. Turn off the TV and read this. Or **read *Huckleberry Finn*. Read Henry Miller. Read F. Scott Fitzgerald. Read a short story—it's just four pages; it'll only take you an hour!"** Yet it's hard to get people to do that when they've got 400 channels, the Internet, little games they can play in their lap—Gameboys. I've never played one and I don't really know what they do, but when you can sell thousands of people a Japanese egg [Tamagotchi] where you get to take care of its chick (people bought *that?!)* then what's it all coming to?

♦ *V:* *I ran into someone from the early punk days and asked him, "What are you reading lately?" He said, "Oh, I don't read much anymore; I go to this place where they sell used videos. If I go buy one of your books, it's like twenty bucks with tax, and for that same $20 I can bring home a big bag of four or five videos."*

♦ **HR:** It's hard to compete with that. If you can go home with like four or five *whatevers* . . . **it's hard to sell a book because you can't dance to it, you can't hit "select" and play all your**

favorite chapters. But it used to be a more literate nation when there weren't so many options that were so *user-friendly.*

Pleasure me!

An English journalist said it very well: "It's wild coming to America from where I'm coming from, because there are so many people out to *pleasure* you." (I'd never heard that as a *verb.*) I said, "What do you mean?" He said, "I came to L.A. and everyone is trying to serve me something. The waitresses are making me feel like I'm a millionaire, and everyone is just trying to pleasure me." He thought it was just surreal: "Everyone is beautiful, the food is good, and there's just so much available to me—it's like I just sit still and it's being dropped into my lap."

Whereas with something like a book you've got to go *after* it. You have to turn the damn pages. It's all *manual.* And these days, your car talks to you, your computer talks to you, there's so much stuff where all you have to do is hit "On" and it just comes to you. You become passive, then it's easy to sell you stuff. It's easy to manipulate you, influence you, make you mediocre, and also fill you with fear and paranoia and reinforce stereotypes.

You know, I think at the end of the day, to put it succinctly, Sony and all those people—*they won.* They put their heads together; they hired some of the best brains in the business, and they won! Because you look at the marketing campaigns and they're *great.* You look at the commercials—they're great. And me: I'm guilty. I do voice-overs for Merrill Lynch. I do voice-overs for GMC Truck. But you know, General Motors made fire trucks before I was born, and Merrill Lynch has been around forever. I make a salary from doing voice-overs for their ads—it's how I pay my rent: I use my voice. I'm one of those people who thinks—well, if they didn't use me, they'd use somebody else. But I think these companies have done a real number. When you can sell, like, two million records of this unbelievable garbage to people, then you *know* the advertising must be great, the video must look great.

I watched some MTV recently. **Most modern bands just really offend me, because they don't have any chops, they don't have any talent and they don't have anything to say. But boy, do those videos look good!** You look at them and go, "Man, I wish that were my video. That was well done." But you realize that the band has nothing to do with it, that Sony (or whoever) is smart enough to put their money where they know it's gonna really talk. They spend $750 grand on a video and it makes them sell 300,000 records in the next two weeks! Soundscan charts a big rise, the next single goes, the back catalog goes, the new album goes, and the record has another six weeks—it's in the Top 100, all for the cost of a fraction of a million bucks.

And boy, they really got it wired. You look at the videos, you look at the album artwork, you hear the album—they're so sterile and so slick. I mean, not one beat belongs to that band. **The guy hits a high note and thanks to the computer the engineer literally turned a knob and the vocal went straight to the right pitch**. There's a very famous pseudo-funk band in Los Angeles whose name I will not mention. I asked someone who *knows,* "Did the singer really sing those notes, or was he pitched?" And the guy says, "Every vocal he did was pitched . . . just like the last album." And so, there's a lot of help.

It's not just in music—*everything's* getting like this now. When things are so airbrushed, when women have contorted their bodies to look like Vargas drawings, when they happily go under the knife to get new boobs, new asses, new cheeks, new noses, new eyes, new ears, less belly fat—*wow!* When men get penile implants, pectoral implants (so they look like they have a chest), I mean—*wow!* That's incredible!

image maintenance: selling out & buying in

I mean, I live in L.A. and I've been out with a bunch of girls in this town. I've had my hands on a lot of fake breasts in my life just from dating girls in this town. You wouldn't encounter that where I come from in D.C.—hell, no. I mean, out here people *without hesitation* (especially in the entertainment business) agree: "Boob job = better part—tell me which doctor you want me to go to, coach." They're right under that knife. "New nose— no problem." "New tits—hey!" "Screw that guy for the part? Fine!" And you can say to them, "You know, you've compromised your art," and they say, "Uh, my dear, next year I can buy Uruguay—and what are you doing? Selling your $150 worth of books at a garage sale?! Ha ha—who won?!" Of course I think, "We'll see how those things look on you in 20 years, and we'll tally it up then . . ."

You know, this country is a way different place than just a few years ago. **With the abundance of communication and increased access to communication, I think we communicate a lot less.** Because I really don't count two-line emails to your friend every once in a while as really communicating. I mean, there are some human beings I do not talk to, who I grew up with . . . take Ian MacKaye, a guy I've known since I was 14. Very rarely do we speak on the phone. Either it's face-to-face (I'm in his town, or he's in mine) or we e-mail each other. I will not hear his human voice, even on the telephone, for like eight months. And he is a guy I keep in touch with! I might not keep in touch with people all the time because I'm on the road or busy, but these days one rarely speaks.

But back in the '80s, we *talked*. And these days—you know, you and I got to this phone call tonight through e-mail. And it's efficient, but . . . Don Bajema, a guy I've known for many years—I talk to Don every once in a while on the phone. We call each other and check in. Usually it's by e-mail. I see him about every 14 months now, and it's when I'm coming through S.F., because he's busy working like a worker ant bringing it home for a wife and kid; he can't come down and hang out with me for a weekend. I don't have time either. And that's just a microcosm. And someone like you or me or Don are people who do value their intellect and all that—and look how *we* gotta scramble!

Think of the guy who has a "real" job—like, he's gonna fix your car. What kind of access does *he* have to books? He's going to buy something at the drugstore right by the cash register. He's gonna buy *Dances With Wolves, Silence of the Lambs.* You show him *Modern Primitives* and he's gonna go, "Get the f... outta here! I can buy something for $8.95; what am I gonna do buying a $20 book about *anything?!"* Unless it's pictures of naked celebrities, or famous people caught in compromising positions, how are you gonna sell that guy a book?

How are you gonna sell a 22-year-old that book? You stand a chance if he lives in Bloomington . . . he might want to get to you if he knew that you existed; you *might* be able to get him interested in the *Industrial Culture Handbook,* or one of my books. But how do you get to him? Yet communication has never been more easily accessible . . . how many people *don't* have a cell phone?! At every intersection in L.A. you can count people on a cell phone in their car: one, two, three, four . . . **Everyone's talking, everyone's e-mailing each other, *and no one knows what's goin' on!***

There are a lot of slobs: "tiny masters of today" (as Nietzsche called them, to quote the Barney Rubble of philosophy) who are in charge of a whole lot of gear. Like in this town—I live in Hollywood, I see a lot of really offensive, pony-tailed outtakes/rejects from some old *Miami Vice* show, driving nice cars going into plush jobs where they really don't do much except make money off artists they're gonna drop in nine months anyway, and somehow it just keeps rollin' in for these people.

Meanwhile, Mike Watt is doing 38 shows, and he's been brilliant for about 20 years now, and I'm sure it's hard for him—I'm sure that guy fixes his own car! He's got duct tape under the hood keeping that thing going, and I'm sure he's never bought a new car in his life. Yet he's made three times the amount of records Guns N' Roses will ever make. He'll be playing music long after the guys in the Offspring just kinda move on to something else . . . all those guys will just kinda retire before they're 35 and have a bland life in the suburbs and wear their surf shorts to the end.

You really tap the nervous system of this country when you get to their wallet . . . you really see where people are at. That's where their soul is now. It's what they'll do with their VISA card that tells you the character of the man. He might not pull you out of a burning building, but man, if he buys, like, four pieces of your gear, he's not all that bad! [laughs]

But you know, on the positive side, I do think you will see a lot of people going, "*F...* this! I'm smarter than this, and I'm not going down" . . . *and creating new ways to communicate.* I meet a lot of wonderful young people on the road. They're not all dull. They're not all buying the Top Ten American records. I meet a lot of little smart-asses—I always liked the geeky smart-asses, y'know. They're pickin' up on our signal. And they're not alone.

My label and the art I've done over the years has always kind of been there for the dysfunctional kid. The jocks never really liked me, but the one who got *pounded* by the jocks—*I* was their hero. Black Flag or Rollins Band or whatever, those records came to your rescue. If you hated the guy who got the cool girl with the cheerleader outfit on, then *our* music was for you—you, who got punched in the stomach by that guy, in front of everybody. Those are the people who sit in rooms and read and learn how to play a wicked guitar because they don't get asked to all the dances. Those are the future Todd Rundgrens [guitarist] who can *really* play. And those are the people who check out what we do. But I also think there are a lot of other people who do have an intellect, who aren't going to go quietly into the American mediocre night, y'know.

I love it that the last Tom Cruise movie [*Eyes Wide Shut*] stiffed. All these people were going, "Oh, it's gonna be The Big One—him and his wife, the Power Couple of L.A." Too bad it was Kubrick's last film. I'd like to ask him if he wanted to use those two in his movie because he thought they were such a screwed-up couple. That was my friend's theory—he thought Kubrick was too smart to use 'em because they're big—he used them because their relationship is so utterly twisted and wanted to try to capture *that.*

But, you know, Kubrick goes out with a whimper and the movie stiffs, and **that to me is always encouraging: when the blockbuster doesn't bust the block**. When the *Blair Witch Project* does, or *Mallrats* does, or even a guy like Adam Sandler who gets panned by every critic still takes it to the End Zone. I think every once in a while there are like *little victories* here and there . . . which shows me there are still signs of life!

♦ *V: Nevertheless, real estate is oppressing everybody now. In San Francisco, because of the Dot-com Gold Rush, really crappy studio apartments start at $1,500.*

♦**HR:** It's becoming like Manhattan; D.C.'s getting that way, too. What's going on? All my friends who were born and raised in D.C. have had to move to Virginia—they can't afford to live in their hometown anymore, even though they have normal jobs. Or, they're a gang getting a house, but there's a guy sleeping in the bathtub—they're ganging up, pooling resources. It's harder all around, and there are bigger and stronger and brighter companies than ours vying for that leisure dollar. And we *are* kind of competing with Sony and Regan Books for that same dollar. Not everyone buys your book because they want to get enlightened; they want to "get off" on it, too. So they're buying a book for "entertainment" (I hate that word)—

♦ **V:** *Like Howard Stern—*

♦ **HR:** Yeah! Howard Stern sells millions of books. The Oprah Winfrey Workout Book sold three million. Pick your favorite book you published—you couldn't sell three million!

♦ **V:** *Maybe our* Pranks *book has the most potential; it has humor in it. Over the past twelve years it's sold about 60,000 copies. Kids buy it now and still love it.*

♦ **HR:** I don't think a book like that ever ages; it just gets kinda cooler. Joe Coleman [in the RE/Search *Pranks!* book] is always going to blow people's minds. Ten years from now people are still going to be looking at those photos thinking, "What a little maniac!" He looks dangerous. I see him every once in a while, like at a book signing or a gig, and I've never spoken to the guy. I just look at him, and he looks like trouble. You could go introduce yourself and he would, like, light himself up and explode next to you or go, "Yeah? F... you!" or just get into your face. I dig him, but he just looks like he's ready to *engage.* He just has it in his eyes, like: chaos. But—I'm a fan. I'm kind of a little awed.

♦ **V:** *There are a few of us still trying to avoid being domesticated—*

keeping it real

♦ **HR:** Yeah, **I keep my trip solo. I kinda like being single anyway**, but . . . as I get older . . . you're older than you were, you think a little differently, and you allow yourself this and that, and go, "NO! I do not do that." Or maybe you used to say, "Only one scoop of ice cream, not three." Now you're like, "Hey man, I worked hard. Give me that third scoop." But **I kind of**

put a governor on myself, to make sure I keep things fairly lean. Just so I can keep my edge. I know this sounds really lame, but one must keep on *terra firma*—see, I'm in a position where I'm around people who all the time tell me I'm great. I go places: "Man, you're The Man!" "Uh, okay . . . Thanks." I go into a TV studio: they all cower—they think I'm gonna go break something. Then they meet me and I'm cool: "Oh . . ." And then they like me even more. So I'm just around people who want to *pleasure* me, as my friend said.

Y'know, I get my ass kissed all the time by people I've never met. I walk into Paramount Recording Studio today: everyone in that studio knows who I am. They all walk up: "Oh man—seen you four times. Always wanted to meet you." "Cool." And they all come up and give me my props and I go to Studio E and start work for the day. But not until I'd heard how great I was from like four different people. And if I ever *bought into* any of that . . .

I mean, I appreciate it. It's nice if someone likes what I do; great. But if I ever bought into that—s..., I'd be *done* in eight months! I get invitations to all the movie premieres and all that—I purposely *don't go!* Even if I want to go, I'll just wait, and then I'll pay $7.50 and sit in the back row of a theater rather than go and shake hands with Richard Gere. I just don't want to be part of it all. Because I think you get *soft.* **I've watched a few people who came in like a lion and went out like a lamb with someone's fist up their ass . . . saying, "Thank you! It doesn't hurt too much; I don't really mind!"** Well, I don't want to go out like that, and I purposely avoid a lot of stuff. In the course of that I've avoided heroin, cocaine, alcohol, speed, pot, tobacco, etc . . . which has been the ruin of a lot of people I know . . . people I was in bands with.

I encountered a former band member the other night in San Diego at my show. Here was this human beanpole of a guy who managed to get fat (alcohol), he was s...-faced drunk and looking bad (looked like he was rode hard and put up wet). And I love him. He used to be a righteous guy—a really good musician who used to be a soulful dude. And I just saw this kind of weakened, drunken buffoon. And he was all over me, like falling on me, [slurred speech] "Hey, man . . ." It just really took the air out of my sails.

Then on the other hand I went, "Okay. I was *right*. I used to take shit from him about being straight-edge—whatever. I'll see you in the End Zone." And here we are, walkin' into the third quarter of life and I'm like, "Yup. I'm still kickin' that ass . . . and what are *you* doin'? Oh. You just *fell* on me . . . and your Heineken spit is now on my shirt."

Y'know, I just try to reconcile that money I make (which is way more than when I first met you) and tryin' to keep it *real* when you're deciding where you want to buy your next piece of property. It's a challenge. I'm not a millionaire or anything, but now I own the roof over my head. Who woulda thought?! But **it's a balancing act to balance your art, your commerce, and your lifestyle, and keep yourself kinda firmly planted while keeping your finger on the pulse . . .**

Also, I've watched a lot of artists just blow it . . . And you see the ones who *did* keep it real: it's the Mike Watts livin' in that van.

♦ *V: He definitely has integrity and our respect—*

♦ **HR:** I haven't toured in a van in eight years . . . unless we're only doing a week of shows or somethin'. But you know what I mean? And I've kept my trip real, too.

To a lotta people, you say you gotta "keep it real" and they go, "Why? So I can starve? So I can live like a jackoff . . . while I watch the guy in Green Day buy half my neighborhood, for playing music that sounds like Dickies' retreads?" It's just a challenge: for the artist, for the label, for all of that. And quite honestly, I haven't seen a manuscript I've wanted to put out for quite a while. *I'm still regrouping my fury . . .* you know, to go back out there and go, "F... you. *Buy* this!"—right now I don't have it. Not

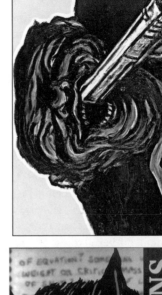

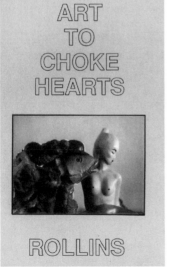

for anything that's not mine.

I'm working on three different book projects now; they're gonna do just fine, I'm sure—well, I *hope.* But as far as a book that's come along that I wanna put out—I read these manuscripts that come in; they don't do anything for me.

♦ *V: Have you been assaulted by manuscripts that try to "push the envelope" of sex and violence with shock-value language but no real content—*

♦ **HR:** Oh yeah! You read this stuff and go, "Wow, you really can put one word after the other. That's great." They write this stuff because they think *I'm* really gonna like it: "Here's a book that's perfect for your label" and you read this ultra-violent misogynistic hateful s... and go, "Man, you have got me so wrong." People email you: "Dude, can I send you my manuscript?" I go, "Please don't! . . . I love you dearly, but we're not putting out books anymore, and there's no staff to read the stuff." A week later you get a one-inch-thick envelope of manic boy's scrawl: [spits out] "In the darkness I can see/you are someone I do not want to be"—all that kinda stuff.

We used to stand on top of our chairs in the office and read these manuscripts out loud, then capsize with laughter. At one point we wanted to put out a book of the worst writing ever sent to us . . . so everyone could have their moment. They would think, "Hey, look at this—I'm in a book!" and they would start reading and by page 10 get the joke . . . just how godawful it all is. In fact, I have *never* been sent a manuscript in the mail that I've ever put out. And I tell kids that: "You know what? I've been getting manuscripts for thirteen years, like up to five a day, and I've never published a single one. So save the trees, save the time, and trust me—there's no one at my place to read it." They go into a pile, then we put them in the paper shredder and use it all for packing material.

♦ *V: I read a big feature about you in a major Sunday newspaper magazine. Did you consider that a good article?*

♦ **HR:** I never read it. There was a slight problem with the writer, in that during the course of her interviewing me, which was over a few-day period, she started hitting on me . . . in my house. We're there working until like 10 PM, and it's time for her to get in her rental car and go back to the Roosevelt Hotel, and she's like, "So, um, I've always wanted . . ." and I think, "Oh, no . . . don't do this, because I'm gonna say No and all of a sudden I'm gonna get a hateful article written by . . . A Woman Scorned." And I did what I'm real good at; I pretended I didn't get it.

I get hit on by girls a lot, and they really mean it, and I don't want to offend. I don't wanna say, "Leave me alone," so I just go, "Duh . . . Well, gosh, it's really nice to meet you, too." They're looking to be kissed and you just stick your hand out [hearty voice], "Well by god it was *great* to meet you and—shucks, I gotta go." I just play like *Leave It To Beaver* . . . like I don't even *know.* And they go, "Gawd, what a geek!" Which is fine—let them think I don't get it. They're thinking, "Here's the chance of a lifetime!" and I'm thinking, "Yeah ... whatever. Whoops— oh well, didn't win the lottery that night, but . . ." So, I suspected there was going to be either this emotional article or a "*F...* this guy" article . . . I don't know, I never read it and I saw her at a Leonard Cohen show a while ago at the Paramount in New York and she was friendly to me. Why—was it a bad article?

♦ *V: The thing that impressed me was: it said you had this house all set up with computers everywhere, and you had 8 or 10 people working there—*

♦ **HR:** At our most full-flaringest we had people working upstairs and downstairs—that place was a little hive. We had one full-time staffer and some part-timers and interns. But now, we don't need a press department—there are no new books. All we need is someone taking calls from PGW [distributor] or taking calls for mail order.

For a while we even had a few writers who would make us

money—to the point where we *needed* a staff. The early Bill Shields books (our Viet vet poet) sold rather well [*Lifetaker, Southeast Asian Book of the Dead*]. When the *Get In The Van* Black Flag book came out, for six months it was like ALL HANDS ON DECK!—we moved like 30,000 books in seven weeks, and they were big, heavy hardbacks. There was a lot of going back and forth to the warehouse, so there were a lot of humans needed. But now, I hate to say it: [grim tone] business is a lot *calmer.*

I always invested my money in office equipment: lamps, computers, desks . . . Now I've got enough office furnishings to sink a battleship!

♦ **V:** *You were in a full-page ad for the Macintosh Powerbook, that appeared in some glossy magazines. A few people I knew attacked that as some kind of sell-out, and I said, "Who would you rather see in that ad: Henry Rollins or a corporate executive?"*

♦ **HR:** I saw that series of ads and saw some professor posing with Todd Rundgren and I went, "Oh, man—I want to get in on this." At the time Terry Ellis was the boss of the label I was on. He was like Mr. Three-Piece Suit and owned half of Chrysalis Records. Actually he was fairly cool; he was the one who produced Aqualung. He used to manage all kinds of people and was "happening" in the music world of the '70s and '80s. He put out Robin Trower records—hey, no enemy of mine. But anyway, I said to him, "Terry, look at these ads. Look at you with your $900 suit, and look at me with my torn-up gym shorts with the bloodstains on them. You and me in a Mac ad"—because we both used the laptops.

Four nights later he was having dinner at some $100-a-plate restaurant and he hears the men at the next table taking about the Mac ad. He said to them, "Gentlemen, I'm interested in those ads." They went, "Great—we're the ones who make them." He said, "I work with Henry Rollins," and they're like, "He's *cool!*" Terry said, "Great—look at me and think of him, and there's your ad." Five days later we were negotiating the photo sessions. They just thought, "Yeah, that's a great idea. We'll take it."

COMPUTERS

♦ **V:** *Did you get paid with a laptop?*

♦ **HR:** Yeah, they said, "You can have a few hundred bucks, or we'll give you gear." I said, "Man, I'll take the gear. What are you giving?" They said, "We'll give you the laptop you're holding in your hand, and we'll give you a three-tray printer. Or, eight hundred bucks." I said, "$800—by the time management, the Tax Man and the business manager gets done, I've got enough for like a trip to Tower Records. I'll take the laptop and printer" . . . which we use to this day.

♦ **V:** *Those Powerbooks were really expensive when that ad came out—*

♦ **HR:** And they sucked; that particular line was really bad. Thank *god* I didn't pay for that one—it was just a dog; it crashed all the time. I need a computer that goes on the road, and that one was not roadworthy.

♦ **V:** *What do you use now?*

♦ **HR:** I use a G3 Powerbook for the road. And I just got a new G3 desktop: the 400Mhz with a whole bunch of RAM, 9 gig hard drive, a new flat-screen monitor. It's interesting: the new G3 first off didn't support a trackball, they don't support an internal JAZ drive. I go, "Gee, your older computers did more cool things. Tell me how you're advancing. I can't even use a *trackball?!*" They go, "Sorry." So I say, "So whack in an internal JAZ and an internal ZIP." They go, "Uh, you'll have to get an external JAZ." I'm like, "Man, what are you thinking? You're giving these computers to people who do audio and video, and you don't have an internal JAZ drive?!"

The computer I use at my desk is that Power Computing line—those clones. Man, that thing rocks! **I saved all my *per diems* from this one tour, came home and had enough money for a new computer**. I bought that Power Computing 275 and I still use it. It's a warhorse. I had an internal JAZ and ZIP put in; it's great. I just needed a new one for my house so I can work, and you can't get those Power Computing ones any-more—Apple took the rights back—so I bought a G3. But it has a lot more memory; they gave me more gigs than I'll ever need— I'm like the Library of Congress or something.

♦ **V:** *So you have a laptop on the road, and a desktop at home—*

♦ **HR:** Yeah. I like a bigger screen. Also, if I'm working on man-uscripts, I need a bigger screen so I can take an old version of a manuscript and a new one and lay them both out side-by-side, cut and paste, etc. Plus I like a bigger keyboard. My eyes aren't so great, so I don't mind a bigger screen. But this laptop is amaz-ing. It's got the 14" screen, the internal modem, it's wicked fast, it's great. I use my laptop more than I use my home computer because I live on the road.

This year I'm gonna be in L.A. for like another 14 days prob-ably for the rest of this year. October I'm in America, November it's Australia and Europe, December is America, Europe, and then probably India and Katmandu after the tour is over. Then next year, the band album comes out, which means nine months immediately on the road. So that laptop is my primary editing, everything, tool.

♦ **V:** *Do you use an organizing program?*

♦ **HR:** I have a really ancient one called Datebook Pro which they probably haven't made since 1996. It's this archaic calen-dar, and I use it because I have five years of dates on it: every gig, every interview, *everything* logged into that calendar. I would love to get something better, faster and more efficient. Actually, I would like one that goes back into the late '70s. I'd like to estab-lish a timeline of my days in D.C. post-high school, pre-Black

Flag, but this program only goes back to 1991 or so.

I'm trying to work on my own personal chronology. I've been finding all the old gig flyers, figuring out where I was on what day, then bugging people like Ian, trying to figure out the 24 months between Summer '79 to Summer '81 . . . when I went from high school boy to singer of Black Flag. Those two years were the last time I had a "normal" life, and I'm interested in seeing what happened. Because I joined Black Flag and—*that's* an alternative lifestyle, right there! **I was living in my car, living on people's couches before that and going, "Hey, this is intense." All of a sudden I'm shoplifting breakfast, like "Hey! Damn!" and hangin' out with punk rock chicks who were selling fake joints so we could eat hamburgers**—you know, this was all very new to me. And I just wanna try and document those two years. So I've been trying to find software so I can do a day-by-day, month-by-month, year-by-year layout and put in all the gigs, the days of work, when I went here and went there, but I can't find the software. So I've just been doing it . . . *longhand,* or in Microsoft Word.

I'm sure there's some bonehead simple calendar software—I just need one that goes back. [Note: our writer friend David Pescovitz suggested *Now Up-To-Date,* which will do the job.]

♦ **V:** *It's funny, I recently got out my '76, '77 and '78 diaries so I could figure out when I saw which band at the Mabuhay . . .*

♦ **HR:** I want to get it all on a calendar so I can see it all . . . almost make it like a graph or a chart! How many gigs I was going to, and where . . .

I think all of us have that "thing" where we'll always have an understanding with each other: people like you and me and others from that scene, because every town had a cool scene for a minute: S.F., D.C., L.A., whatever. And **those early shows were where you met people whom you still work with to this day. That was where you formed opinions that really defined**

you. It was music that you hear and it still makes your heart swell up.

For me, those early days in D.C. were so *defining*. So you wanna at least remember them somehow, because they were really important. And I know *you* have those memories, too. Because gigs aren't the same anymore. You used to be able to go to gigs and there was *no* violence. It was people who didn't want to be jocks, who didn't want to get in fights, who went to those gigs. And after the show you'd go hang out at someone's house and play the Velvet Underground and drink coffee and *talk* all night.

♦ *V: Yes, because there were hardly any punk records available, and we'd already played those to death.*

♦ **HR:** In D.C. there were like forty punk rockers, and we were all kooks, intellectuals: people who thought, people who wanted to write, people who were poets who would show you their notebook and you'd show them yours, and you'd put on weird music and you'd hang out all night. It wasn't about "Let's go f... this girl!" or "Let's go break something!", it was "Let's go to your house and be totally sleep-deprived and talk some weird surrealist s... until dawn."

♦ *V: And also show each other stuff we'd gotten.*

♦ **HR:** Yeah. I really miss those days. I don't like going to gigs where I'm watching *Mortal Kombat*. Sometimes it's hard for me to justify my audience. I see these people and I'm like, "You know, you are people I would never want to be around: [hoarse Cro-Magnon roar] "F... you! Look, Henry, this dude's a f...in' faggot, man!" and I think, "What am I doing?" **In the early punk rock days, half of your damn friends in the punk rock scene *were* gay—it's the only place they could go. All your friends were misfits and *you* were a misfit too ... and so glad to be it!**

I really miss those days, so I'm trying to at least be able to chart them. I hate going backwards in time; it makes me feel, "Ohmigod, am I having a *crisis* or something? Or, was it truly such a really great time that I want to at least have a handle on it?"

♦ **V:** *Exactly: we want to have a handle on that . . .*

♦ **HR:** That's why I bought a CD-R. I took all my rare tapes from D.C. and burned them onto CD. I went to everybody's house—all the guys from Fugazi, Ian MacKaye—I said, "Give up your tapes. They're all coming to L.A. I'm going to make analog and digital backups." I had people going, "Gawddamnit—stop bugging me!" But you know, when they got like 15 CDs in the mail, of like the second-ever Bad Brains show and *their* first-ever show that they had lost 15 years ago (but *I* still had a copy of), *then* they thanked me: "Man, you did the right thing."

♦ **V:** *I have dozens of tapes I made with a crappy tape recorder held up to the Mabuhay sound system—*

♦ **HR:** All that stuff you should at least make analog dubs of.

collecting, archiving & live tapes

♦ **V:** *Actually, I wanted to transfer them to DAT and put them through a computer noise-reduction program—*

♦ **HR:** Yeah, there's all kinds of software for that now. You can do de-clicking, de-popping, compression, reverb, all right in your computer. It's pretty amazing.

I bought a thousand blank CDs two years ago; I'm now down to 125. (My friend in a music store got them; he had a sale and I bought 500, then he called me: "They just went down a dime each," and I said, "Get me another 500," knowing I'm gonna use them. Because a lot of times, the courtesy thing I do is: I borrow your tape, you get a CD out of the deal. So I put probably 50 Nick Cave shows on CD, all the D.C. stuff like that second-ever Bad Brains show, all the early demos of everybody, and everyone's basement tapes—which they no longer have! They let me borrow them and dub them back in '83, asking, "Why do you want this stuff?" "Because you guys are great and this is important. The music you're making and we're making is important." Every Minutemen show Joe Carducci would tape, I dubbed all those tapes. I saved my food money to buy TDK SA-90s. And I duped them, and all that stuff has gone on CD. I'm meeting people all the time and they say, "Hey man, my friend has this tape of blah-blah-blah" and I go, [abrupt] "GIVE ME HIS PHONE NUMBER!"

I'm trying to make my own library of my history of music: the history *I* think is important. So **I'm kinda doing my own Alan Lomax field recording. I just get tapes from everywhere and archive them: everything from Van Halen to the Germs.** I go to Tower Records regularly and buy lots of cassettes and at the very least make real-time analog dupes. I have a whole bank of very high-quality dubbing decks—you give me a dozen tapes and the next afternoon I'm done! Because I don't want to stress anyone out.

Ian MacKaye just lent me all the original live tapes of his early band, the Teen Idles. Last time I saw him, I said, "Ian, let me borrow 20 of your rarest tapes to take to L.A." and he went, "Man . . ." and I said, "Dude, trust me!" I backed them all up, analog and digital onto CD, cataloged it all, and FedEx'd it back in five days. I lost sleep doing the project but at least it's now on a CD.

First I make an analog dupe off a cassette, then repeat the process with a DAT and go from DAT to CD. So my office is literally milk-crates of cassettes, closets of master tapes, DATS, reference CDs, every rough mix, every other thing. Someone's gotta get this right!

When I play these tapes back, I'm so glad I did it. These tapes are so cool. I can hear people who are now dead, or you meet some guy in a band who tells you, "I've always been looking for this show I did," and I go, "What? Give me your address—I can help you." Penelope Houston from the Avengers called me looking for anything, so now I'm on the lookout. All these people in the '80s who gave me s… for doing this are all calling me now: "Dude, you know that jam we did?" I go, "Yeah. I have it. Gimme a week; I'll get it out to you." This documentation is important for us to do—no one else cares!

I'm eventually hoping that at the end of the day I'll donate my whole archive to a library. I'm not looking to sell any of it. I just want to have access, and give other people access. I would hope that students could use my place. Like you, I've got a ton of books—stuff you're never gonna see again. Records that were made in pressings of only 300. There's 7" 45s that are little gems, and no one can find the master tapes. I've been trying to buy the master tapes of the Negative Trend EP for years, conspiring with Steve DePace of Flipper: "Look, make the deal. I'll put up the money. Buy it and let's put it out." Boy, what a record! I would pay just to be able to back it up.

You know, I backed up and restored Iggy Pop's *Raw Power!* We'd heard that the multi-track had been stolen from England and had ended up in Belgium. We ran into a friend who was in Tuxedo Moon, Steven Brown, and asked him about this and he said, "Yeah, it's in my friend's studio." We went there and I said, "On Iggy's behalf, we'd like it back," and the studio guy said, "Here, take it!" I took it back to Iggy and he went, "What am *I* going to do with it?" so I said, "Then give it to me." I took it to Westlake [in L.A.], we had to bring in another 2-inch 16-track machine (took awhile to track one down), then we made a super-high-quality analog copy as well as two digital copies. We made some rough mixes off the dupe masters and vaulted all of it. Luckily, the master is in good shape, but thank god it's digitally backed up and analog backed up and it's in storage. I said, "Iggy, never give this back to Sony. It got ripped off; they didn't even *know,* and they didn't bother to tell you—screw 'em, it's yours." And he says, "Well, *you* take it," and I said, "Fine, even better." I have this closet that has this air filtration system so everything in it is dry, cool, and clean.

You know Alan Vega from Suicide? I have all of his solo masters. I took them all from New York. He had them stacked like pancakes in his living room, and I saw them and said, "Alan, just give me your tapes." He went, "Okay; take it." I took them to Westlake, we made DATs of all the quarter-inches; cataloged everything in the computer—maybe no one's gonna care, but s… man, I know where it all is, and you can hear 13 different takes of *whatever* because we have it down. That's what it's all about.

PUNK ROCK HISTORY & DOCUMENTATION

This documentation is my hobby: photos—if it's from music I'm interested in, people I'm interested in —I keep all the letters, all the emails, faxes, whatever. Otherwise, there's this beautiful part of history that just gets covered up by the Danielle Steels and the Bruce Willises of the world . . . **this really *cool* history gets covered over by a lot of high-sugar fluff . . .**

♦ *V: My fantasy is to put an incredible counterculture archive free on the Net, accessible to anyone who wants to download it.*

♦ **HR:** Yeah! It would be great to have a hands-on thing where you pay three bucks to get in, and you can Xerox, and there are dupe masters you can play, there are letters you can view from who to who, there are old fanzines . . . *ACCESS TO INFORMATION.* At least have a situation where you could make enough money to keep it open and keep yourself going . . . be able to pay a curator to curate.

♦ *V: True; it would be bad to miss a month's payment to your server and suddenly this whole site just disappears—*

♦ **HR:** Yeah, I spend a lot of my own money on this documentation . . . buying all this stereo gear for duping, endless mountains of blank tape, blank CDs, postage—basically *paying* to preserve other people's work! It's worth it to me, and it's great when you uncover some really cool vein of stuff, like you meet someone from the band: "Man, I got eighty of those!" I go, "Oh, boy!"

This one guy was working on a Lenny Bruce project; he's the one who had to bounce all these quarter-inch tapes and cassettes and whatever onto DAT. He's got over 100 hours of Lenny Bruce. I told him, "You know, all I need is a week with those tapes. I would really like to back them all up. And I'll have my lawyer put it in writing that they'll never go anywhere." He said, "You want to hear a hundred hours?" and I said, "Yes, I want to hear *two hundred* hours! I mean, Lenny Bruce is one of my heroes. I want to *know."* Or, "The next time you're rolling one of those tapes, let me come over and sit in the corner. Whatever. *GET ME TO THE TAPES!"*

♦ *V: It was my idea to put on the Web the most massive counterculture history I could think of, going back to Lenny Bruce, Lord Buckley and Buster Keaton before him and—*

♦ **HR:** I was about to say Charlie Chaplin; he's another one who was punk.

♦ *V: Especially in the movie* Modern Times, *his critique of the factory system. You may not like every single Chaplin movie, but—*

♦ **HR: There are a lot of people who had these great moments: a lot of writers with a bunch of bad books and two good ones. But those two good ones are so great** . . .

♦ *V: It's amazing when you can actually meet (and even publish) writers who influenced you when you were young. One of my biggest influences was* Those About To Die, *a history of the Roman games by Daniel P. Mannix. It was such a thrill to be able to actually spend a week with Mannix on his farm; plus, I got to republish some of his books. J.G. Ballard is another such writer—*

♦ **HR:** A girl I was going out with earlier this year really loved J.G. Ballard. She was Irish and living in England and was saying, "I read this book, and that book" (naming about four titles) and

I went, "Wait a minute, there's a whole bunch more" and I showed her a book you gave me—a million years ago you gave me some of his books and I still have them all. She went, "What are *these?*" and I realized, "They must all be out of print." So I think he's got titles that are now rare, like the ones that were basically falling apart when you gave them to me. They were dime store novels—

♦ *V: Pulps, like* The Drought. *St. Martins recently reprinted some of his books, but who knows how long they'll stay in print. Books are like magazines—if you see something you like, you'd better grab it immediately.*

♦ **HR:** What's really funny is, my band are all record fanatics; we hit every record store—I mean, we wear each other out on trivia; we're just into it. And we have found in the last few years that the most collectible thing now is *CDs!* Because record companies put out the wrong stuff all the time. They put out the wrong version of Sly Stone's "Fresh" album—the entire album in sequence: alternate takes! Sly heard it and hit the roof, and the record company said "Whoops!" and pulled it. We managed to get one, so of course I duped it (went from CD to CD).

There are Miles Davis CDs that came out with the wrong takes . . . all kinds of mistakes like that! Or just cool CDs by the Meters, Sam and Dave—stuff that came out for a minute and went out-of-print. Most Chuck Berry is out of print! And every once in a while you find those old MCA CDs from like '87, and they're rare! Who woulda thought that CDs would become rare? There's all kinds of music like that . . . and it's fun. So you go out in the middle of nowhere and all of a sudden you hear one of the guys in the band going, "YES!"—he just scored some compact disc that is now rare, like a stamp.

I'm used to vinyl; I'm used to paying way too much for like Beatles vinyl or what have you. But finding CDs that are rare is amazing. Because record companies would put it out and go, "Whoops—it didn't sell!" and they'd just delete it. Big bands, too. Of course, small labels often put out a thousand copies of something and then just didn't bother anymore.

There's even stuff by bands the size of Motorhead that are really rare records. If you see that rare Motorhead CD and you're halfway interested, you pay your $5.99 and get it used because you're never gonna see it again. It's kinda cool. And it's interesting how stuff really does come and go—you gotta grab it!

♦ *V: I'd heard about this, but hadn't really focused on the topic of rare CDs. It's funny you mentioned the Meters. I used to love the Meters, and have their early albums. I don't have 45s, but . . .*

♦ **HR:** If you have the Warner Bros. *Rejuvenation* or one called *Cabbage Alley*—

♦ *V: Oh yeah, I have that—*

♦ **HR:** That is worth a fuckin' ton. Hundreds.

♦ *V: I was really into them, before punk—*

♦ **HR:** Well, they're really good. They're good now.

♦ *V: The drummer, Zigaboo Modeliste, lives here in the Bay Area. You can see him play for free at Pier 23 cafe. Years ago he and Earl Palmer were almost my favorite drummers. I used to like these really spare, crisp drummers like Eddie Blackwell (when he played with Don Cherry)—*

♦ **HR: Eddie Blackwell has way more balls than any punk rocker—talk about playing music to starve by?!** Him, Albert Ayler, Don Cherry, all those guys are like "Hello. Starve me to death." They went for the music first. All died prestigious, legendary, and probably *skinnt.* Don Cherry probably did okay because he survived, but poor Albert tossed himself into the East River. Maybe he had religion issues; I don't know, but . . . Yeah!

There's vinyl that commands massive amounts of money: Meters, any good condition Beatles mono (hundreds of dollars), Doowop 45s, a lotta country 45s—ridiculous! And you find them—every once in a while you find something for $3.99 and you eBay it for a hundred bucks.

The guys in my band are eBay-happy; they go to every record

store and they're finding like P-Funk 45s, Miles Davis jukebox 45s and they eBay the stuff—they support themselves by that! They get in their car and go on buying trips; garage sales: Granny is dumping out her attic, she just uncovered her old husband's 78s . . . you can get money for every Fats Waller 78 or Duke Ellington 10" you can find: *Bank!* It's all pricey now.

You'd be surprised at how much stuff is worth, even punk rock stuff. I've never gone on eBay; I've heard about it. I've heard stuff signed by me fetches quite a sum; the guys in the band say, "Yeah, autographed books by you just go!"

We just did a show in West Virginia; it got eBayed and got sold for $91!

♦ **V:** *What do you mean?*

♦ **HR:** A copy of the video! It was probably made by a handheld mini-DV digicam from the back of this club we were in: sounds like hell, looks like jittery *pogo-cam*—who knows?

♦ **V:** *Oh, so there's a whole market for bootleg videos shot surreptitiously in clubs—*

COLLECTIBLES and BOOTLEGS

♦ **HR:** Are you kidding? I've got a ton of them. Whenever I go to Japan I go to the bootleg video store, grab like five of the ones they did of me, show them to the clerk and he gets terrified and I go, "Okay, I'd like one each of all my stuff" and they just give me a paper bag and point at the store, like "Take whatever you want—don't hit me!" I take one of each of my thing (I figure that's fair) and I grab two or three other ones. I heard that Metallica cleaned out this store one time. There were like fifty different Metallica videos and the guy said, "Take whatever you want," and they said "Okay, pack up the crates!" and the road crew took like *one* of everything in the store.

I find stuff all the time at the Japanese bootleg stores. **There are whole stores in Shinjuku that are nothing but bootlegs. Like not one legit CD in the store.** And there are specialty shops. There's one shop that's nothing but "British Invasion." Then there's a shop: one wall is Dylan, one wall is Zeppelin, and one wall is Clapton-Beck-Hendrix—you know, guitar heroes. The back is Beatles . . . whatever. And it's amazing! You walk out of there with your VISA card just expiring!

I *save* for Japan. If I know I'm going, I just start salting it away. Last time I was there I had to buy an extra suitcase for all the CDs I found. Captain Beyond live CDs! Like, five different Black Flag CDs of gigs I didn't even remember *doing*. Stuff like that. A radio session I never even got to hear—I found it on CD in Tokyo. Yeah . . . fascinating.

I have probably over 75 Beatles bootleg CDs. I have that many Hendrix ones—there's a whole market, and it's good stuff, too. The Beatles stuff is amazing. Someone broke into the EMI vaults and just took everything and it's waxed onto CD: *every* alternate take, every conversation—it's mind-boggling. It's perfect sound quality; it's like Rykodisc put it out or something. And **to hear Paul McCartney sing off-key is just amazing. Like, he made a *mistake?!*** It's incredible. Yeah, there's a whole bunch of that. I'm sure that eventually there'll be bootleg *books* too: stuff you can't get anymore, so there'll be a demand.

A lot of record labels are seeing gold in their back catalog. The reissue market has never been bigger: repackaging old stuff, making it look really cool. **For Duke Ellington's centennial they repackaged Duke 'til he probably came out of the grave and told them to quit!** I bought a lot of it because it contained unreleased stuff—I *love* Duke Ellington. So they probably got three or four hundred dollars off me! They probably got a few hundred bucks off me when Sinatra died, too. All the remasters of the alternates, with extra cuts—I'm there! I loved that guy.

♦ **V:** *There's amazing technology available now for improving old recordings as well as making new ones. I read how the producers spliced together hundreds of takes to make a "perfect" Whitney Houston Number One hit.*

♦ **HR:** Oh, sure. My old drummer was down the hall from Mariah Carey, who was doing her vocals on 64-track digital. And she does her own comping. She kicks everyone out of the studio, goes in the vocal booth, and she comps her own vocals. It's all digital: you press a button and you are recording. She does a vocal, then hits another track, does a verse, hits another track, does a line, does a word, and the producers comp from thirty or more vocal takes.

Now, *I'm* comped. I'll do like three vocal takes of a song, and if I really *rock* that one verse, and a chorus from over there sounds good—well, I've comped from a couple of different vocal takes—that's common. But when you're comping from thirty tracks, and you're splicing fractions of a word together, and then processing it through computers, you're not getting *music*, you're getting this "thing." Whatever it is, it's no longer music; it's no longer human. When it enters the digital domain; there's no longer a human on that tape—it's literally a computer rendering of an analog signal. That's why all the vinyl-heads go, "Look, *f...* *you*, there's no one on your CD. There are no humans on your CD." And they're right, if you want to get technical.

♦ **V:** *You're using the word "comp"—what does it mean?*

♦ **HR:** "Comp" is short for "composite"; the shortened active verb for "to make a composite" is "to comp." **When you take one take of a song and bounce it over to the other take—that's called comping a vocal.** So if Whitney Houston is doing 60 takes, they're doing 60 separate tracks and if she said "the" really good on take 20 and she sang "I will always love you" really well on take 38, then they whack all that together in Pro Tools. They comp everything now. They comp bass lines, vocals; different takes of a song. But that's not *new:* the Beatles were comped, left and right. Even on a "normal" record, you can hear some really bad edits. Like on "Help" and albums like that, you hear one take at one speed and in the middle of one chorus suddenly it's going at another speed and the cymbal sound is different—that's George Martin trying to get "one take" out of these guys.

♦ *V: Even though they only had four tracks back then, at the most—*

♦ **HR:** Oh yeah. He would be grafting on . . . if you hear the bootlegs, you hear him doing one verse; he cuts it into the middle . . . or has them do the outro again, then he edits it on. Sometimes if the edit is good, you can't hear the tape splice. With Pro Tools you definitely can't hear it; it's seamless. It's digital; you just connect one thing to another; there is no seam. Numbers don't know a seam, they just read the information. And it's handy. Like **when I do my talking records now, I throw it all into Pro Tools and get rid of the "umms" and the "ah-ha's"—I sound like one concise motherf...er!** The gig may have been this rambling stewpot of verbiage, whereas on the CD I sound like I'm *slammin'!* I sound like I'm reading from a script and my wit is oh so razor sharp—

♦ *V: That's good—*

♦ **HR:** Oh yeah! You basically just remove the *schmoot* for the listener so they can get the damn point I was trying to make.

♦ *V: That's what I try to do with interviews: make them as concise as possible without removing the speaker's idiosyncratic style—*

♦ **HR:** Yeah; you don't want to take them out of context. *I* interview people, for magazines and whatnot, and sometimes I clean their language up. Like when I interviewed John Lee Hooker, he talks in a real . . . *rural* way.

♦ *V: A super-accurate transcription would probably make people disrespect him—*

♦ **HR:** Exactly. So, I don't white-ize it, nor do I sanitize it, I just kinda make the sentences a little stronger. I did that with Jerry Lee Lewis. Here's a guy who never even knew what MTV was until I took him *in* to MTV, to interview him. I've interviewed him a couple of times; I've been to his house . . . and he's not *dumb,* by any stretch of the imagination, but when he talks, he's a man from Mississippi, and some of the sentences . . . you can go, "Well, *that's* an interesting way to use a verb. How about we just move that to the back of the sentence, so it's more active instead of passive?" I would just do stuff like that every once in a while.

♦ *V: I do things like that, so I started sending people edited transcripts—*

♦**HR:** I just *do* it. And you know, it's so minute that the artist reading his own interview wouldn't even notice; he'd think, "*MAN!* I was *ON* that day!" Because I want the *reader* to get it, and not go, "Oh, ha ha ha," but rather go, "Wow, that's cool!" I don't change the point the guy's trying to make, I'm talking about a word here or a word there. But if every "ing" word is "in' ", you just get tired of looking at that.

♦ *V: You have to almost do a "translation" from spoken word to written word—*

INTERVIEWS, EDITING & PUBLISHING

♦**HR:** Yeah, I do that so it ends up being more readable than the actual transcription, which is like, "Okay, thanks for the field recording—on paper. Can you please help me translate this?" I do it, just so you can get the info and maybe become *interested* in the guy.

♦ *V: Exactly. We try to never interview people we don't like.*

♦**HR:** Yeah; I wouldn't want to be in a position of having to interview someone I didn't like, because I always want to be sympathetic. I always wanna be on *their* side. I try to put them in the best light. I did a whole book with a lot of interviews in it:

Do I Come Here Often? I interviewed Isaac Hayes, Jerry Lee Lewis, David Lee Roth, Roky Erickson, John Lee Hooker—it's cool. David Lee Roth—he's fine on his own. The guy *knows* how to do an interview. **But John Lee Hooker? He'll talk to you, but he doesn't want to "do an interview." And so he begrudgingly kind of grunts and gives you these very laconic replies.** Like I asked him, "You ever meet Jimi Hendrix?" and he's kinda funny; he goes, "NO. Who's that man at the crossroads?" I go, "Robert Johnson." He said, "*Yeah!* I never did meet him neither." He talks like that, and you have to kinda go, "Okay." So I had him say, "Who's that man who wrote 'At the Crossroads'?" I changed it so the reader would get what he meant, and then maybe you've turned someone on to John Lee Hooker *and* Robert Johnson—which is no bad place to be . . .

♦ *V: You're trying to inspire people—*

♦ **HR:** Yeah, and communicate . . . get it across. Because when you talk to someone, you translate anyway. You know, when you meet someone from Germany, and they're speaking the best English they can, you're hearing it and immediately you're putting it through a filter, and you're flipping the verb and you're understanding it *anyhow.*

♦ *V: That happens with everyone, on some level or other—*

♦ **HR:** It's your perception, anyway. But especially, if you meet a lot of people . . . I meet people in every country I go to. I talk to people all the time. So when you're in a place like Russia, these people are burning lean tissue trying to tell you how much they love your music. But *English*—they don't speak English! So they're like, "Uh, much liking ya" translates to "I like your music!"

One of the best letters I ever got was from a guy named Igor Ivan. He said, **"I have some take photos of you 2 X" (like, "the two times you played in Prague"), "but fatball technologist be insane,"** which means: the guy at the print shop ruined the film. I just loved that sentence! Man, that's so cool:

obviously, the guy at Rite-Aid screwed up and the film came back dark, you know. But what a way to say it!

♦ **V:** *Right; you can enjoy original language anywhere you can find it—*

♦ **HR:** Yeah. My old roommate was talking to a Korean fellow—this was in the early '90s—and she said, "I had the greatest conversation today. This guy told me that his friend didn't have his s… together, and what he said was, "My friend, his s… is all apart." We just started using it: "Oh Man, his s…'s all apart." Whaddaya mean? "His s…'s not together." "Oh dude—that's so cool!" Or, **in this one Japanese hotel, by the sink it said, "Be drinkable." And that became our phrase for "Deal with it"**: "There's no soundcheck today!" "Hey, be drinkable"—you know, deal with it, be liquid, be cool, flow with it. It's perfect.

♦ **V:** *You started publishing as a labor of love, yet how successful did it become?*

♦ **HR:** Well, for several years we turned a profit and then we had some bad luck with some photo books we made that were seriously cost-intensive, like a couple hundred thousand dollars for a print run . . . that stiffed. Our Led Zeppelin photo book—we just climbed out of debt last year from that; lost over $100,000. And for a company our size to lose a hundred grand—that might as well just have blown us up. So that single book made me think that Jimmy Page probably really *is* the Devil! He took one of the books, actually, and wrote me a letter inside the opening page: "Man, it's a great book; thanks a lot" and gave it back to me, like, "Thanks." That single book, and some other photo books we did which were very beautiful, didn't sell. And they cost me so much money.

♦ **V:** *Didn't you do one on Heavy Metal?*

♦ **HR:** We did a Metallica photo book. That actually sold out its print run; it did okay. We basically broke even. But our book by Stephanie Chernikowski; all her great punk rock shots at CBGBs, like early shots of the Cramps, Sid Vicious, Johnny

Lydon, Tom Verlaine, Talking Heads, Suicide, Ramones—just *godhead* photos—beautiful book, great shots of Warhol, you name it, they're all in it, beautiful black-and-white—it stiffed. We had to put them on Broadway [NYC] on those rickety tables where they sell all the ten-pound art books for five bucks.

♦ **V:** *You had to remainder them. How much do they give you?*

♦ **HR:** *Dick.* You have a book that was retailing for $29, you're now selling it for $14.50. Our Zeppelin book was retailing for $100, we put it back into the stores for $24.95. So basically, we're only losing $8 a book instead of $19. **It was a lose-lose proposition: you could lose a little *less*.** And it was such a weird position to be in: "Either we'll take your spleen and your lung, or we'll just take two fingers." "Uhh…take the two fingers! Wow, what a good deal! Boy, we were lucky!"

Basically, you get the books taken off your hands—you get nothing. Unfortunately, from a marketing standpoint those books were very poorly researched. I really let people on my staff have too much responsibility. With the most cursory, rudimentary little bit of business research, we never would have put out the Zeppelin book. If we'd just looked at what other Zeppelin books were doing, what photo books do in general, you find out **no one makes money on photo books. They're gestures; they're made by the Guggenheim as a write-off.** No one makes money on photo books, and we put out like four without even thinking. Because I loved 'em: they're beautiful books! Those who bought them said, "Man, that thing is great!" and I'm like, "Thank you for getting that book—you and forty other people!" We made them really nice, used really good paper, they all went off to Hong Kong, and we lost our ass. It's those photo books I've been digging myself out from until last year.

In the meantime, my other titles that aren't "me" don't sell much . . . little poetry books . . . you do a print run for X, and you end up losing .7X on it: "Wow, that's great! Uh, let's learn a lesson here." And I love these writers and I'd like to do their next book—I just can't afford it. I think it's bad business to keep running up the opportunities to lose another seven grand. And in a way I feel like I'm failing, in that I *wasn't* able to sell these books, but you know, we took out a lot of ads. We put out a lot of flyers. We gave away a lot of little inserts and stuff. We had PGW. It's not like you can't get to the books—people just aren't interested. And some of the artists are pissed: "Hey, how come—?" "Look . . . get real. This is how it is."

You could probably make more money if you put out some movie star's crappy poetry.

♦ *V: Oh yeah, like the book by Jewel—*

♦ **HR:** Right. If you had the Jewel book; if you had the Hootie & the Blowfish or Eddie Vedder lyric book five years ago, you could have bought Uruguay. And good reviews don't seem to matter, either. One of the last books we put out, *The Cowardice of Amnesia,* was by Ellyn Maybe, one of the coolest poets you'll ever read or see perform—she's magic. She got every wet-dream review ever. Like, she's a woman—they love her; Exene championed her; everyone loves this woman. She does these poetry slams; everyone is in love with Ellyn at the end of the show. She's wonderful. Her books sold dick. And her book is so good, too. And I hate going up to her saying, "Hi Ellyn, uh, you're never gonna recoup . . . I can't *give* these books away." And she's so good—you see her, you're a fan.

So do we try and get her in front of more people? Maybe. But *no one* goes to poetry readings—not even for the big people. Even if you're Ginsberg, it's still: Beyond Baroque [small L.A. arts center]. It's still a polite group of fifty people and you'll sell twelve books after that show. And they love you, too—*that's* your target audience. They're all substitute school teachers—they don't have any money. They're still wearing corduroys, driving an old Charger . . . it's tough. And so we just stopped.

It broke my heart to stop making books; to say, "Yeah, we're not making them right now." And for me it's always, "We're not making them right *now.*" Because if Don Bajema [San Francisco author] squeezes out another manuscript, well, I'm gonna put it out. Because it's *Don!* God, he's done two beautiful books for us—neither one made any money, but boy are they good, especially the second one. He's amazing. And I'm kind of duty-bound to "Serve The Truth" in that way; to put it out. But it's really hard to go and lose that money; it's not like it's hung on trees for me to grab. I'm going out and "doing it" onstage to earn money to put out these books, and I just kinda got worn out from running around the track, y'know.

I'm putting out all these books, yet I don't have a car. My manager begged me: "As an experiment, how about just a year of, like, getting something for yourself? Let's get you a car. Let's buy you a bed." I've only had a bed for eight months. Even when I met you, years ago, I didn't have a bed. I slept on a futon on the floor or on a couch, wherever. And my manager said, "Wait a minute, stop being Mother Theresa for a second. Let's get you a car, a place to live—it's not like you don't work hard enough." And I said, very begrudgingly, "Okay." And so I did all that. And it's cool.

♦ *V: Did any of your spoken-word CD series sell at all?*

♦**HR:** Mine sold great: 50-75,000. And the overhead for those records, well, I'm taping live shows, it's two days in the studio of Pro Tooling and the record's done.

♦ *V: Can't you do that Pro Tools work at home?*

♦**HR:** No . . . but I can now, with the new computer I got with all the gigabytes—plus, it's easy software, too. While I was in the studio, the engineer was kinda moping along, so I just watched him for ten minutes and said, "Let *me* do this." I started doing it. It's cut-and-paste, pretty easy. There are a lot of little nuances to it, like cross-fades and whatnot, but it's not unlearnable. I mean, the guy I was working with—if *he* can learn it, I can learn it— that's for sure! That dude was totally entry-level.

Great Records That
Don't Sell . . .

♦ **V:** *That phrase "totally entry-level" seems to describe most of the population now; they don't know the most elementary history or culture—*

♦ **HR:** And we're suffering for it. Guns N' Roses invented rock-'n'roll, Cameron Diaz is the first beautiful woman in a movie—that's all you need to know!

Exene's talking record, Hubert Selby's talking record, stiffed—and they're both great. Exene's thing is magic—no one cares. Selby's thing—he's *Hubert Selby;* it's awesome, and those who did buy it loved it. Who cares? No one cares. So I lost money on that, lost money on all my little jazz records, lost a ton of money on my Alan Vega record (his electronic, synthesizer things: *Deuce Avenue, New Raceion*) . . . I put up a chunk of dough to put out his last studio record which is like, amazing . . . I lost all the money, and then some. Like, enough to where I still have to *steady* myself when I remember the figure . . . but you know, I still play the record, and it's great. I just wish I could have gotten more than 400 people to agree with me!

When you see what people *do* buy, I think, "Man—I've got something so much better that I wanna give you." But all that stuff pretty much stiffed.

As far as my back catalog goes, **one of my books, a book of *fake* letters to me written by a friend of mine, made money!** He had my name on it; my picture's on the front, and that did fine—and the guy's a great writer, he's wickedly funny.

I don't know if you know the Ducks' Breath Mystery Theater, but Merle Kessler, the Ian Shoales character, does a long-running thing on NPR called "I Gotta Go." It's a 90-second, high-speed rant, "The thing I hate about supermarkets . . ."—wickedly funny, devastating humor which he caps with, "I gotta go." We did an "I Gotta Go" CD which is just *crippling*, as well as an "I Gotta Go" book which is the best of the "I Gotta Go's" from '84 to two years ago. It's great, it's flawless, it should have been one of those things that every dickhead buys from the airplane shop before he gets on the plane. It's what P.J. O'Rourke wishes he could be. And it sold *nothing*. Except that the people who *did* buy it went, "Man, he's a genius." I went, "Thank you—get your sister to buy one too." We lost money on Merle. And it breaks my heart.

♦ **V:** *You'd think that because he was on NPR, it would have sold.*

♦ **HR:** Yeah. Coyle & Sharpe; we eventually sold out the run, but . . . All that stuff I've actually been pretty unsuccessful with, unfortunately. Besides my personal titles, I never had anything go like your *Modern Primitives* book. I was kinda going a smaller route; you're never gonna sell a bunch of poetry books by anybody—

♦ **V:** *Unless it's* Howl; *that's keeping City Lights alive.*

♦ **HR:** Well, you know I think that's one of the best pieces of American literature ever. I've tried to write my own version a couple of times!

♦ **V:** *That's a great idea; we need a new* Howl—

♦ **HR:** I wrote a thing called "Everything" in a book of mine called *Eye Scream*. It's my version of just inhaling America, and exhaling my wounded, jaundiced air onto the page. There's like one last wail—it's like a *howl*. And I wrote it for two years. I did it in a book, and I also did a double CD—it took two CDs to read the whole piece. And I got Rashied Ali, Coltrane's last drummer, and Charles Gayle, saxophone player, to do duets—that was the music that would go in and out of both CDs. I stuck a microphone out of the studio window at Houston and Broadway in New York and we recorded rush hour. **So you hear rush hour traffic with me reading over it, with these incredible sax and**

drum duets. It sounds great. In fact we did it live two times, me and Charles. We did it in Europe, and in Chicago for the ABA [American Booksellers Association convention] . . . and it *stiffed!*

I did an audio book of *Black Coffee Blues*—I think *that* did okay, because the book does so well. But, you know [sighs] . . . *aggravating.*

I did a spoken-word double CD of *Get In The Van,* the Black Flag book—it won a Grammy . . . but it *stiffed.* It got a lot of great reviews and a lot of great letters, but, like, Time-Warner went out of business doing audio books, and I got the title back. So someday I may foolishly re-release it to non-applause: the sound of no hand clapping, as opposed to two—or even one.

♦ **V:** *Hey, that could be an "Internet Only" special!*

♦ **HR:** Well, you know, that'd be the way to go. In fact, we just did our first "Internet Only" spoken CD—it came out three weeks ago, and it's selling like hotcakes.

♦ **V:** *People love rare and autographed things—*

♦ **HR:** Well, like I told you, we go on tour, I come home with like a hundred tour posters. I came home with 150 Australian tour posters from my tour earlier this year, and I signed them all, and they lasted just a few days. We went, **"Ohmigod—let's make posters!" Like, how are we going to keep the lights on in this place?** We're just hoping that from one of those poster sales someone may go, "Hey, what the hell—let's buy a *book!*" I'm hoping this makes them buy a book . . . maybe *not* of me, maybe one of our poets, maybe Don Bajema. Everyone who reads Don loves Don. If they can get to the book they go, "Man, that dude Don Bajema is just amazing!" I'm like, "Huh . . . thank you! (You caught on.)"

♦ **V:** *I'm thinking of putting out a line of quotations books, because they're shorter and easier to digest.*

♦ **HR:** And they don't necessarily have to be from books, either. The rich, the famous, the infamous, and just the really cool . . . people whose names you *don't* know saying something really great. There's a very rare book I found for ten dollars—a hardback edition of the *Notes of F. Scott Fitzgerald,* and it's worth about fifty bucks. I love F. Scott; he's one of my heroes. He made copious notes, like 15-page character descriptions. He was really into this and kept these ledgers—book upon book of notes. And these are everything from little bits of dialogue to funny one-liners to just aphorisms, and it is great reading.

♦ *V: I love insider material like that, which illuminates the creative process—*

♦ **HR:** Sure. A great quote: **"Great art is a great man's contempt for small art." Just reading that one line put such a *fire* under me to be a better writer, singer, whatever** . . . where you can take "I want to be really good" but you can turn it into *contempt for the bulls---*. It's a rallying cry! It's such a beautiful phrase.

♦ *V: I read* The Great Gatsby *and* Tender Is the Night *ages ago—*

♦ **HR:** Find any collection of his short stories. There's a new $15 edition out: *The Short Stories of F. Scott Fitzgerald: A New Collection.* I've never read anyone with a better gift for dialogue. The short stories are just brilliant; they're from the '30s and '40s—it's a different time. It's handholding, no sex before marriage, guys waiting six months just to have a date with a girl — it's really painfully romantic. And there's a lot of heavy alcoholism and death in his writing. He's basing it on his own life: wife in the loony bin, his own alcoholism, and this painful genius that he possessed. I mean flat-out literary *god.*

I've been reading Fitzgerald, Hemingway and Thomas Wolfe for the last two and a half years fairly exclusively. Thomas Wolfe—that'll take you two years to read. **He died at age thirty-eight and wrote so much. His books of letters are like more than I've ever written all put together!** That's all he did: *he wrote and he died.* I've been reading him, and rereading Hemingway, and tearing through all the F. Scott, and it's been a great ride.

♦ **V:** *I've been reading Nabokov—English was his second language—and he seems to be a real genius—*

♦ **HR:** Yup.

♦ **V:** *And I've been rereading Charles Willeford, who has great dialogue, idiosyncratic characterization and astounding plotting.*

♦ **HR:** It's amazing how some people can weave a tale—even a guy like James Ellroy. I love his books; they're so much fun.

♦ **V:** *Even though he's popular—*

♦ **HR:** Yeah! But you know, sometimes people are popular because they're really f---in' good. I read *anything* Ellroy puts out, because it's just a damn good time. And he's a mean muthaf----a; he does whatever he wants.

♦ **V:** *I saw the film on him—*

♦ **HR:** *James Ellroy: Demon Dog of American Crime Fiction* [1998]. He's not a friendly guy; he's really prickly. He hates rock musicians. And apparently all these rockers read his stuff. I've seen him in interviews go, **"All these f---in' rock bands come up to me and say, 'I love your stuff,' and they tell me they're in a rock band and I tell them to leave me alone or I'll have my dog bite them!"** You look at this guy: half G. Gordon Liddy, half ex-drug addict/lunatic. But boy, he writes a damn good book.

I like Dominick Dunne too: *A Season In Purgatory*—what a great read! His fictional take on O.J. Simpson, *Another City Not My Own:* brilliant! He can really write; his magazine articles are great—he's fun. I save his books for the Trans-Atlantic, Trans-Pacific flights. He makes eight hours go right by. So does Michael Crichton. Certain guys I read. Because you can't read a Samuel Beckett novel for two hours—I've tried. I'll sit there wrestling with *Molloy* or *Malone* . . . and I *love* Beckett—he's funny, he's wicked . . . but it just wears me out!

I love the Russians; I love Dostoyevsky, but after ten pages I'm winded, because it's so heavy I need a break. I was taking a break from reading Thomas Wolfe by reading F. Scott, and F. Scott got so neurotic I was having to take a break from him by reading Hemingway, which is like jumping into cold water! "I hit him. He fell. It was a good day"—all that bulls---. [laughs] Simple declarative sentences. But anyway, I should jam; I have to be up in a few hours. Did you get your questions answered?

♦ **V:** *Yes, more or less.*

♦ **HR:** It is the truth; I hate to admit it: my publishing has basically been a grand failure, financially. But in my own defense, I don't think that is solely how it should be judged. I think the "art" should also have a place, because that is why we started the whole thing in the first place. **It was *never* about money; it was always about the art. And just because it didn't work financially doesn't mean the art wasn't good.**

Planet Joe . . .

♦ **V:** *I was really glad you published the book by Joe Cole,* Planet Joe—

♦ **HR:** Which actually . . . believe it or not, I guess because he was my friend and he was murdered [during a hold-up of Henry and Joe in Venice, California] makes it a little bit more interesting, but his book sells like hotcakes, and for years.

♦ **V:** *He was such a sweet guy. Can't remember if he stayed at my house or not—*

♦ **HR:** He always took all my RE/Search stuff into his room and read it. He was well into your trip. Definitely gave you respect. Yeah, an interesting guy, a real different individual. Sonic Youth did a couple songs about him on their record that came out right after he died. Hole dedicated their first album to him. A lot of people like that gave him respect. He was really different; he was a kook! One of those guys, like, "Where do you come from?"

A biography of Joe Cole would be interesting. He had a very intriguing upbringing. His father was Dennis Cole, the sleazy TV actor. His stepmother was Jacqueline Smith of Charlie's

Angels. Joe used to tell stories, like, "I'd come home from like, eleventh grade, and there's Heather Locklear toweling off. My dad had just finished f---ing her . . . I come home from school and there's Cher coked out on my couch. He f---ed everyone in the *Knott's Landing* cast, everyone in the *Dallas* cast"—I mean, that was Dennis Cole! Just womanizing.

In the '70s and early '80s, before AIDS, he was just wheelin' and dealin'. Total pussy hound. And nailin' it, too: the parade. And Joe as a kid had Bruce Lee's autograph when he was the Green Hornet; went to the Hefner mansion all the time with his dad as a kid. Fascinating stories . . . which he just kinda tossed off without any affectation—he wasn't bragging. You'd watch *Apocalypse Now* with Joe, and see the chick coming out of the helicopter with Bill Graham, and Joe totally deadpan would say, "He f---ed *her* . . . *her* . . . but not her." "Joe, you're blowin' my mind!" "Yup! That's my dad!"

Joe had a helluva take on life because he saw all this weird s---; by the time he was sixteen, he had seen *so much* . . . kinda like chemical excess. When I first met his dad, he was fifty or something and was with this 19-year-old moron Canadian stripper. He introduced her [deep stage voice]: "Boys, this is Candy!" We're like, *ohmigod*. And she went [chirpy voice], "Hi!" They left and I said, "Joe . . ." and he went, "Yeah; my dad's Satan!" I said, "Damn; that was gross!" and he said, "Yeah! Welcome to hell!"

We were at his dad's Beverly Hills house and it is just the grossest leather, silver, big rug, seventies, frosted-hair palace. Medallions and chest hair and cologne and hair dye . . . unbelievable. His dad was out of a TV show, literally. And he's like [deep voice], "Hi, Henry!" "Hey man, what's happening? Hail Satan." The guy was like surreal, so whenever you laid a weird vibe on him, he was cool.

Manson wrote to Joe all the time. Joe originally wrote Charlie a letter (you can look up any convict's number and address):

"Hey, my name's Joe Cole. I'm kickin' it here in L.A. I live in hell. How's it for you?" They had a massive correspondence for years. I have it all; all the letters he wrote Joe: 20, 30 letters . . . multi-page. Joe connected with people like that. Like there'd be some weird guy gibbering to himself on the street, some homeless guy totally out of his mind . . .within minutes, him and Joe are in deep conversation, totally bonded. "Hey Joe, how'd you do that?" and he'd go, "What do you mean? We're from the same planet." Like, "Damn, I guess you are."

I never met a guy like him. And so, when he died, there were a lot of people like me who were really kinda blown away. It was a real tragedy. But his book is a really good read. It's totally psychedelic. Halfway through the book he took his first-ever hit of acid; the book is such a "Young Person's Guide to Lysergic Diethylamide." And it's right in the middle of a Black Flag tour, so you get all the day-to-day tour feel—

♦ *V: Maybe that helped sell it.*

♦ **HR:** Yeah, it has Black Flag, it has Henry Rollins in it—and the guy was murdered. And a picture of me and Joe on the back of the book. Every Rollins fan has it.

♦ *V: Well, all those factors add up to help it sell—*

♦ **HR:** But on its own, it's a helluva of a read. I get people all the time telling me how much they love that book: "When are you going to release *Planet Joe #2?* Is there any more?" I go, "Yeah!" I don't think I can sit there and edit it down, though. I can't go there. But it's a great read.

Okay, I gotta go—tomorrow morning I have to get up and do a PSA [public service announcement] for an anti-tobacco campaign, then I gotta go across the street and finish this album. I'll be going up North within the next three or four months, so I'll see you soon, I'm sure. Really great to talk to you. ♦ ♦ ♦

BOOK RECOMMENDATIONS

Here are some writers who mean a lot to me:

NELSON ALGREN: Mostly known for his books *Man with a Golden Arm* and *Walk on the Wild Side*. Chicago writer. My favorite book of his is very hard to find these days—until it comes back in print. It's called *Somebody in Boots* and it's about the Depression. It was written six years before Steinbeck's *Grapes of Wrath* and I think it's a better book. Algren's short story collection *The Neon Wilderness* is a great read as well.

FERDINAND CELINE: I like his power and humor. He didn't have a lot to laugh about living in France through WWI and WWII. He's brilliant. Thankfully, most of his work is in print. Some titles: *Death on the Installment Plan, Journey to the End of the Night.*

JIM CORBETT: the great tiger hunter of India. He lived in India at the beginning of the last century. At that time, there were regions of India that were losing up to 500 people a year to tigers and leopards. They called in Corbett. His books chronicle life on the hunt. He never takes pleasure in killing the animals—he'd rather be photographing them. His descriptions of all-night stake-outs, having to bring whatever piece of the kill he could find back to the village so it could be burned and the ashes put in the river, the sounds of the animals and the sheer physicality of his work…Twenty-mile hikes were all too frequent. Some titles: *Man-eaters, Man-Eaters of Kumaon, Jungle Lore.*

KOBO ABE: What incredible and strange stuff he writes. Have not read all of his work but I will. *The Ruined Map* blew my mind. I read it while in **MADAGASCAR AND KENYA;** the book and the surroundings really did a number on me. I am sure the work would be potent enough in more everyday settings.

JOAN DIDION: I really like how her mind works. Her books of essays *Slouching towards Bethlehem* and *The White Album* are great; her novel *Play it as it Lays* is damaging stuff.

I could go on but I think that should do it.—Henry Rollins

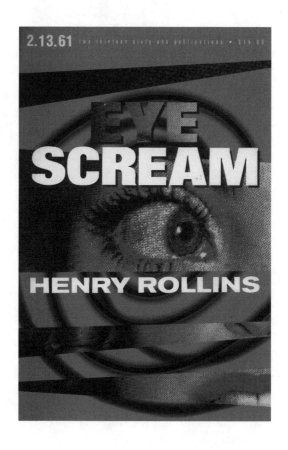

B I L L Y   C H I L D I S H

Billy Childish is a British cult hero—a painter, punk rocker, poet, and publisher [Hangman Books] who since 1977 has produced over 150 LPs, CDs, cassettes and 7" 45s; 40 books; several zines; and thousands of drawings and paintings. His bands include Thee Milkshakes, Thee Headcoats, Thee Mighty Caesars and The Buff Medways. His books include *My Fault* and *Notebooks of a Naked Youth*.

Thee Headcoats at Bimbo's 365 Club, San Francisco. Photo: V. Vale

Billy's official website is *www.theebillychildish.com*. See also *www.stuckism.com* for information on Stuckism, the first Remodernist art group, which Childish founded with Charles Thomson, Sexton Ming and other artists. Billy Childish lives in Chatham, Kent, England.

EARLY PUNK BEGINNINGS

♦ **VALE:** *Let's start from the beginning: the same year I began publishing* Search & Destroy *(1977) you started The Pop Rivets—*

♦**BILLY CHILDISH:** We played our first gig in September '77 and actually made a reel-to-reel recording, but it got destroyed. Awhile ago I found a cassette of this and reissued it. Bruce Brand [original guitarist] and I played together with Thee Headcoats right up until the summer of 2000.

♦ *V: That's amazing. I wonder why I never heard of you back then.*

♦**BC:** Well, we didn't play London—we were a proper suburb group down in Chatham, which is halfway to Canterbury, North Kent (30 miles outside of London). There were hardly any punk bands down there—just the Names from Canterbury and the Gash from Chatham. And us, of course.

♦ *V: Living in the suburbs, how did you know about punk?*

♦**BC:** Well, I was a punk before I was asked to play in a group. I didn't like seventies music; I just listened to '50s and '60s rock-'n'roll. I learned how to play guitar by listening to Bo Diddley. When punk rock came along I thought, *"This* is for me."

I was 17 then—a good age—when I started going to London and seeing the groups. I had a job as an apprentice stone mason in a dockyard in Chatham, so I had to go to building college in London, where I stayed in a squat with my brother in Chalk Farm near Camden. Then I went to art college, and that's where the group was formed. We were doing "Hippie Hippie Shake," "White Riot," "Whatcha Gonna Do About It," "Fireball XL-5"— we always had a lot of rock'n'roll in our set. Although nobody seems to know this, **I think we released the first independent punk *album*, around the end of 1978. We recorded it with a friend's dole money**; it was called *The Pop Rivets' Greatest Hits.*

♦ *V: That LP didn't get exported to America—*

♦ **BC:** Oh, no—we only pressed 500. It had handmade sleeves and handmade labels.

♦ *V: You acted according to the early punk principle, D.I.Y. ["Do It Yourself"]—*

♦ **BC:** Yeah. We did another album in '79, and then split up in 1980 because we couldn't get anything to sound exciting—the studios destroyed our sound. During our "career" we played in Germany excessively; we had a big German connection! We only played London—the center where punk was happening—once, because our idea was that "they should come to *us.*" Of course, it didn't work that way! We always made our own clothes—painted them up—and had our own look, and never became fashion-punks wearing leathers. Consequently, we weren't considered a punk-rock group.

I saw the Sex Pistols play their last show in England and by then punk had become nasty and unfriendly; skinheads were going to shows. It seemed like it would be downhill from then on, so I stopped going to gigs as often. Then in 1980 I was part of Thee Milkshakes, with my friend Micky, who was The Pop Rivets' driver. Next thing you know, the "New Romantics" fad was here where bands didn't use guitar anymore, and people like David Bowie (who we had hoped were dead and gone forever) had started re-emerging. Meanwhile, Thee Milkshakes played three-chord rock'n'roll music, like we had heard when we were kids. Over the years we just carried on from there: we went from Thee Milkshakes to Thee Mighty Caesars to Thee Headcoats. We always changed the band name when the songwriting per-sonnel changed or if an important member left—we thought it was a con to pretend we were the same band.

♦ *V: Unlike a lot of groups—*

♦ **BC:** Yeah, for us a name change meant we'd had a big change of line-up. But Bruce, the guitarist in The Pop Rivets, was the drummer in Thee Headcoats.

♦ *V: What's the secret of working with someone for twenty years?*

♦ **BC:** I don't know. For one thing, Bruce is notoriously late—I always say that he owes me about twenty years! I met him at a Damned gig, summer of '77, at the Sundown on Charing Cross Road. It was the Damned and the Adverts—whom I thought were good. You know, all these groups have one or two really good songs, and that's enough! The Adverts didn't last long. I used to see Siouxsie and the Banshees a lot at the Vortex which was only open Monday and Tuesday nights. It was a place where when you're 17, you can meet your hero, and everyone's there.

♦ *V: Well, in punk there wasn't supposed to be that separation between audience and performers. In early punk, most of the audience were in bands, making posters, making zines, making their own clothes—*

♦ **BC:** Right; that's why when we play in England we don't use the house PA (in America we have to, however). We like to use 30-year-old gear (like a 100-watt tube P.A.) so we're not blasting the audience. We don't believe the sound has to be loud to be impressive. People equate power with volume, whereas my feeling of punk rock is more like the blues of Robert Johnson, Leadbelly, and Bo Diddley through the rock'n'roll of the early Stones and early Kinks. We always thought they sounded so exciting—why doesn't their later music sound as good?

♦ *V: Right; those early Stones and Kinks albums were raw and unselfconscious, up to "Satisfaction."*

♦ **BC:** Yeah, well, it's before people start believing their own publicity. In the sixties, groups were able to survive one or two albums. These days, groups don't have enough time to develop to even do *one* album that's good all the way through (and if they do, it's often killed by the producer). At that time, the sound was primitive and more real—not too dressed up.

The first two Kinks albums were big inspirations. That's what we listened to as kids. But if I say, "I'm a fan of the Kinks," it means I like about 5 % of their output—just a few things. I also like Alternative TV; their first album, "The Image Is Cracked" is one of the greatest rock'n'roll records ever. We played a couple of their songs in our set. I think Mark Perry dismantled ATV because he was afraid of turning into what the Stones had turned into.

CHILDISH
RECORD PRODUCTION

You have to go by your first instincts, never believe your own publicity, and try not to become a parody of yourself. Rather than trying to change my music, I try to make it sound like our first album each time we record. I'm very fortunate in that I don't have much musical ability—consequently we don't "develop" too much or get too involved in "musicianship"!

We don't record at a pricey studio; we still record an album in two days. I do a lot of the backing tracks at home on an old valve recorder, a half-track Revox G36; the drum, bass and guitar are recorded "live." Then we put on a vocal in the studio. Lots of our albums are half home-recorded; they cost the same now as they did when we first started! You see, we're not trying to *develop*—we've got too much sense!

♦ *V: It doesn't seem like recording has gotten much "better" since that 1957 monaural one-take 78rpm recording of The Phantom singing "Love Me"—how many records can match that passion?*

♦ **BC:** Yeah! I think trying to get *feeling* into what you're doing means that you have to shy away from technology. The more technology that's involved, the more money you spend, and the bigger distance there is between you and your reality. **I'm not a career artist; I'm an amateur.** I don't have anything at stake, so I don't have to go into expensive recording studios worrying about my "career"—'cuz I don't want one!

♦ **V:** *If you think of punk as folk music, then it should have a catchy tune you can easily remember and sing along with. Initially, I was attracted to punk because the lyrics were political and dealt with "real" concerns.*

♦ **BC:** Yes, but paradoxically, when they're sort of *crap* and don't really mean anything, I like that as well. Like the nonsense ones. Johnny Moped & the Mopeds was one of my favorite groups. The group were friends with the Damned; they were also from Croydon. Johnny Moped was totally, absolutely, naturally strange. His mother would dress him, and he'd go to gigs where he was supposed to play and wouldn't be able to get in because nobody would believe he was in the band.

♦ **V:** *If he were doing paintings, you'd call him a "naïve artist"*—
BC: Yeah, and he wasn't even trying to be. The Mopeds were absolutely the funniest group to see. They were brilliant, them and the Damned—talk about people who write a load of nonsense! I mean, bands like the Clash were really exciting, but after seeing the Damned or the Mopeds I'd go home with an aching jaw because they'd just make you laugh with childish delight.

♦ **V:** *The Mopeds are a legendary early punk group that never got famous.*

♦ **BC:** But they left behind a really good album and a couple of good singles. You know, I don't like playing too often. **You don't want to become too *serious*. You don't want to be a professional in anything you do because professionals destroy everything.**

♦ **V:** *Especially in art.*

♦ **BC:** Right, because professionalism has nothing to do with creativity. I'm not talking about things like showing up on time—that's just being *decent*. I mean people who've got this notion of controlling a whole scene and excluding amateurs— and of course amateurs are the ones who are truly creative. Take fanzines, for instance. I did a fanzine in '77 before I was in a group—that's how I started *doing* stuff; I didn't have a clue. The first one was titled "Chatham's Burning" [pun on "London's Burning"], then "Bostik Haze," [pun on "Purple Haze"], then "Fab 69," and then "The Kray Twins' Summer Special"—I did *that* one every summer. My friend Sexton Ming and I started Phyroid Press [1980], which became Hangman Books around 1982. We put out at least 30 little booklets with titles like "The Old Onion of the Mountain," "The Wild Breed Is Here," "Bizarre Oxen," and "The Cheesy Bug Gazette."

♦ *V: Why do you think you did all this? So many people don't do much of anything, or they just go to jobs.*

♦ **BC:** I can't understand that. All I could do was paint pictures, so I painted, and then I went into—

♦ *V: Right—haven't you done about 1,000 paintings?*

♦ **BC:** Oh christ, those are just figures people make up, but I've easily done more than that. I paint every week—*THAT'S* my main thing. I've painted since I was a kid and never stopped. It was only when I was 17 I started getting into music and writing poetry.

♦ *V: And never quit, unlike most people.*

♦ **BC:** Right. And it's really good our band didn't became famous, because if someone had "discovered" the Pop Rivets, that could have destroyed our creativity. Kids are stupid—you get a load of money and you can't keep your head together. Everyone wants to be a millionaire, even if they pretend they don't, and they'll end up doing all sorts of undignified things.

♦ *V: Not to mention repeating themselves creatively.*

♦ **BC:** Well, supposedly I repeat myself creatively all the time—but I'm not so sure about that. **I think some people don't understand the sophistication in simplicity.**

♦ *V: Yes; it's deceptively difficult to come up with a simple song that is "original"—*

♦ **BC:** Actually, **the quest for originality stops people moving, so I just don't bother with *originality*.** You can strive for originality but there will always be someone who did something similar. So you use whatever's there; besides, you can never repeat anything exactly the same. And even if you *try* to do something similar, somehow it will strangely turn out to be different. Ray Davies [Kinks] said that "You Really Got Me" was meant to be a copy of "Louie Louie"—yet it couldn't sound more different! If you're going through a period where you're working in a *mechanical* mode trying to sort out some problem, the next part tends to appear all on its own, just by dint of doggedly working.

♦ *V: I'm glad you attacked the concept of originality, because that constipates so many people: "Am I really being original?"*

♦ **BC: In Japanese the word for "copy" is the same as the word for "learn"—I really like that.** Van Gogh couldn't draw, so he forced himself to copy other people's drawings for five or six years. All that heritage is there to provide inspiration; it wasn't copying, it was learning.

Sometimes I help young writers put a book together and then someone says, "Oh, that writing's just like Billy Childish's." I say, "Sure. But if you work at it long enough, it won't be. Everyone takes a bit from here and a bit from there."

Someone's always saying, "You can't do that—it's like so-and-so" just to *stop* people. We had a group called Thee Headcoatees, featuring my old girlfriend and other girls who had never sung before, and we recorded an album. My girlfriend took the album to play for her mother who, before she even heard it, said, "But *YOU* can't sing."

♦ *V: That's so typical!*

♦ **BC:** You know, parents and teachers are the ones who always tell kids they can't do things; I wasn't allowed to sing at school because I'm tone-deaf. I think that's a reason to *allow* me to sing; children should be encouraged, not stopped. They don't stop you studying math because you can't do it. I'm somebody who likes projects; I do these things to entertain myself—as far as I'm concerned, art and music are all children's games anyway!

Billy Childish in the halcyon punk days of yore, circa 1977, U.K.

Everyone's got ability to some degree, and if you don't use whatever you've got, you're never going to develop anything. And why *not* do something, even if you're bad at doing it? When punk rock happened, suddenly all these crappy groups started up and miraculously produced all these brilliant singles— they've all got one great song in them. **People believed the idea, so they made the punk scene exist; they made songs exist.** A bunch of people got together, picked up instruments, and all of a sudden they were making great music because they didn't know how to do it. If the punk thing hadn't happened, these people might never have done it.

♦ **V:** *They don't know the rules.*

♦ **BC:** They don't know they're not allowed to do that!

♦ **V:** *They're creative by breaking rules they didn't even know existed.*

♦ **BC:** Exactly. That's how culture that matters gets created. This notion of "good taste" destroys any creativity, just like the notion of professionalism: the idea that you can't do it, that because you're not good at it you shouldn't do it. Which is absolutely the most ridiculous idea going. People who don't know about music are always talking about their friend in a group who's a "great musician," and I always say, "Well, what use have great musicians ever been to anyone?"

The good thing about groups like the Stones and the Kinks is: when you see early footage of them, you can see they weren't great. But once they started getting a bit better— *that's* when the problems came in . . . You get your Eric Claptons coming along, where people start thinking, "I could never play that good"—

♦ **V:** *And then decadence sets in, like heroin addiction—*

♦ **BC:** And this is a very important point: when punk started, we really were against that "drug culture" of getting stoned and laid back and not doing anything.

♦ **V:** *I hate when music "histories" romanticize drug use. In San Francisco's early punk days, if anyone was doing heroin, they kept it very private.*

♦ **BC:** The thing is, if you're trying to *relate* to people, or communicate—and that's the bottom line with all music and writing—a lot of drug abuse and drinking is about *not* communicating. So they really work against each other. When I stopped drinking seven years ago, I started feeling like when I was 17 on stage playing. The thing about "professionalism" is: if you're on the road for a year, that'll drive you to drug use or being an alcoholic, because of all the rubbish involved. Even on my small scale, when I once did a lot of touring, I found it very necessary to be drunk all the time. Entertaining people through your own destruction is an expensive way to get recognition!

♦ **V:** *The romanticization of drug use and alcoholism never seems to end. The* Please Kill Me *punk memoir was full of that—*

♦ **BC:** Having been a real drinker for so many years, I say: it's a fine place to visit, but a terrible place to live. I watched a video of Charles Bukowski prattling on about his alcoholic exploits, and if his poems had been as off-target and dumb as the conclusions he was making when he talked, no one would have read him! It would have been a good idea for him *not* to have done this interview. It was entertaining and a bit funny, but also a bit sad—like laughing at someone who's pathetic.

A lot of musicians go through this cycle: at one point you need a drink to get onstage and loosen up. Then you became jaded by it, and you're hiding, when the whole thing is supposed to be about *exposure:* exposing what you're hiding, laying open your soul. It's about direct communication: you're trying to get rid of the mask—not putting it on. That is, if what you do is going to be of value to people, for them to be able to relate to it . . .

♦ **V:** *That's true, people don't want to read or listen to phony B.S.—*

♦ **BC:** Well, actually they *do,* but you just don't give it to them! I mean, people are continually trying to shut you up if you're too open.

♦ **V:** *Media since the 90's has been full of confessional, bare-all memoirs and incest revelations that purport to be "telling the truth"—*

♦ **BC:** The trouble is: just because people say something is true doesn't make it so. If *anything* becomes a fashion or a movement, it's not going to be pure anymore. Just because you call something punk rock doesn't make it punk rock. Just because you call something a "true confession"—you know, all these things can be put on like clothes. **You can say "I'm a Buddhist" or "I'm a punk rocker" but the truth is: you know things by** *action,* **not by words.**

♦ **V:** *A lot of people SAY they're going to do something; then to them it's as though they've done it!*

♦ **BC:** Exactly, all the time. It's always important NOT to talk about books you're going to write—only talk about ones you've actually written.

♦ **V:** *Back to D.I.Y.: now anyone can make music and record it. For a few hundred dollars you can buy a four-track and make your own recordings at home. With a CD recorder, you can burn CDs as you get orders.*

♦ **BC:** There's a very healthy music scene—garage music—going on which is ignored by the music press: a lot more people are "Doing It Themselves." In a way it's healthier than during the punk rock period. People are realizing they don't need a posh studio . . . that they'll actually get a better sound by *not* having a posh studio, not having that controlled, filtered sound—the kind that's acceptable to the mainstream.

The important thing in all this is the *interaction* going on: you put two really dumb people together and something interesting can come of it! (This is why I'm not so keen on deejay stuff, which is solo or solitary.) In an interaction, two can play off each other and it's not controlled; random interesting things can happen. Real drummers, as opposed to drum machines, are great because they're *irregular.* Anyone can pick up a guitar and make interesting sounds that are different—whereas with synthesizers covered with buttons, it sounds the same no matter who's pressing them.

♦ **V:** *Right; the value of interaction itself is underrated. Just two people getting together can create something that transcends the two of them . . . From surrealism I got the idea that everyone could be an artist, because everyone is born with the machinery in their brain that produces dreams and imagination, which is all you need to be an artist—*

♦ **BC:** Yes, but this is shut down when you're at school. At first, creativity is encouraged, but after kindergarten, creativity becomes less and less important. To pass exams you aren't asked your opinion, you aren't asked to creatively think; you're just forced to memorize. Creativity is the greatest thing we've got—and it's the most underrated. **I couldn't believe I was at school with kids who could paint and draw brilliantly, and they just *stopped* doing it.** They were never encouraged to do it, yet creativity is the most saving thing, the most decent thing that people do.

Thanks to the imagination, you can feel what other people are feeling. Then you know what pain is, you begin to understand suffering—and if you understand that, you have compassion, and you can begin to get along with people rather than just hating all the bastards!

♦ **V:** *—Or treating them like objects or something to be used.*

♦ **BC:** Yeah. I've treated people like things many many times, and I've gradually learned not to; to try to respect others . . . that's why I don't steal teacups from Japanese restaurants anymore! You've got to try to be decent—the thing is, you can't be *partially* honest, can you?

Communication is really the bottom line. *Not* mass communication—this is really the paradox when people say, "Oh yeah, we've signed up with a major label so we can reach a bigger audience and communicate with more people." Yeah, you're communicating with them, *sort of,* on a McDonald's level, but to do that you have to be bland, producing just mass communication that people can listen to while they're driving their car. As opposed to really being spoken to.

♦ **V:** *Corporations rarely permit uncensored language—*

♦ **BC:** I met this bloke from Paramount Studios who was into literature. He'd read my *My Fault* and said, "This is a brilliant book—it's fantastic and exactly the sort of thing *'they'* wouldn't ever touch." I thought, "Oh, I'm doing something right." Then I said [jokingly], "Well, can't we get some Hollywood actors, set it in New York, and stick a few guns in there?"

SHOCK "VALUE"

♦ **V:** *Obviously, violence sells—*

♦ **BC:** No matter how vile the subject matter, it's all out there, going on and being discussed . . . I like movies like *Touch of Evil.* Hitchcock's films are incredibly tight: people can act and you can hear the dialogue. *Mean Streets* and *Taxi Driver* get you emotionally involved; there are characters that things happen to and "A leads to B leads to C" so you can understand *why* somebody gets their head blown off; there's some sort of morality. I saw *Reservoir Dogs* by Tarantino and thought it was all just "stylistic death"—graceful, beautifully-shot murder scenes, but no core meaningfulness—who needs it? And Scorsese's *Casino* was absolutely beautifully shot, incredibly paced and had no core meaning either—so he's given up, too.

♦ **V:** *The trend is gratuitous violence and shock value just for its own sake—*

♦ **BC: I think all shocking material needs to be brought up and spoken about—*discussed*—not just presented as surface, shock-value imagery.** You want to be spoken to in a respectful way.

The great thing that was not recognized in punk was its *intelligence.* Punk allowed room for all sorts of expression. Take Mark Perry of ATV—there was nothing dumb going on with him. Or the Clash, who were right preachers and very serious young men (even though I don't think they achieved much after their first album). Punk was at least trying to communicate ideas intelligently. **Like the blues, punk music was trying to relate a personal view of the world in a real way.**

♦ **V:** *—and political as well.*

♦ **BC:** Yeah, well—that's the same thing. "Political" for me always comes through the personal . . . a view which has authority because it's personal, experiential. Rather than the Clash, who had some good ideas but it was more theory—party politics. They fell into the trap of using politics mostly as a soapbox.

♦ *V: College students used to join Marxist groups and then think they had all the answers—*

♦ **BC:** —people looking for an identity within a group, which is fine, I suppose, for kids—they have to do it. But I always want something with a bit more practical use. You meet people who've got a lot of great answers, but then you find out that they don't like talking to women. Or people who are right-wing who don't want their beliefs questioned, because then they might have to *expose* themselves; reveal what they don't know. A lot of people are like that . . .

♦ *V: Let's talk about the original founding or propelling principles behind punk: how we're still trying to live them, and how we've had to modify some—*

♦ **BC:** Certainly a lot of garbage has been written. Your *Search & Destroy* books just contained what people who were *doing* it said. When I saw them I thought, "Great—it's not just someone's opinion." Journalists: *christ.* I really liked Dada when I was a kid, and **Kurt Schwitters said, "The artist creates, the critic bleats."** He always had a great sense of humor which he brought to his art, and he never took himself seriously—*that's* punk rock. And he was a bloody businessman who ran his own printing shop, invented his own art, invented everything himself. He was my hero when I was about 16. That probably says a lot.

♦ *V: How did you know about him at the age of 16?*

♦ **BC:** I used to make collages for my fanzine covers, and somebody said, "Look at Kurt Schwitters." I instantly loved his work, and still do—I have a tattoo on my left buttock that says, "I don't bother with *ideal;* I eat the apple with the peel" which is a line from a Kurt Schwitters poem. I did thousands of collages like his; I used to call myself "Kurt Schwitters." Thee Milkshakes took out a bank account in his name where we put all the band's income. We didn't pay ourselves, and everything went toward putting out the next record—which no one would buy!

Edward Lear (famous for "The Owl and the Pussycat" and nonsense limericks) was another favorite—this was before I started writing about my own world. I didn't like "literature" because they all have their heads up their arses; I didn't know yet that I could invent my own language, so I hit on nonsense as being the best option. I suppose that's how I ended up with the last name "Childish"; I was calling myself "Gus Claudius" on my first fanzine (after the 1976 British television series which I liked a lot) and a friend of mine named Button-Nosed Steve said, "No you're not—you're Billy Childish." The name stuck.

♦ *V: Does your art have a "childish" quality?*

♦ **BC: When painting, what I try to do is to not edit myself.** I spent years painting to please myself and not to please other people. Then a couple of years ago I realized that if I want to do this properly, I've got to stop trying to please myself as well! Because . . . I edit myself too strongly, so I thought I'd better do some stuff that *isn't good enough,* to loosen up a bit. Picasso made some brilliant statements; he said it took him sixteen years to learn to draw like Raphael, and *sixty* to learn to draw like a kid. He also said that **good taste is the enemy of all creativity**, and that's a true punk motto. (Picasso was also a complete bastard!)

♦ *V: It seems that the label "art" has extended into everything, and everything has become "art." Duchamp said, "Anything is a work of art if an artist says it is." What does that mean? Who's to say who is an artist?*

♦ **BC:** These idiots who run galleries seem to think that art is something that has monetary value, which has nothing to do with what art really is. That's where the problems come in. It's okay to sell things and make a living, but when something becomes really overblown . . . like, I know someone involved in Damien Hirst's group. The collectors of this "new" art in England claim the artists are "punk artists" (and they ain't at all). And Saatchi, the advertising agency that put the conservatives in power, buys, collects and bankrolls these artists. You can't be more mainstream than that—it's a bit like the CIA involvement in the American Abstract Expressionist movement. (The CIA were trying to establish an "American" art market, so they were jacking up prices and otherwise generating interest in it. I learned this from a British TV documentary.)

♦ *V: Right—prior to World War II Paris was the world's art capital. Now it's New York; the CIA succeeded!*

♦ **BC: The mainstream always tries to absorb anything "on the edge"—and the easiest way to absorb something is to buy it.** Why? Because everyone wants money, because money gives you space and power (supposedly)—a delusion of freedom, like: "If I have this studio, or extra money for canvas and supplies, then I'll be able to paint." Whereas I think, "If you want to paint, you'll paint on the floor or the back of a door—whatever you've got. If you need to paint, then *paint!"*

♦ *V: So you've thought about what you wanted to avoid. Musicians often get into bad business situations. The singer from Flipper said that the band didn't read the fine print on their major label contract. So the label had the rights to anything they recorded, even as individuals—but didn't HAVE to release it. Consequently, they couldn't record even for a small label. Most bands get so excited when they get offered an advance ...*

♦ **BC:** All a big advance is, is an ego puff for the group—you never actually *see* the money. Usually that money is already spent for recording or tour support. If I sign to a record label, I want money in my bank account—that's real—and I don't want a producer. If you're going to sign away all your rights and all your life and your creativity, you'd better make sure you've actually got the bloody money!

♦ *V: It's very dicey to sign with some mega-corporation and think you can still have 100 % control and freedom.*

♦ **BC:** Yeah, after all these years of seeing so many people go down that path, I'm quite aware how unlikely it is that I'll ever achieve that: a major label contract with complete control. But, the only way they've got you is if they've got something you want.

◆ **V:** *It's best to be happy with a smaller, quality audience, as opposed to a McDonald's audience.*

◆ **BC:** One label representative said to me, "You have to be radio-friendly if you want to get on a big label or do MTV, but *you* wouldn't ever do MTV anyway." My reply was, "I have no problem with doing MTV—it's just that we want to make the video *ourselves.*"

But these **corporate people are terrified of not having control. The first thing they always do is try to split the song-writer off from the group—isolate him.** They don't want him with his friends, working together and raising questions: "What are these bastards doing?" They'll flatter him, tell him he's a "genius," that he doesn't need these sidemen, that they're holding him back. The interesting thing is, they don't care so much if a thing is marketable; they're interested in having their two-bit creative ambitions fulfilled by pretending that *they've* created the act. They don't let a group create and get on with it; they *don't* say, "Here's some money, do what you do and we'll sell it." They want to pretend *they've* invented this thing, and usually they have invented it—that's why it's so anemic and useless! It's been drained of any verve or life or instinct.

PUNK PRINCIPLES

◆ **V:** *"Corporate" often means decision by committee and focus group . . . Let's try and recap some punk principles: 1) Do it yourself, 2) Anyone can do it, 3) Everyone can be an artist—*

◆ **BC:** There's one thing I always like, whether you're looking at a painting or seeing a band or reading a piece of literature or poetry: it's when you think, *"I could have done that!"*

♦ **V:** *A lot of people saw the Ramones and thought, "I know those three chords; I could write a song like that."*

♦ **BC:** People can see a painting by Picasso and go, "Anyone can do *that*." But the trouble is, they don't go out and do it. They don't try to be that "anyone."

♦ **V:** *People said the same thing about Jackson Pollock: "I could splatter paint on a canvas like that!"*

♦ **BC:** But they don't realize that's the point: *they should!* **I'm really into forgeries; I've done some "Schwitters" artworks.** I had a friend working at an auctioneer's in London. It never came to pass, but I went into their art storeroom a few times and we were looking into the possibility of placing counterfeit art in there. I just love that idea—especially since it only takes a pop at those idiots who want to *own* this stuff. How can the original be worth so much more than the fake? It doesn't matter. That's what so good about photocopiers: one copy of a zine is just as original as another. But when things get monetary value attached, it stops people having access. I should add that I didn't do it, because that would be lying.

EVERYTHING should be empowering, shouldn't it? The one book that really empowered me to be a writer was *Ask the Dust* by John Fante. I read that when I was 20 and it made me think, "I know I can do it; I can write a novel." It's best if you read something and it's impressive in its ability to empower—not in its style. You think, "This is possible, it's simple—I could do this." You can understand the fabric of it and how it works. It's not from some inaccessible, intellectual world that you can't be a part of.

When you see something you feel a connection with, you want it to be friendly and open—you want to be a part of it.

♦ **V:** *But isn't some distance inevitable? It's pretty hard to escape the fact that you're the performer on a stage, and there's the audience a foot below you.*

♦ **BC:** There's always some of that, but it's a matter of not *glorifying* that distance—and when you bridge it, everyone knows.

That's when it works.

This is my big principle (I don't know if it's a punk one): **"You can only win by failing."** When you win, there's always a problem. If I'd had success the way most people define it, I'd have really failed drastically. All the small failures—when you don't get what you want—make you check everything and work harder on everything. Instead of a preoccupation with success, people should have a preoccupation with failure!

♦ *V: A lot of people lose their creative souls becoming financially successful—*

♦ **BC:** Yeah, the ego can't take it; it gets really overblown. This is what happened to groups like the Stones, the Kinks and the Beatles—they started thinking, "Well, obviously we've become famous because we're so much cleverer than everyone else." And that's when the deterioration sets in, and the records become bad. Even a "religious" view is better than that: believing that it's the grace of God, rather than *you,* that is responsible.

♦ *V: Sometimes it seems that artists are "channeling"—that they're in touch with and expressing what's on a lot of people's minds. Like the early Bob Dylan—*

DYLAN AND SINATRA

♦ **BC:** I think that since everything is interconnected in this world (and nothing exists in separation), who's to say that certain artists aren't tapping into a universal unconscious? It actually seems more likely than not. It's interesting that you mention Dylan, because *I* always mention him when talking to people about punk rock: "Yeah, I love his first two albums. He's great— he can't sing and he can't play but he does it." And sometimes Dylan fans get insulted and say, "He's a fantastic musician, he's a great writer." He's *not* a great singer or writer—he couldn't do it, but he did. That's what's great about him: the fact that he wasn't great.

♦ **V:** *His voice used to be almost intolerable, but now it sounds almost commercial—*

♦ **BC:** Yeah, that's weird, isn't it? I was brought up on the Stones and Dylan—my father played them when I was about three (he left home when I was about six). My mother always thought Dylan was depressing, so she'd play Frank Sinatra. But I found him far more depressing.

♦ **V:** *Sinatra seemed like a true existentialist; he had completely capitulated to all the corruption in the world—all the bankrupt values. He was singing with a bit of irony, but he wasn't really trying to change anything.*

♦ **BC:** Well, I'm talking just about the emotional level of a three-year-old. The sun's shining through the blinds, your mother's ironing and Sinatra's playing in the background while you're thinking, "Ohmigod, I'm in hell!" Sinatra is music for alcoholics, in a way. Actually, Sinatra's a bit punk because he does sing flat once in a while.

♦ **V:** *Wasn't Sinatra allegedly Mafia-involved, as well as abusive to women? I think Mia Farrow said that.*

♦ **BC:** But who knows the complexity of Frank Sinatra's life and his relationships and what formed the man and why? Even if he is exactly all those awful things, people aren't *totally* anything—they're formed by their experience and often by their upbringing. You shouldn't condone evil actions, but I think it's completely possible to listen to someone and not have their biography rule out other redeeming qualities, like a nice voice or a sense of rhythm.

But you know, people always need an enemy. Even good, kind people need enemies—they need somebody to represent the evil in the world, to personify it. *Why?* Because of the difficulty of facing that aspect in ourselves that may be capable of the same things!

◆ **V:** *Right...There's an argument that punk was the last unselfconscious underground.*

◆ **BC:** I do believe that punk was the last unselfconscious social-change movement. Those corporate ["cool-hunter"] scouts are preempting anything that might happen. They maintain their position at the top by assimilating what they see happening on the street as quickly as possible—thereby destroying it. **The big corporations missed the boat with punk rock and they're not going to let that happen again.**

But garage music—a worldwide movement that we're part of—is completely ignored in the British music press. The poetry we do is ignored by the literary press. Ignored is good. Maybe it won't ever be part of a big movement, but what good did being part of a movement ever do anyone, anyway?

◆ **V:** *At least being part of a categorized, branded movement. Right now there are literally thousands of smaller-level bands who don't have much money, yet are constantly traveling. They make and sell their own T-shirts and zines and records. So there's a whole "alternative" economy managing to perpetuate itself. It's not exactly a star system; it's hard to be a star when you're sleeping on someone's floor.*

◆ **BC:** That's exactly what we've been doing for the past few nights. We've done this for 20 years and in a way I'm sort of a celebrity—I'm a celebrity sleeping on the floor! And with an ego like mine, this is probably good for me . . . a few floors are what I need!

◆ **V:** *You've put out a lot of records; are most out-of-print?*

◆ **BC:** Yes. A lot of them are selling for astronomical amounts of money, but of course I don't see any of that. I'm not bothered by kids who just like the records and want to know everything about them, but the big collectors who want control . . . trying to keep the world at bay by owning as much as they can, trying to make everything "safe" by having a complete barrier of material things around them—that's the collecting syndrome. And I totally understand that, I just work against it because I realize it's not productive.

I've got the same fears, phobias and worries as everyone else, but that doesn't mean I have to embrace them. **There is always a choice . . . *always*. The only time there isn't, is when you don't believe there is.** The idea that "you always have a choice" is beaten out of people early—and that's a tragedy. You can decide to be a painter; you can decide anything. Every moment, there's a choice.

In England, the art colleges are starved for cash—and in a way they deserve everything that's happening to them, because of the attitude of the tutors within these colleges: always trying to save their own arses, never standing up to fight as one against these budget cuts. A lot of people are down on painting at the art colleges: "What use is painting?" And the conservatives were the first to be down on it. Of course, the painters are the ones with the most imagination, the ones who go out and create all the small business. Everything comes from creativity and imagination. "They" don't realize that the more you encourage creativity, the better *their* crappy world works, actually.

Everything seems to be moving toward a smaller scale of people doing it themselves, like with organic foods—why eat crap that's mass-produced? Everything's got to break down and become smaller.

♦ *V: And back to more personal relations, bands should give up the dream of selling millions of records—*

♦ **BC:** When we perform or record our way, using old equipment, some people think we're copping out. Whereas actually, to use modern equipment and do things the way everyone else does is the easy way. If we just went along with the system it would be an easier ride.

♦ *V: Your vision of "success" is different from the norm—*

♦ **BC:** I think about what happened to SubPop Records. After their first success, they nearly went bankrupt and then [allegedly] withheld money from bands like Mudhoney for about a year, just so they could hold out long enough to sell the rights to Nirvana and make themselves millionaires. Luckily they only sold 49 % to Warner Bros., so they kept a controlling share. But they got $20 million—and then they offered Thee Headcoats $2,000 for a three-LP, worldwide deal!

Greed was there, and **when you have greed (where someone else has got what you want), you're giving away your power.** If you don't have greed (or, if you recognize it, but don't play up to it), then no one can have power over you. If you have greed, then you have a problem, because to satisfy your greed you might have to sell out certain people down the road and capitulate on certain principles that will damage the whole fabric of, say, what *I* do, which is all about relationships.

COMMUNICATION

Relationships come down to communication, so you damage the communication. I think that communication is the real key to everything. We make books, we make records, and all of it involves communicating—that's the bottom line. If you produce books in a language nobody can understand, you may as well burn them! That's why modern art is crap.

♦ *V: But communication has been so corrupted by mass media. I never watch television, yet its soundbites have infiltrated my own speech—*

♦ **BC:** All that has a bit to do with how you view yourself. Like, you catch yourself using these catch phrases without even thinking about it. For a brief second the language takes you over, then you realize what happened, and this reminds you how susceptible to *everything* you are, and how you can just fall into things without any conscious control. You're there, being an idiot along with everyone else!

♦ **V:** *I hate that.*

♦**BC:** Because it makes us think that maybe we're not quite as special as we think we are. The brilliant thing about the world is that everything is in flux, nothing is solid. Everyone wants everything to be solid, because they're scared of change. Everyone wants the world to stay the same forever, and it resolutely refuses to. The more people try and control it out of fear—like these right-wingers—the more it sprouts out in other ways.

A few years ago Prince Charles made some really stupid remarks calling for people to speak "proper English" (in England, there's a lot of snobbery about diction). But the thing is, language has always been totally eclectic. There are always new words, and language is always moving and shifting. Whoever we are and whatever time we're cursed to be living in (or blessed, depending on your point of view), you're looking over the edge of oblivion. We see ourselves at the forefront of time as we stumble over each new moment.

We think of the past as all sorted out—safe and accountable. And this brings up all kinds of paranoia and fear and neurotic behavior. We may think, "I'm saying things out of a sit-com; this is dangerous." Or, "What's going to happen to language if everybody talks in catch phrases?" None of this is ever going to happen; there's always going to be diversity, and there are always going to be new ways of saying the same thing.

♦ **V:** *We're trying to resist "colonization"—*

♦**BC:** But colonization is continual; maybe in this case it's a fake concept. Language is uncontrollable, and as long as we're trying to control all that stuff, we're not really dealing with the issues. **Everything is in flux and will always change and there's *bugger-all* you can do about it!**

♦ **V:** *Still, language is a principal instrument of the control process, which is preventing any major social "Revolution"—*

♦**BC:** Yeah, definitely. But "The Revolution" is all about blame; it always has to do with the "Others." And as long as it's to do with the others it will always be, "How can we control these sods?" If it's down to control, then you know the revolution, no matter what its principles, is going to be fascistic in its outcome. That's the abhorrent thing about right-wingers: the need to control . . . and that's their big similarity to the left; it's all about *control.* That's why there's always been this romance with anarchism. It's the idea that "If everyone else were like us, the world would be fine"—yet we'd still have exactly the same problems.

Even anarchy needs people to go along with it. *Everything* comes down to fear, and the fear is of what we feel we're capable. That's what we feel we must control; this is the whole issue: understanding and knowing your own *motives.* Most of the time we're trying to obliterate that by watching television: "Do not feel what you feel." Who wants to sit and feel bored all day? What lies behind that boredom? It's too difficult and too unsettling to deal with; it's easier for people to think it's outside themselves and someone else's fault.

♦ *V: In an ideal society everyone would be an artist—then perhaps people wouldn't feel such a need to control others, or be always orchestrating manipulation—*

♦ **BC: The great problem in societies is this need to control people, thereby robbing them of their autonomy.** Then people become resentful and blame others. **With control you've always got conflict, all the time.** The only chance a person has of respecting somebody else and not hurting other people and not wanting to do harm to others, is if they have an understanding of their own value. Because everyone has this terrible fear of these urges, they've got to rape, murder, and control.

♦ *V: Advertising is based upon people's feelings of low self-esteem and inadequacy—*

♦ **BC:** Yeah, self-esteem is so important. As soon as you like yourself (which I've managed to do to a very small degree; it's taken me over 30 years to begin to like myself and give myself a slight break) . . . when you become able to like yourself, you become incapable of hurting people the way you used to be capable of. Like the Christian catch phrase, "Love your neighbor as you love yourself."

♦ *V: Oh—that's a lie.*

♦ **BC:** It is, because it means that you have to *force* yourself to love somebody—you're *pretending,* therefore you're not loving them. It might be better to say: **As much as you love yourself, you can love others.** The thing about loving yourself, or beginning to like yourself, isn't a matter of having great ideas about yourself. It's accepting all the bullshit that's in you, and letting yourself off the hook for not being perfect. We're an amalgam of opposites and extremes . . .

In the Charles Bukowski interview I saw, he always talked in absolutes and always had to be right—which is a real shame for such an intelligent bloke who can write so well. His idea was: because he was capable of all these evil thoughts—all this evil he was supposedly capable of doing—that's what *everyone* is really like, and anything else is a lie. Rather than: both are simultaneously true, and you can accept all that negativity without damning any goodness.

♦ *V: Our childhood training is deficient, and these days discipline is a major problem—*

♦ **BC:** The most important things you can teach a kid are: real boundaries (so they can feel a sense of security), and not always having instantaneous gratification. **That "instantaneous gratification" syndrome screws us all up: "I've gotta have it, and I've gotta have it NOW!"** Success—anything. The work and the process aren't important; only the result.

work schedule

♦ *V: Right; everyone focuses on results and not on process. So . . . what are your work habits like?*

♦ **BC:** Well, I paint once a week, and usually do two or three paintings at a time. I write either all the time or never—I've got a notebook which I keep for my poetry, and I write on the move whenever I've got ideas. **When writing prose you work on your own *emotional* view of the world.** I usually write songs in batches, like I'll write an album in a week or two and then not do anything for six months. I rewrote *My Fault* every summer for 13 years or so. *Notebooks of a Naked Youth* I wrote in two weeks. The painting is sort of a discipline that I do every week, but everything else I do in blocks.

♦ *V: If this were a society where everyone produced paintings weekly, you'd have to give them away just to have room. My friend Philip Lamantia said, "Imagine everyone regularly giving each other poetic imagery, poems—"*

♦ **BC:** Well, we're back on the topic of communication again . . . communion.

♦ *V: In academic circles the word "communion" has been discussed as something which is somehow more sacred, more meaningful, more crucial and community-enhancing. Through the media, we're inundated now with false communication . . . usually to promote some consumer lifestyle—*

♦ **BC:** McDonald's style.

♦ *V: Now, there are corporate billboards and logos everywhere "branding" (as though we're cattle) their message into our skulls. Communication is so devalued now; almost all of what's out there is junk food. What we're trying to do is to preserve and perpetuate—*

♦ **BC:** I think you should change that from "preserve and perpetuate" to "create." Because if we're just perpetuating or preserving, that's a bit boring and fearful. But if we're creating, we're just doing it . . . creating meaningful communication, or communion. Again, **everything that's meaningful in life comes down to just one word: communication.**

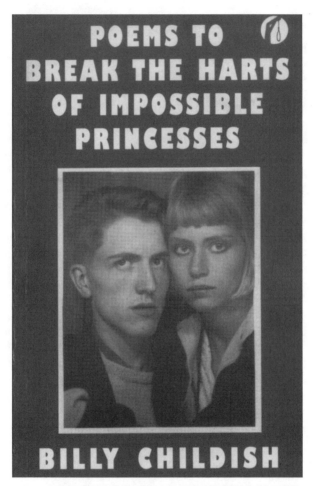

POEMS TO BREAK THE HARTS OF IMPOSSIBLE PRINCESSES

BILLY CHILDISH

With Sanchia, photo booth, Richmond. 29th Sept 1979
"but the camera has clicked and now they will never
question/that they were indeed the smiling and the chosen/the
butiful and the young."—"the face" (excerpt from above book)

SUCCESS

♦ **V:** *I recently spoke with Henry Rollins. He's another person who in my opinion hasn't "sold out" over the years—*

♦ **BC:** I'm not that familiar with Henry Rollins, although I saw him do a reading in Holland. He was talking about doing stadium rock festivals in South America and knocking himself out with his microphone and bleeding on the audience (he said it was an accident). It was a story to undermine himself—it was witty! Whereas my main ambition isn't to play big places; we don't see getting bigger as getting *better*.

I wouldn't mind if somebody gave us money to do what *we* want to do—I've always had that view. But I wouldn't sign with somebody and then have to tour when I didn't want to, or make records I didn't want to, or be forced to be produced by certain people.

♦ **V:** *Let's discuss the problem of "selling out"—*

♦ **BC:** Someone asked me the other day whether I would allow one of my recordings to be used on a commercial. I said that if I didn't have a particular problem with the product, it might not bother me. Like, Michael Jackson owns a number of Beatles songs. The Beatles stated they didn't want their songs used in commercials, but he overruled them and licensed the songs out of greed. That makes the Beatles more radical than these modern groups who are trying to write things that they *want* to be used in commercials—they are greedy. But Michael Jackson is ultra-greedy, and disrespectful to boot.

♦ **V:** *Let's discuss the Dead Kennedys' lawsuit [1999-2001]. Levi's offered $70,000 to use part of their big hit, "Holiday in Cambodia," in a commercial. The other three members were desperate for money, but Biafra refused, so they sued him. (There were other issues involved as well.)*

♦ **BC:** I don't blame Biafra, because I think Levi's offered far too little money—that's disgusting! It's insulting! If someone wanted to ruin a piece of music I'd done and turn it into an advertisement, I'd expect to be paid properly—a helluva lot more.

♦ *V: Biafra cares about his "street credibility."*

♦ **BC:** I'm not bothered about that. I think money is a very important and powerful thing—a tool—that can be used for useful purposes or bad purposes. I don't have much money, so it could be quite useful to me. It would depend on which song.

If Levi's wants to use one of my songs because they think it's really good, they can pay me for it. You don't sell your birthright for a mess of pottage; who'd want to lose their street cred for $70,000, or even $270,000?!

♦ *V: So $70,000 wouldn't be acceptable, but $270,000 would be okay?*

♦ **BC:** Don't know. I definitely would want a helluva lot more than $70,000.

♦ *V: So it's the* amount *that's the pivotal factor?*

♦ **BC:** Yeah, because it's power, isn't it? Money is very useful, and you can do a lot of things with money. I could run a small press and publish what I want to for x amount of money. I'm not going to undermine Levi's by not letting them use a song—and they're not going to ask me anyway, so it doesn't matter! Also, I would probably find out how they run their operation—like, I found out that 90% of the Gap's merchandise is made by people who are overworked and underpaid in the Third World (sometimes only 35 cents an hour), and who don't have any rights. If I knew that about the company, I'd strike a deal with them on some sort of level where I could do a nice interview about their work practices!

Ten years ago *NME* [*New Musical Express,* a British music weekly] asked to interview me when I was on the SubPop label. I agreed on the condition we discuss the fact that they were doing this interview because SubPop had a publicist, rather than because I'd been doing ten years of independent music. They declined, so I refused. So if you do something with Levi's and they're doing something shady, maybe you can take their money and do an interview with somebody exposing their shoddy practices, so you can have *both:* you can have their money, *and* use that position as another piece of power to expose what you think is wrong with what they do. Or, you can be very principled and not take any of their money and still get some coverage on that. I mean, if you think you want to change the world or bring to light some practice you disagree with—I don't know what Biafra's position was . . .

♦ **V:** *"Holiday in Cambodia" is a political song, and for a corporation to use it to promote their corporate brand—well, Biafra felt this wouldn't have any integrity—*

♦ **BC:** I think that's to be respected, if that's his view. But it wouldn't be mine. The Clash licensed one of their songs for a Levi's advertisement, so for fun we wrote a version of their song "I'm So Bored with the USA" that went "I'm Selling Jeans for the USA"—and we credited it to "The Stash"! And the "B" side had a song, "CBS: Should I Suck or Should I Blow?" But that's because the Clash set themselves up as a great "political" band. I don't consider our band to be a political animal like that. But money is a very powerful tool. I'd like to have it, but I won't do *anything* just to get it. I'll find another way to get what I need, just like I've done everything to date. I've got faith that there's enough out there, and it'll all turn out fine.

We still don't have a producer, and we've done over *ninety* LPs. Record companies give you money and command you to make silly videos for silly television programs. If that's going to come about, then *I'm* going to do the silly video for the silly program so that I personally can be responsible afterward for what a load of rubbish it is!

♦ **V:** *Unfortunately, videos dictate which music sells.*

♦ **BC:** Yeah, but what sells doesn't really matter, does it?

♦ **V:** *Well, I personally don't buy the Top Forty—*

♦ **BC:** And that's not a game we could really win at—we haven't got any *armaments* in that area. We don't belong to the "professional" league. They've got their mortgages and their careers and their expensive hairstyles to worry about.

♦ **V:** *You don't own your own house? I thought that was a lot cheaper in England.*

♦ **BC:** No, I don't—it's more expensive. *Everything* is more expensive in England than in America. But **I'm not interested in turning creativity into a 9 to 5 *job*, and music does that very easily. It may be nine at night 'til five in the morning, but it's still 9 to 5!**

The longest tour I've ever done is four weeks, when I was about nineteen . . . and the shortest was a couple of days. When we come to America we do about ten dates. We don't have management, we don't have record label backing, and we don't have an official agent. We do exactly what we want, where we want.

♦ **V:** *So you have fun when you visit here?*

♦ **BC:** That's the idea! The goal is to still *want* to play the music for the most primal reason: to express yourself. And that's difficult, even after a few days, without drink and drugs. But as I said before, drink and drugs actually take you further away from the area of true expression rather than nearer, especially after repeated use. We don't tolerate the "rock'n'roll lifestyle"—it's one giant yawn. I'm not interested in people's drug habits, and that's why a lot of "Beat" writing sucks—including Mr. Kerouac's bad travelogue, *On The Road!*

♦ **V:** *What do you mean? Look at the influence he had, to this day. He could really capture an out-of-control character like Neal Cassady.*

♦ **BC:** *I* don't think so. But I must admit—I only read one page of *On the Road* when I was a kid, and I've only heard highlights read by David Carradine! But if you read Gogol or Knut Hamsun— *that's* what Beat writers should have been achieving in the fifties. Compare Dostoyevsky's *Crime and Punishment* to Kerouac's *On*

the Road, and you think "This is just travel writing—very dull."
I suppose it's sweet, though. Kerouac's got a naïve optimism
that's actually quite nice.

♦ **V:** *Also, it had ideas of independence—a   restless, truth-seeking
way of life—that still appeals to people. Well, I'll say this: in*
Hunger, *Knut Hamsun vividly communicated his own interiority—*

♦ **BC:** Yes, subjectivity, and **without subjectivity, the work is
useless—the *only* thing that's interesting in art is the subjectivity—seen objectively.**

♦ **V:** *Literature, quite uniquely, allows you to look at life through someone else's eyes . . . you can burst the confines of your own "identity"—*

♦ **BC:** Yes. Celine absolutely pisses all over most Beat writers—
and he's writing thirty years before! So does John Fante, writing
in the thirties—he talks from his *heart.*

Maybe I'm spoiled because I've read a lot of good European
writing. You read the opening lines of *Moby Dick* (I know—he's
an *American!*) and immediately you're thrust into the main
character's mind-set: when he's compelled to start going around
knocking people's hats off, he knows it's time to go to sea! Then
he gets into bed with some strange cannibal . . . this is the kind
of travel writing I can relate to.

♦ **V:** *Well,* On the Road *is absolutely required reading. It vividly
describes white people talking like "hipsters," imitating the blacks'
speech and "digging" their music. A matrix for the Beat movement
was the bebop jazz scene where Charlie Parker was THE icon, and
he was totally "cool": he would come out, not acknowledge anyone,
get up onstage and start wailing.*

AGAINST "SCENES"

♦ **BC:** He probably thought, "I'm not talking to these squares!"
[laughs] Anyway, I don't like "cool."

♦ **V:** *"Cool" can easily become "elitist"—*

♦ **BC:** I'm not interested in *scenes,* you see. You look at Hamsun and read *Hunger* and there's no "scene" going on. This person's life is on the line and he's *doing* something. I suppose it's wrong to compare *On the Road* and *Hunger,* but **for me, art that isn't intrinsically subjective has very little value, because you've got to GIVE of yourself.**

♦ **V:** *Not only can you feel Hamsun's hunger, but it's like he just washed your windshield—you see everything more clearly, with hallucinatory clarity.*

♦ **BC:** But mainly there's not a big "scene" around the book, or the author. Whereas with someone like Burroughs, you're forced to be around all these *stamp-collectors* who are into him. I've met these anal-retentive Northern Europeans—German chaps— who love *anything* Beat. They think it's all so risky and wild.

♦ **V:** *Of course, you're generalizing here. The so-called "Beats" are really all very different, as writers and personalities—*

[two guests arrive, Johnny & Giselle Brewton]

♦ **JOHNNY BREWTON:** I think Bob Kaufman was on top of all of those Beats; what he achieved was pretty amazing. I also think some of Harold Norse's poetry is astounding. But they're outsiders.

♦ **GISELLE BREWTON:** And what about Jack Micheline [lesser-known, later Beat poet who died recently in San Francisco]?

♦ **BC:** But Micheline's poetry is subjective, and he's a genuine Outsider. Maybe he desperately wanted to belong somewhere, but he probably benefited from not getting famous or overexposed, because fame and exposure doesn't do anyone—writers, poets, musicians—any good at all. Yet that's what most of them are striving for.

I mean, nothing is as good as people say it is; it's all hype. Artists aren't as important as they (or their fans) say they are. Jack Micheline never had a cult, like Burroughs, so he's unknown. Besides, who's interested in someone's drug habits, for chrissake?!

♦ *V: You're reducing Burroughs to "drug habits"?! Well, what I enjoyed most was* The Job *[interview book], plus the scores of interviews he did. I'd read* Naked Lunch *much earlier, but didn't get fanatically interested in Burroughs until* The Job *came out.*

BOWIE AND DUCHAMP

♦ **BC:** Why are we talking about the Beats? **I think it's the "Cult of the Ego Artist" that is the problem.** We seem to be stuck with this situation where cults and the fan base are the important issue. Take David Bowie: nobody says to him, "David, your hair looks ridiculous, and your music's been crap and getting worse for the last twenty years. It wasn't too bad when you did those R&B records—straighten yourself out, you tit!" You know he doesn't surround himself with people who might speak to him like that. No, he surrounds himself with people who say, "Nice perm, David . . . You're a genius. Carry on assimilating modern youth culture and trying to beat them to the punch, charting even before *they* do. Congratulations—you're a star!" Of course he prefers that. But that doesn't really do your creativity a lot of good, does it?

♦ *V: Taking a longer view, I think Marcel Duchamp is the single most original artist of the 20th century—*

♦ **BC:** Well, I think he had a good sense of *humor.* But I think the people who followed him, doing all this "Conceptual" art, are dull. Duchamp was trying to take the piss out of the establishment, whereas now the establishment is peddling that sort of thing as mainstream. Duchamp would be intelligent enough not to have anything to do with these twats producing so-called cutting-edge art these days, like the so-called "Brit-Art Pack"—I think if he were around now, he'd get on with some *painting* again.

I propose that it's important not to chase after success, but to instead concentrate on *PROCESS* . . . and that brings us back to Duchamp and readymades. Duchamp said, "Something is art when an artist says it's art"—i.e., **you take something that wasn't previously considered "art" and by saying it *is*, you con people into believing that. And that means you're clever, because then you've had an "original" idea,** and originality apparently is very important. Fortunately, people seem to know that most artists' ideas nowadays are worthless—

♦ *V: Except for Duchamp—*

♦ **BC:** But he thought up the joke! I think he had nothing but contempt for the people who considered things like his urinal to be art. Because as soon as you take them out of the gallery, they're not art. I can understand Duchamp doing it, but after that, there's no reason to do it ever again!

In my opinion, the only thing that makes something "art" is when you do something deeply subjective and risk "baring your soul." And of course you might fail, and do some useless pictures, and people might think you're stupid.

♦ *V: Well, I still like the idea of "appropriation," which Duchamp pioneered. He took a cheap reproduction of the Mona Lisa, wrote "L.H.O.O.Q." on it and signed it—*

♦ **JB:** Which meant "she has a hot ass"—

♦ **BC:** It's great making jokes like that and working against a gallery system like it was at that time. But Charles Saatchi put on his exhibition, "Sensation," in New York, mainly to inflate the value of his collection. Saatchi is a very influential ad agency businessman who helped bring the conservative party and Margaret Thatcher into power. And the kind of "controversial" work he's selling us is really mainstream—I doubt Duchamp would go near it. A lot of artists today consider their work to be very advanced and really good if it can be assimilated and turned into advertising *immediately.* And supposedly all alternative culture can be turned around within months and used for advertising—

♦ **V:** *Within days, you mean, thanks to cool hunters—*

♦ **BC:** Whereas previously it could take twenty years for that to happen. I think it's wise to be aware of that and actually work in the opposite direction: try to do work which is absolutely *impossible* to use in advertising!

♦ **V:** *Well, the ad agencies refined the concept of the "focus group" with the testers behind invisible windows, videotaping emotions and body signals (like an eyebrow raising). They study the physical signs of us reacting as machines: the involuntary responses we don't have control over mirror our inner reactions more truthfully than you might pencil in on a form.*

♦ **BC:** That's interesting . . . but I think all you can really do is go into your own work, your own process, and do your own "thing." You know: **Becoming a Painter is the Answer! Risk doing bad pictures!**

♦ **V:** *And bad poems, I suppose. And while doing this, aren't we all supposed to be evolving, on our own personal evolutionary paths?*

♦ **BC:** Actually, I think that might be one of the big problems: the idea of the evolutionary path; the idea that we're going somewhere along some linear upward road. Why is it that every music group on god's earth makes one good album and then it's all downhill? In the sixties, if groups were *lucky* they got to make two or three, because marketing wasn't as sophisticated and the musicians didn't learn they were "geniuses" quite so quickly.

Whenever I do anything, I'm always trying to remember why I did it in the first place. I want to release records that people think were done by talentless fifteen-year-olds. That's the thing: to stay *there,* in an area where you're not really trying to be involved in the technicalities, like trying to be a genius guitarist. **Everything now is style over content.**

The goal is to try to recapture your original creative energy, keep your "channel" open—not to impress people with *technique:*

that's dull. That's like a scale model of the Titanic built out of matchsticks: you think, "Fantastic—that must have taken a long time." Then you leave the room. Or rather, you wonder if it's flammable! [laughs]

♦ *V: Actually, I have a liking for scale models like that.*

♦ **BC:** I love scale models—they're little worlds.

♦ *V: One of my favorite San Francisco cultural legacies is beneath the Cliff House at the Musée Mécanique: a scale model of an old carnival built of matchsticks by a prisoner in the early 20th century.*

AMATEURISM

♦ **BC:** You can still look at and admire technique, but it's not something to *aim* for. It doesn't have anything to do with art, or furthering anything. It's nice for a little fantasy world—I love fantasy worlds; I live in one. But I basically feel that exalting craft or technique is objectionable.

It's really weird: you're walking this tightrope between two poles: *you've got to realize how unimportant your work is, and also make it the most important thing you do,* all the while respecting it enough not to turn it into a *job* at the same time! That's why the Amateur will always win. The Amateur is in the best position to do anything, since you're doing it because of love rather than your mortgage!

AMATEURISM is so underrated in this society. **When you're working at an amateur level all the time, you've got this massive advantage over everybody else, because you enjoy a certain level of *freedom***—whereas the professional has all these constraints: "It's my job! I *have* to do it like that." And all the newspapers and everybody are trying to make you a professional. You just have to fight them tooth and nail. Why? Because we love that punk rock spirit. All those groups that came in and didn't know what they were doing—that's what was fantastic. Because then they might do something other people don't do.

I was really only in punk rock about six months; then I got out in 1977. Once the mohawks and black leather clothes and drugs came in, it was finished as far as I was concerned. Also, it started to turn into "rock music." The Sex Pistols were a punk band that was basically a rock group, and when the "rock" element began taking over the "punk"—well, let them take the "rock"; I'll keep the "punk"!

♦ **JB:** People started saying, "You're not supposed to do this!" and all these rules emerged. But in the early days there were people dressed all sorts of ways; you didn't have to have a certain haircut. It was a bunch of *individuals,* and that's what drew me to it.

♦ **BC:** When you went to see the Damned, Captain Sensible would be wearing his nurse's costume or his ballerina outfit . . .

♦ *V: There were gays, weirdos and all ages involved. At early punk shows in San Francisco there was a woman in her seventies named Lenore, who was always elegantly dressed, and that was fine.*

♦ **BC: Once any movement starts becoming homogenized, it becomes clichéd.**

♦ *V: When teenagers from the suburbs started pouring in (because they'd seen violent-appearing "punk rock" on NBC Weekend), the original generation just vanished.*

♦ **BC:** Well, I think that's the thing to do: *vanish* is the answer.

♦ *V: Yes, but then what do you do for fun? Stay home? I don't consider that much of an improvement. The word "coyote" comes to mind: become a trickster or a camouflage artist just to keep some kind of integrity—*

♦ **BC:** In a world of professionals, the artist must forever be a moving target. **You've got to stay a moving target all the time—absolutely. When undergrounds keep going long enough, the emphasis seems to change from "content" to**

"form." And once people start dwelling on "form," they lose interest in "process" or dealing with their own neuroses.

♦ *V: Poetry used to be a very solitary occupation before it became "PoetrySlam!" While hiphop has been applauded for "turning kids toward poetry," sometimes I question the* process *involved: having rhyming dictionaries and using the mechanism of the forced rhyme to almost dictate the* content. *Because to me that is not interiority, which is the crux, the core, the essence. It's as though there were some conspiracy to take away our inner lives—*

♦ **BC:** Yeah, but I don't think anyone's taking anything away from anyone. I think things have always been the same; you're always faced with the problem of getting on with your *own* process.

STUCKISM

I'm part of this anti-Conceptualist group in England called the "Stuckists" (or "Stuckism"). We have a manifesto at *www.stuckism.com.* The term derives from an insult by an old girlfriend, Tracey Emin, a painter who used to be involved in Hangman Books. She's now a famous Conceptualist artist. She said that my music was stuck, my painting was stuck (meaning I'm not doing "new" clever, conceptual ideas).

One of the Stuckists' more contentious points is: **"Artists who don't paint aren't artists. Art that has to be in a gallery to be art, isn't art.** The Stuckist paints pictures because painting pictures is what matters." Again, the "genius" of so many contemporary "artists" *apparently* is: they invent something new by saying that something that isn't art, IS!—which I don't think is actually that clever, once one person has thought of it. And at the moment, that's what people in the Brit-Art Pack *specialize* in.

In the holiday sun: June (mom), Nickollas (brother), Steven (Billy)

With this Stuckist group I've done interviews with the national press in England, partly because we were against the Turner Prize and art prizes in general. They said: "You're in danger of going mainstream; what do you do if that happens?" I said, "That would just be another set of problems. *No* interest gives you problems, and *too much* interest gives you a different set of problems. But **the important thing is to surround yourself with people who think you're an idiot, rather than people who think you're a genius.**"

♦ *V: I wouldn't say it's easy to achieve recognition as an artist in any field. And there are "professionals" who are laudatory, like Shakespeare, J.S. Bach, Maria Callas and Luis Bunuel. But coming out of punk, I do think one of the hardest things is to "keep an edge." You've always got to be questioning yourself, and nourishing that creative, critical fire inside of you. But at the same time, we have brains that keep on learning. So technically, you might get better as a painter.*

♦ **BC:** But that's the thing you really have to be on guard against. "Technique" doesn't always mean "better quality." I mean, technique's okay as long as it's a tool that works. But if it's a tool for its own sake, then you start getting into the area of "Form Over Content." Because getting better at something often *isn't* getting better at something! Actually, what you've got to get better at is *exposing yourself.* Like, in music or in playing a game of chess, there's the idea that *more is less.*

♦ *V: Or vice versa. Chess always reminds me of Duchamp. So many of his aphorisms I've tried to live by, like: "Never repeat, despite the encores."*

THE CONCEPT OF "GOD"?!

♦ **BC:** Yeah, but also, you've got this idea of "never repeat" reinforcing the bane of creativity, which is "originality." Duchamp, as far as I'm concerned, can take a running jump—give me Van Gogh any day! Because Van Gogh was aware of "god," aware of the need for human contact, and acutely aware of universal suffering (expressing that, and rising above that suffering). He wasn't playing any games; he had deep faith and belief in humanity. *You've got to have the guts to look for god!* And possibly fail, but have the guts to look.

When Van Gogh made his art he wasn't worrying about "originality." He didn't worry about the problem of "Don't do the encore" . . . whereas Duchamp's boxing clever all the time—*always* trying to be clever. Van Gogh had reverence for other people's work; he would copy that work to try and understand how that person thought and felt—but always bringing in his own feeling and vision, because he was a true visionary.

Modern art is entertaining and witty—but it has no humanity in it; it doesn't make you laugh, it makes you titter. People like Blake and Van Gogh are the people who matter; they're looking for how we're all in the same world together.

♦ *V: I still think Duchamp's ideas shaped the creativity of the 20th century. He introduced the idea of appropriation into art. He tried to live a simple life with minimal consumer needs, and relished sex. He announced that retinal painting was dead, and gave it up (sort of)—*

♦ **BC:** But that means he just joined in with all the teachers and other creeps who stop kids from being creative. I mean: **Painting is fundamental to the human condition. Everyone should try painting, because it's a fundamental expression—just like talking.**

♦ *V: I find Duchamp's observation that "the spectator completes the work of art" illuminating. Actually, the way I interpret that statement is: the real "art" is not in the painting itself, but in the "experience" that lights up a person's brain when they respond to a work of art.*

♦ **BC:** It can't be one or the other; it has to be *both*. There's a *process* that goes on there. Our Stuckist manifesto states: "Painting is mysterious. It creates worlds within worlds, giving access to the unseen psychological realities that we inhabit."

♦ *V: There's something to that. When you see small children painting in a kindergarten, it really seems like a primal urge is being expressed.*

This past year I've been thinking about the I.W.W., the great early 20th-century labor union that was trying to unify all workers so they wouldn't remain isolated in their special interests but have a more universal outlook. Their credo could have derived from Buddhism: "An injury to one is an injury to all." That's not just for labor unions; it's a statement of the human condition. This is why we react so strongly when somebody gets murdered—

♦ **BC:** I totally agree.

♦ *V: We're all connected. That is the thing that people have forgotten.*

♦**BC:** This is why it's important to have the *guts* to look for god in art! . . . because that's what we are looking for.

♦ *V: You're on risky territory. No one's dared to use the word "god" for decades, especially in "counterculture" circles.*

♦**BC:** Yes, but that's the problem. If you read Dostoyevsky, he's not afraid of god; he's not afraid to mention it. Van Gogh certainly wasn't; he had a very clear idea in mind.

♦ *V: But you're using a word associated with thousands of years of patriarchy, hierarchy, hegemony and oppression—*

♦**BC:** I know. But you've got to have a lot of guts to be an artist as well.

♦ *V: I think that instead of "Stuckism," you'd be better off using "Amateurism."*

♦**BC:** Maybe. [continues reading] "**Painting is the medium of self-discovery. It engages the person fully with the process of action, emotion, thought and vision**, revealing all of these with intimate and unforgiving breadth and detail." The idea being: painting doesn't hide anything, especially if you haven't learned technique. By the way, your friend Klaus Maeck from Hamburg is painting now. [reads] "The Stuckist gives up the laborious task of playing games of novelty, shock and gimmick."

♦ *V: All the so-called "cutting-edge" art of the past decades has been preoccupied with shock for its own sake.*

♦**BC:** And it's all godless rubbish!

♦ *V: I like the idea that painting is necessary; a necessary process of self-discovery. That's half of what life is about: self-discovery. We also want to know how the world works: its laws and principles, plus all the important history that has been hidden from us.*

♦**BC: I would say that self-discovery is the primal reason for being alive: to discover ourselves, and in the end love ourselves**, and thereby be able to relate realistically and communicate in as "real" a way as possible who we are, and what our beliefs and dreams are, so that we *can* make the world a better place!

♦ *V: Do you think you've always had a sense of entitlement?*

♦ **BC:** Yeah—although I'm not very well educated, and I'm dyslexic, and was sexually abused. People always used to ask, "Do you think you're different from everybody else: special?" and I'd go, "Yes, I do." But **the truth of the matter is: either all of us are special, or none of us is, so we're *all* special!** I'm lucky in the sense that I have some sort of "handle" on that idea. It's all right for me to do what I want, but that's also everybody's right.

♦ *V: Don't you think people have a drive to know the world, and have the biggest possible picture of the way the world works?*

♦ **BC:** I think so. But in the end, self-discovery actually IS discovery of the outer world. **Knowing yourself IS knowing somebody else . . . but knowing somebody else is NOT knowing yourself!** [laughs]

♦ *V: At the same time, I'm interested in knowing, period.*

♦ **BC:** But you're an archivist. You think you can accumulate enough knowledge to "know" things: list them, catalog them, put them in libraries, and thereby think you know about life. You've got a real collector mentality. You think you can somehow capture the world or capture the knowledge, in books and records. You think you can *record* it all and thereby have it at your disposal or at your beck and call, as if you've *assimilated* that knowledge. It's a bit like tourism: traveling somewhere and "doing" places. That's the feeling I get from the way you put things together: you're sort of like the ultimate collector.

♦ *V: I think my books (e.g., the* PRANKS *book of thirty interviews with pranksters) present widely diverse viewpoints—de-centering and de-hierarchizing the single monolithic voice that dictates most narratives.*

♦ **BC:** I think doing some painting would do you good—a lot more good than cataloging what other people say. [laughs]

♦ *V: The reason I do what I do is: I felt there was a shortage of "real conversations" in the world. In the mass media, all so-called "conversations" are tailored to fit certain agendas, formulaic structures, or "edited"—the polite word for censorship. Part of my motivation is: I think history is very important, and I believe that much of the "real" history was not preserved, or is not being preserved now.*

♦ **BC:** Is it an obsession?

♦ *V: Just one of many obsessions. I certainly won't live long enough to know everything I want to know—there's not enough time.*

♦ **BC:** I think we distract ourselves all the time from our "true" purposes by intellectual pursuits involving mainly books and ideas. I think ideas are *so* overrated.

♦ *V: What do you mean? I'm constantly questioning how our thoughts are shaped by structural mechanics of language, like the "either/or" syllogism which William Burroughs got from Korzybski. So many people think, "Well, it's either THIS or THAT," when in reality there could be a hundred choices. Yet it's so easy for humans to be persuaded by rhetoric that they only have two choices.*

♦ **BC:** Oh yeah, I can totally see that. "Either/or" is fantastic for arguments, as are all generalizations. But, if you're really interested in "truth," and if we're all "one," then all of this dualistic world is an illusion. I think in Buddhism the idea is that *all concepts are errors,* in the end.

♦ *V: Including the concept of "Buddhism," I suppose!*

♦ **BC: It seems very likely that we *are* interconnected; it seems very likely there *is* a collective unconscious.** It seems very likely that we're all cut from the same basic cloth. Nothing exists outside of anything else; everything is interconnected, because as soon as you know something exists, it's already included in the "connectedness."

♦ *V: Yet we're all different. It's hard not to believe that extraordinary consciousness exists, when you read about idiot savants who can divide a twenty-digit number by a ten-digit number almost immediately.*

♦ **BC:** I believe in the Law of Cause and Effect and I believe that probably there is Reincarnation.

♦ *V: Let's change the topic. How come you're not attacking the main bane of our life: the corporate, capitalist mind-set that says the highest justification for doing anything is the profit motive—*

♦ **BC:** What do you mean by "attacking" it? I think that an attack probably is more useless than not attacking it.

I'm not interested in movements or groups. Communism doesn't hold any interest for me, and neither does fascism—none of them seem to work particularly well. I don't really subscribe to any dogma, so capitalism bores me, communism bores me—I just don't want to belong to any artificial group of people. I think we all belong together anyway, and I don't want to gang up with one gang against another gang!

I never did that, even when I was younger—that's why I was very disillusioned with punk rock stuff, and I never went on any "Rock Against Racism" gigs or any of those things—I just was never interested in it. And liberalism interests me less. I've never been involved in any religion—I mean, I've been *interested* in Christian and Buddhist and Taoist and Sufi ideas and some New-Agey American Indian-type ideas—*if* there are tools or things within those that are useful. But not as a way of living or being *separate*.

♦ **V:** *That's a good way to look at all these religions and philosophical systems—as providing* tools, say, *against fear. Fear is such a crippling emotion; it keeps us from being creative and enjoying life. I'm always interested in trying to imagine a better world.*

♦ **BC:** Yeah, but I think that a better world would involve de-evolution. I mean: *not* having to have *growth*—say, in national product. To have smaller regional governments. **I believe in organic farming, in organic painting, in organic bookmaking—*everything* organic, everything back to corner shops.**

♦ **V:** *Yet the main goal most small business people have is to gain larger market share—*

♦ **BC:** But how do you do that? You become like McDonald's. If you're an organic corner grocery, you're an organic corner grocery—it's not scalable. Either you've got quality intimate communication, or you've got mass communication which is basically all *marketing*—junk food. The thing is, **if you want to make**

homemade cooking, you can't actually *do* that *en masse*. It's best to try to communicate in a real way to a few people—properly—rather than give millions of people McDonald's fare.

♦ *V: We're talking about creating our "own" culture here, and for that maybe we need to start our own city. I gave a talk at Cleveland's Rock'n'Roll Hall of Fame on the early 20th century Harlem Renaissance. Harlem was promoted by word-of-mouth as "the first negro city," and rebellious, creative black Americans from all over the U.S. migrated there. All these geographical upstarts coming together caused an unprecedented flowering of language, poetry, music, dance, clothes (in every color of the rainbow, because everyone had tailors then; clothing wasn't "off the rack"). About ten years later (1936) this turned into the "Swing Movement" when the white American populace finally discovered and embraced it—*

♦ **BC:** Speaking of black culture, I saw an interview with the blues musician Muddy Waters, who I think was a very great man. Muddy Waters wasn't some sort of dogmatic preacher, yet one of the things he said was, "You can't do this music without god."

♦ *V: And god equals love, I suppose.*

♦ **BC:** Love *is* what everybody desires. **Our deepest wish would be for unconditional love, unconditional acceptance.** In a poem entitled "The Excesses of God" the poet Robinson Jeffers said [paraphrased], "You know god by his great *superfluousness.*" Because who else would make deep sea fishes tinged with amazing colors, or secret rainbows on the domes of deep seashells that most people are never going to see? Why would the act of reproduction have all these amazing feelings and all this richness? So much in Nature gives off this seemingly superfluous beauty—

♦ *V: To Sufis, perfumes were the proof of divinity—*

♦ **BC:** Day-to-day you can go out and feel that everything's meaningless, but another day you can go out and be struck by the beauty of so many different sights: the sky, the sunset, trees, birds—any number of things. Then you may realize that it's *all* an incredible mystery, isn't it?

◆ **V:** *I like the analogy of a fish which has lived all its life in water. Suddenly an eagle snatches it up into the dimension of air which the fish had no concept of. Likewise, "god"—like that eagle—may exist in some dimension we can't imagine. I feel the words time and space are equally indecipherable. Heisenberg said that time is not linear but more like a Moebius strip or a kind of spiral. Such a time concept might also help explain the notion of karma.*

◆ **BC:** Yeah, I don't believe in only linear time—if simply because the unconscious doesn't have a concept of time at all. And karma: obviously, what you put out will come back in—it's the Law of Cause and Effect. You can't outwit nature!

◆ **V:** *So many strange things have happened to me that I don't believe in coincidence, either… Your "god" concept still bothers me. Do you actually believe there's a white-bearded male patriarch/god up in the sky? Way back in time, your British ancestors were Pagans. Recently I've been reading about the Gaia theory, that the entire earth and universe are alive and are one big unified organism, even the rocks. Do you go along with that notion?*

◆ **BC:** Oh, certainly! **There's no doubt** *that's* **what "god" is; that makes complete sense to me. I don't really like organized religions very much. I read that book,** *The Gaia Theory* **when it came out about 13 years ago**; I was very impressed with it. There was also a very good TV program on the Gaia hypothesis in England.

I don't have any problem with Wicca or how that works. I don't need to become a Pagan because I already *am* one—I'm just not one to join groups; I'd rather start my own! I don't have a dogma about what people should, or should not, do. But I do like the basic Christian ethic about trying to treat people right and be forthright and honest, as well as: Don't judge, or be judgmental. Some of the best Christians don't know they're Christians, and some people who say they're Christians are among the most dangerous (and deluded) people alive! In the end, we've all got our own conscience.

Again, all that matters in life is *communication:* genuine, meaningful communication with other humans. It's the only thing that gives our lives meaning. Because without other people, there's nothing. We really are all in this together.

♦ *V: Yet today there are so many people whose communication skills are damaged. And communication can be much more than words— dance is a form of communication, and so is gesture.*

♦ **BC:** Obviously, just as much as words.

♦ *V: So if we're talking about restoring society, it means greatly enhancing our communication models—being more actively truthful and less passive. It's important for everyone to actively reinvent their language—*

♦ **BC:** Yes, passivity is absolutely useless . . .

♦ *V: The language of politicians is all about form, not content: "I'm for the American people."*

♦ **BC:** The "Form Over Content" idea goes right through society now and is part of bureaucracies everywhere. And business has become all about "image" or "branding" or "positioning"—just *façade.* I think that conceptual art goes hand-in-hand with that. Before, the avant-garde really *was* avant-garde—it was *leading* society. Now the so-called avant-gardistes are dragging their feet and are actually *behind.*

♦ *V: It's funny how you have to always be reassessing your views, and even reversing them, sometimes.*

♦ **BC:** That's essential, isn't it?

♦ *V: Partly because society's mechanisms of co-optation are so fast now. It's not necessarily radical to have a mohawk and look punk rock, now.*

♦ **BC:** We have to live *now;* I think everything starts now. Every person alive has been born into the present; every person born is living on the edge of their own destruction. **It's up to you to take responsibility as quickly and as ably as you can, and live your life according to your vision—find out what your vision *is,* and live your life by that.** That's each person's duty. ♦ ♦ ♦

RECOMMENDATIONS

Some books on Billy's bookshelf:

All Charles Bukowski, especially *Ham on Rye* and *Burning in Water, Drowning in Flame*

All John Fante, including *Wait Until Spring, Bandini* and *Ask The Dust*

Celine: *Death on the Installment Plan*

Mark Twain: *Huckleberry Finn*

Selected Odes of Pablo Neruda

Tom Kromer: *Waiting For Nothing*

Gogol: *The Overcoat*

Knut Hamsun: *Hunger, Pan, Mysteries*

Dostoyevsky: *Brothers Karamazov, The Idiot, Crime and Punishment, Notes from the Underground*

Herman Melville: *Moby Dick*

Chogyam Trungpa: *Born in Tibet, Cutting Through Spiritual Materialism, The Myth of Freedom*

Ronald De Leeuw, ed: *Letters of Van Gogh*

Irving Stone: *Lust for Life* (biography of Van Gogh)

Hans Fallada: *Little Man, What Now?*

Freiherr Von Mullenheim-Rechberg Burkard: *Battleship Bismarck*

Theodore W. Goosen, ed: *Oxford Book of Japanese Short Stories*

Iona Opie: *Oxford Nursery Rhyme Book*

Black Elk: *Black Elk Speaks*

Dee Brown: *Bury My Heart at Wounded Knee*

Paul Radin: *The Trickster*

Julia M. White: *Hokkusai and Hiroshige* (Japanese painters)

Charles Mingus: *Beneath the Underdog*

Amadea Morningstar: *The Ayurvedic Cookbook* ("I like cooking!")

Walt Whitman: *Collected Poems*

Alfred Lansing: *Endurance* ("about Ernest Shackleton; I like triumph over adversity")

Robert Walser: *Institute Benjamenta*

Bruce Bernard: *Vincent by Himself* (Van Gogh)

Arne Eggum, B. Holm: *Munch and Photography*

Stephen Mitchell: *Tao Te Ching* and *The Gospel According to Jesus; The Book of Job* (he tries to work out what Jesus was historically, without the B.S.)

Francois Villon: *Poems*

Biographies

Film Favorites:

Night of the Hunter
Goodbye, Mr Chips
Ben Hur
Dial M for Murder

Published by Codex, 1996, U.K.

Michael Powell: *Stairway to Heaven, Peeping Tom, Life and Death of Colonel Blimp* (banned in the U.K.; Churchill didn't like it because it showed friendship between British and German citizens)

Jason and the Argonauts
A Christmas Carol (with Alistair Sim)
All Laurel & Hardy
It's a Wonderful Life

Documentaries ("especially about animals, archeology, real history, World War I and World War II")

"I don't like films that glorify violence, are too hateful or spiteful, or horror films—my life's too much like that already!"

        —Billy Childish

JELLO BIAFRA

Jello in the year 2000

J ello Biafra was the lead singer/songwriter of the early San Francisco punk band Dead Kennedys. Unlike most punk musicians, he was one of the first to go up against the music industry itself, forming Alternative Tentacles Records over 20 years ago. He remains musically active today in groups such as Lard.

In 1986 his *Frankenchrist* trial (the first record in history charged with obscenity) forced him into international limelight as a gadfly speaking out on censorship and First-Amendment violations. Thus began his career as a spoken-word firebrand. Biafra has a way of penetrating political and corporate media smokescreens to spotlight the *real* issues festering beneath. His radical insights inform a dozen music albums and six spoken-word albums on the Alternative Tentacles label, which is currently under legal attack. It seems he has paid dearly for sticking to his original anti-corporate vision, ethics, and principles of the band.

Jello Biafra's newest recordings include *Become the Media* (a 3-CD set) and *The No WTO Combo,* available from *www.alternativetentacles.com* or PO Box 419092, SF, CA 94141-9092 USA (send $1 for catalog). This is also the contact address for the Alternative Tentacles Legal Defense Fund; contributions are needed to help ensure the independent punk label's survival.

This interview began after a Tomata Du Plenty painting show/reading at Vesuvio's in North Beach, San Francisco. A second interview took place by phone from Biafra's hometown, Boulder, Colorado.

WELCOME TO THE NEW CORPORATE FEUDALISM

♦**JELLO BIAFRA:** [having just been panhandled] Even the homeless have corporate logos on them—what does THAT say about what we're turning into?!

♦ *VALE: That's because in the past 20 years the corporations have learned the importance of branding, and they give away lots of clothing prominently displaying their brand or logo—*

♦**JB:** Oh, they make you pay for it. You *buy* T-shirts with your favorite band's logo on the front—you're *paying* to advertise *them!* And I traffic in it, too—I admit it—because our record label sells T-shirts.

I was part of the 30th Anniversary of the Summer of Love concert in Golden Gate Park (1997). I walked up to the microphone thinking, "Oh, s..., I'm by far the youngest person on the bill. *What* am I gonna say? . . . I know . . ." So I said, "I'll bet you the difference between the original, 'real' Summer of Love and this, is there were not all those corporate logos and banners by the concession stands. I'll bet that giant blow-up Miller beer can balloon wouldn't have been there." And by the end of the Jefferson Airplane set, someone had popped that balloon!

So Miller, after the fact, called up Chet Helms [promoter] and said, "We're pulling $15,000 in funding from your event because you failed to guarantee that no artists would attack our products from the stage." Dirk Dirksen [Mabuhay Gardens impresario] called and told me how livid the promoters were over this, adding, "Please don't go to the press with this, Biafra—it'll make it worse." So I played ball and didn't go to the press, and finally Miller was shamed into coughing up the promised money. Part of the agreement was that the promoters had to patch the balloon so Miller could take it to their next event—an amusing ending to this that shows why **these bastards must be fought when they try to . . . not exactly "steal" our culture so much as *stamp ownership* on it—kind of like the Mark of the Beast!**

♦ *V: It's finally time to examine how advertising, marketing and branding have gotten so much better, to the point where it's almost impossible to have any kind of "counterculture" anymore—*

♦**JB:** The *San Francisco Bay Guardian* ran an article about Pepsi trying to buy into the school district here. Soda companies and Frito-Lay will offer millions to a school district that has had its tax money taken away (by the very same people whom the soda companies "funded," I suppose), then say, "We'll give you ten million bucks if we're the exclusive beverage in all of your schools." And they get to advertise. Like in Colorado Springs: instead of pep banners in the gym, there are Pepsi banners, Pepsi machines the minute you walk in the front door, Pepsi ads on the sides of school buses, posters, etc. And even though they passed a law against it here in California, the companies are trying to do it anyway.

♦ *V: It's the mind-set of the corporate state: Do whatever it takes to make maximum profits as quickly as possible, ignoring people's welfare and the environment—*

♦**JB:** Actually, the corporate state has no mind, because there are too many people (and too much money) involved, who fight with each other because they want total control over everybody else—and no one can have it all, not even Bill Gates! When you get to that level, it's like *wealth addiction* rather than crack addiction—a far more dangerous drug, in my opinion. That's why I seized on the Green Party's idea for MAXIMUM WAGE and trumpeted it everywhere. The Green Party didn't set a maximum, but here's mine: six figures, and then cut everybody off! And the benefit would be FREE SCHOOLS, FREE MEDICAL CARE, FREE CHILD CARE— things that are a *given* as a human right in other "civilized" countries. And FREE TRANSPORTATION . . .

I like the idea of abolishing the stock market entirely.

That's a major element of wealth addiction. Once somebody gets their first million, what more is there to gain? Obviously, there's a very deep drive to succeed, and success is measured in money, and people figure they have to keep playing the game and play for higher and higher stakes to make more and more money to feed their wealth addiction habit. And if it means screwing over everybody else, so much the better—thus Ross Perot, Donald Trump, Dianne Feinstein's husband, etc., etc., etc. That's why the best way to put wealth addicts in rehab is to take their money away. [laughs]

When I went on "Politically Incorrect" and introduced the idea of maximum wage, I was booed by hosts, guests and audience alike. When I called Michael Jordan a wealthy parasite, another guest (the star of the TV version of "Clueless") whined, "But *wait,* he was a good basketball player. He deserved all that money" and other pearls of wisdom.

Part of what I did in Seattle during the anti-WTO protests was just to say: Step One is to divorce oneself from corporate feudalism as much as humanly possible—not to mention *sabotage* it, if you possibly can. Unfortunately, there's just one way to completely divorce yourself from corporate feudalism—I know of only one person who ever pulled that off, remaining pure and politically correct as the driven snow, and that's Ted Kaczynski. But he suffered dearly for his art statement, didn't he? He lived in a little cabin with no windows, so miserable that he sent mail bombs for 20 years to people he didn't even know, because he couldn't get laid. There's got to be a better way!

So what I try to tell people is: **Just think about what you're doing, what you're buying, and start trying to divorce yourself from *crap* as much as possible. Don't go to chain stores, don't buy corporate products.** To some degree we all have to—I happen to like cars, and there's no nice organic woodsy oil company out there to supply us with politically correct gasoline. So a compromise is being made right there.

SUVs = Yuppie Tanks

♦ *V: You don't drive a new SUV, do you?*

♦**JB:** Hell, no—those things just radiate evil. They're yuppie Cadillacs; tanks—that's the whole mentality behind them. I saved a magazine ad for the Lexus model that shows all these look-alike houses in suburbia with tanks in the driveways, and the smart shopper front-and-center with a Lexus SUV in the driveway instead. And then the Lincoln Navigator ad proclaimed it as an "Urban Assault Vehicle" with "luxury" written above in pink cursive writing with a little pointer. I mean, what kind of self-important, paranoid a--hole thinks they need a Humvee to commute back and forth in L.A.? And those drivers just cut in front of everybody. You heard about the SUV Nazi who cut in front of a woman near the San Jose airport? When she bumped into his back bumper, he got out of the SUV, pulled her dog out of her car and flung it into oncoming traffic and killed it. When you drive one of those SUVs, what you're saying to the rest of the world is, "I'm an a--hole, and I'm an a--hole because I can afford to be—*ha ha ha."*

♦ *V: What's your take on the incredible amounts of money being spent on prisons? Venture capitalists (VCs) are big investors here; it's a growth industry. And all these prison employees are happy to be getting such high-paying jobs—*

♦**JB:** Well, **what does it say about our "family values" when a prison guard makes twice as much as a schoolteacher?** I'm sure you've heard the term "prison-industrial complex." That's exactly what's happening. The reason to keep building more and more jails and locking up more and more people is *money,* pure and simple. Private prisons is the fastest-growing sector of the American economy; Corrections Corporation of America was one of the top five stocks on Wall Street. They're expanding into Australia and other countries now, too. As far as I know, their closest competitor is Wackenhut, which is long reported to have been owned and operated by the CIA. The *Baffler #12* had an excellent article on this.

It's a way to treat poor kids and black kids the way Germany treated the Jews, and make money off it at the same time. Plus, the prison guards' union is the most powerful in the state, and they pour huge amounts of money into the political campaigns. They knew enough to fund Gray Davis instead of Dan Lundgren, so they basically pull his strings now. I mean, it costs way less to rehabilitate somebody than to lock them up for drugs, but we're locking everybody up. It's all a matter of who's making the money.

♦ **V:** *Lobbying is just another kind of corporate payola at work—*

♦**JB:** The word "scam" comes to mind. There aren't Communists to fight anymore, so now those same military executives make their money waging war on the American people. That's why there are so many SWAT teams now, and why so much military hardware is given to local police departments by the Pentagon. How many small-town cops really need grenade launchers? And the kind of armored personnel anti-riot vehicles that were invented for South Africa—I've read that they're giving them to our police departments for free because they can't find any dictator who wants them. Bush wants to replace a lot of our stockpiled weaponry because it's "too old"!

♦ **V:** *Wonder who profits from that? I just saw a photo in the* New York Times, *taken in Israel, of an armored bulldozer—I didn't even know these things existed. They just crash through into a house when somebody's holding someone hostage.*

♦**JB:** No, what they do is—like in Indianapolis and L.A.—they declare a house a "crack house" based on somebody's rumor, bulldoze it, and ask questions later. Kind of like how the Israeli Army treats Palestinians.

♦ **V:** *This is an era where corporations have more power than governments. Isn't the corporation the ultimate extension of capitalism?*

CORPORATE FEUDALISM

♦JB: It's not capitalism anymore, it's *feudalism:* techno-feudalism, cyber-feudalism, new feudalism—call it whatever you want.

♦ V: *Feudalism? The way that it used to be was: you had the man in the high castle and the serfs all around tilling the fields for him—*

♦JB: —a moat in between, and the guy in the castle had the gestapo in shining armor. **Every time we buy Budweiser, go to Wal-Mart, Blockbuster, or McDonald's, or consume a Time-Warner product—we're their serfs! Every time. That's how today's feudalism works.** NAFTA, GATT, the World Economic Forum, that MAI treaty they tried to put in, the WTO, etc.— that's all sealing in writing the dictatorial enforcement arm of corporate feudalism.

The term "capitalism" applies to small business owners like us, just trying to pay our bills while putting out ideas that the corporations don't want in circulation. But feudalism is what's running things now. Feudalism is naming that new San Francisco stadium after the Pac Bell phone company instead of Willie Mays.

♦ V: *As well as changing the name of Candlestick Park to 3-Com Park—*

♦JB: The funny thing was, our then-mayor Frank Jordan was so dumb that he sold the name of Candlestick to 3-Com for a little over $400 grand, while in Denver, Coors paid $40 million-plus for the privilege of naming "Coors Field." Jordan really didn't make a very good deal.

♦ V: *Switching topics a little, the big chains Borders and Barnes & Noble have won—they've driven most of the independent bookstores out of business.*

♦JB: But what about Amazon?

♦ V: *At least they make our books available, unlike the chains. But* *for their "Advantage" program (offering to ship books to customers within 24 hours), they demand a 55% wholesale discount, and publisher pays shipping. Then they start ordering, like, six copies at a time.*

♦**JB:** Wow. Music chains aren't quite so consolidated. But what happened with the chains is: if you want your stuff displayed or even stocked, you have to *bribe* them to do it, like pay the individual manager of the store a buck a CD.

♦ *V: In order to get Borders to order more than a few copies of my book* Swing! The New Retro Renaissance, *I had to buy a $1,500 ad in their in-house catalog. They ordered 5,000 copies and then returned about 2,500—all damaged. Books are fragile; the corners are easily bent.*

♦**JB:** Gawd! And Borders was at one time a supposedly "hip" company. They've been very good against censorship over the years, but not so good on employee unions.

♦ *V: They've changed. The corporations themselves are being squeezed by competition. There never was that much money in the book business anyway. And when you have Barnes & Noble—*

♦**JB:** Oh—you must mean "Buns & Nubile"! The chains' impact on the music business is not as severe. The worst area hit, I think, is toy stores. Remember when some of the weirdest people in the world ran toy stores—eccentrics who still had factory-sealed 20- and 30-year-old toys in the back room, forgotten? They've all been paved over by Toys "R" Us. There are no more toy stores except Toys "R" Us—unless you buy somebody a toy gun at Wal-Mart, or something like that. **The "strange people running toy stores" species is extinct!**

♦ *V: Whenever I went to a small town or different city, I'd always look for small, musty old used bookstores. It seems they were always run by bookwormish, dowdy people, and you could make great discoveries. Now they're all gone.*

♦**JB:** It's happening with used record stores: "Oh, you can't buy that—I'm going to sell that on eBay!" All over the country all the

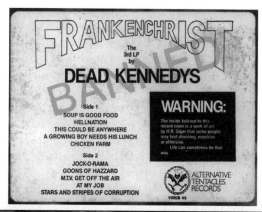

The first album busted for "obscenity" in history. The trial gained Biafra international renown, helping sell old DKs albums.

cool stuff is being pulled behind the counters and put up on evilBay. **EvilBay is the Great Satan of Record Collecting! It also encourages that many more people to think of their records as "speculative stocks" rather than music.**

♦ **V:** *There are "good" chains like Tower, which started out as one record store in Sacramento and over the years branched out all over the world. Tower, more than anyone else, got my books out to the heartland. But now they're under intense competitive siege from Virgin, Borders, Costco, Wal-Mart, etc. So they've drastically cut back their square feet of bookshelves, because in terms of linear shelf footage books don't return as much profit as CDs. They probably have MBAs calculating all this.*

♦ **JB:** A lot more people are doing mail orders now because of the crappy selection in stores. When we put up our Web site and started taking credit cards, mail order multiplied by a factor of five or six and is still growing. Has that made up for the trouble we have getting into stores? No. But it has certainly helped.

I don't know who it is, but somebody already registered *jellobiafra.com* and *jbiafra.com*. Are these well-meaning fans or junior venture capitalists trying to make me buy back my own name?! Although . . . **I love the guy who got *georgewbush.com* and put up an anti-Bush Web site—that was great!**

♦ **V:** *That's the other side of the coin. Just in the past week, two people out of my distant past found me by searching the Web. Tonight, Tomata Du Plenty said he lived in Hollywood in the early '70s, and discovered Mae West was listed in the phone book. So he called her up and visited her! She told him, "I think a star should be accessible to her fans."*

♦ **JB:** I told Tomata that if I ever had my phone number listed in the book like Mae West, I would never have any peace or get any work done.

♦ **V:** *It's great you just did this reading at Tomata's Jack Kerouac memorial, and for free—*

♦ **JB:** I do lots of things for free. But I'm not sure I would have

Biafra with Tomata Du Plenty of the Screamers, a legendary L.A. punk band. Tomata died Aug. 21, 2000 in San Francisco.

—Tomata, 1977. Photo: Judy Sitz

carved out time for it if it hadn't been Tomata who asked. I mean, that's payback in a way—because of how much the Screamers mean to me.

FAME & Its Repercussions

♦ **V:** *They never got famous, yet they were so amazingly original— L.A.'s first all-synthesizer punk band. They had such great songs and stage dynamism. Speaking of fame—how do you think you've handled fame?*

♦ **JB:** It depends on who you talk to. I mean, if I get cornered at the wrong time when I want to be left alone, I've been known to snap at people—which in one case got written up as a hit piece in some Seattle weekly. Years ago, some journalist barged into my dressing room—I was trying to warm up my voice before going onstage—and I refused to drop everything and do an interview right then and there, when I was supposed to be going straight out onto a stage. This person apparently felt that he took priority over the hundreds who were waiting for the show to start. People like that try my patience, and sometimes I'm pretty direct about that.

If you're a known performer on any kind of level, people judge you very harshly and look for flaws when they meet you; they start shopping for them, especially in punk rock. **Nobody likes to eat their young—or eat their own—the way punk rock people do. Nothing is ever good enough for the harder-core-than-thou. They're just like parents; they devour their own.**

♦ **V:** *You've had to deal for twenty years with the problem of fame. You just tell people to go away, right?*

♦ **JB:** No, not like that. Not exactly. Uh . . . it's hard. There was a little bit of that tonight at Tomata's show. I was cornered by somebody who obviously just wanted to be able to talk about spotting Jello Biafra in the bar (like I'm a rare wildlife specimen) and be seen talking to him. That's treating me like an "it."

The other ice-breaker I never know how to handle is, "Wow, Dead Kennedys was really cool when I was in high school." Is that supposed to be a compliment or not? Does it mean, "Now that I'm out of high school, I've outgrown you—and I listen to Phish"? It can be demeaning if that's all people want to hear, and they won't listen to my other stuff—I point out I have another dozen music albums and six spoken-word albums out. I mean, **I really get thorny about this myopic, rose-colored "Happy Days" version of the early punk scene that has been so effectively marketed and regurgitated** by bands who had no business reuniting. I don't get down on a band reuniting if they enjoy playing again, but a lot of people are doing it for other reasons, and don't even bother writing any new songs. Guess who doesn't go to the show? Me!

One of the things that I hated about the seventies at the time of punk, was *fifties* nostalgia: "Oh, the fifties are back! Wasn't the Eisenhower era great? Gee, isn't Fonzie funny every week on TV? Why don't we all be like that instead?" And the punks at the time were like, "We're never gonna fall for that s...; we're never gonna participate in that stupid nostalgia." And now you go to just about any punk—or for that matter, metal—show, and what do you find but row upon row of punk rock Fonzies! And the more cartoony they get—especially in appearance—the more they think they're really rebelling against something by adopting a twenty-year-old uniform, complete with logos of old obscure British bands they may never have even listened to. And that just irritates the hell out of me on one level.

On another level, I assume they're just trying to find some kind of an identity that separates them from all the wannabe yuppies and jocks and bimbos and Gap kids—the Flintstone children or whatever. But to grasp onto a cartoon and a mirage without caring about meaning—to me, it's just sad. And some-times they try to force it on somebody else, like booing a band that's far more interesting than the one whose logo is on the back of their jacket—or get down on me because I don't want to play the same Dead Kennedys songs over and over again until the end of time. They were not the people I was playing for in the first place; they're the modern equivalent of the Stones and Lynyrd Skynyrd fans who took swings at me and tried to boo us off the stage!

♦ **V:** *Back to the issue of celebrity—well, it really seems to interfere with romance. Most movie stars seem to only go out with other movie stars—*

♦**JB:** Not all of them. The ones you don't hear about find hap-piness and you never find out who the spouse is—they keep it private; there's no blood for the junk-food media to lap up. I mean, there was the same Mrs. Robert Mitchum during Mitchum's entire life—as far as I know. There *are* people like that; Jack Nicholson just doesn't happen to be one of them!

I sometimes wonder if some of the so-called stars the tabloids keep raking over the coals *arrange* for this through their publi-cists, just to keep their insecure names in the papers. It sure did wonders for Axl Rose and Oasis. The dumber their remarks, the more the tabloids played it up, and the bigger they got. Where would Eminem be without all that naughty-star pin-cushion publicity?

When you meet women, they don't necessarily see *you;* they see "it." And in my case it's mostly not women, it's guys—not for romantic or sexual purposes but for Jello the "it" purpose. So yes, that can be painful, because my social skills haven't improved much since before I got into punk. They had to improve *some,* because I had to get a band together and hustle shows. Then we got very successful real quick, so there was this calling card to hide behind. But hey—better that than sitting home growing bitter, *wishing* I'd done these things!

Another thing that happened is: as you know, I did the lion's share of the work in my band. And so when other people were going out, hanging out and partying, or even—in the case of 29th and Mission [where Biafra lived], partying in other parts of the *house*—I had band work to do. Get the songs written, get the shows happening, keep my body in one piece—

♦ **V:** —*and write up the set lists of songs to perform*—

♦**JB:** Set lists are written pretty fast, usually just before the show. Ideally, I like to sniff out the audience *before* doing the set list . . . which means some frantic writing backstage, sometimes. Unlike a lot of bands—especially British bands—Dead Kennedys never played the same set twice. If we got a good groove going on tour, I'd only vary one or two songs, but I always took a fresh look. If it was San Francisco, we'd change every time. And we always knew all of our songs—if I'd suddenly call out "Ill in the Head" as an encore a year after we'd last practiced it, we could still play it.

♦ **V:** *What's your take on marriage? My theory is: if you can prove you're a fertile couple (and have a child), THEN get married!*

♦**JB:** Fertility is measured in many more ways than one, such as: is there enough *there* to sustain the relationship? **I'm totally against this Christian thing of people not living together before marriage—***of course* **you should cohabit and screw before marriage, otherwise you might get a rude surprise when you're married!** Give yourself a year or two to get sick of each other; then and only then consider getting married.

♦ **V:** *I went to a tiny town in upstate New York and my 14-year-old niece said, "Guess what happened in theater class today? This kid did a Jello Biafra spoken-word imitation!" Apparently, he memorized one of your pieces and emulated your voice and delivery exactly. And this is a boy who's fourteen, out in the middle of nowhere. You're still influencing the younger generation—*

♦**JB:** I heard about a girl in a friend's daughter's class, about that same age, who wanted to do a report on me. And her fundamentalist Christian parents were so angry that they took all my albums away from her, pulled her out of public school and put her in a fundamentalist school.

♦ *V: Hopefully, she'll keep her integrity and rebel—*

♦**JB:** If she doesn't end up hanging herself first.

♦ *V: At least she's in a fundamentalist, rather than a Catholic, religion. The Catholics have had many more centuries to perfect their control process. They annexed Pagan imagery and icons to help sink their hooks deep into the backbrain, bragging, "Give us a child until the age of seven and he/she will be ours forever."*

♦**JB:** In their rituals they employ blood, gore and sado-masochism—no wonder they have such an impact!

♦ *V: I remember when you played a suburban high school in Moraga—*

♦**JB:** Did you go to that—the "Creamsicles" show? It was put on by this whole clique of kids who went to this wealthy suburban high school, who had been going to the Mabuhay. They found a club that was an official, sanctioned, "Rah Rah" glee club that was so square nobody ever joined it. So they all joined the Whittlers Club and voted themselves the directors. The Whittlers Club got to put on a dance every year, so they got us, the Zeros and the Liars (*aka* Sudden Fun) for the Whittlers' Christmas Ball. And no one on the PTA or faculty knew it was us until right when we walked onstage—but by then, it was too late. (We had been billed as the Creamsicles.)

We tried this again as the "Pink Twinkies" a couple years later at another high school in Contra Costa county. But by that time things were more polarized, and another punk band from there called Deadly Reign opened for us and began dissing the cowboys, which was a redneck faction at the school. The cowboys, unable to fight Deadly Reign, were about ready to fight anybody—at which point the faculty booted us off the school grounds, and we didn't get to play. But by then, enough of the redneck, reactionary jock-types at school knew that "punk rock faggots" were something to beat up on, so that we couldn't do that anymore. I mean, the beauty of the Moraga show at Campo Lindo High School was that punk was so new, we could call ourselves a new wave band like the Creamsicles and not only did the parents and faculty fall for it, but so did most of the student body. It was hilarious seeing the cheerleader types with purple bubble gum bouncing up and down with glee to the Liars and the Zeros! Everybody had a great time. It wouldn't surprise me if that was the height of Dennis's (the lead singer of the Liars) life. These young kids didn't know what hit them, but they *liked* it.

♦ *V: It seems impossible for anything like that to ever happen again—*

♦**JB:** Well, they said "never again" after the Summer of Love, but then punk happened. And then from a whole different part of our culture that major labels forgot about, hip-hop happened. But they didn't give a damn about what ghetto black youth wanted to hear. And before they knew it, the independent rap scene was strong and hugely influential. So they began trying to buy it out and/or sic Tipper Gore on both the major label and independent artists who were getting too graphically political. It was only after two or three years of this that the majors began signing authentically underground bands for the first time since the Dickies. Hüsker Dü was the experiment that didn't quite take off, and then the band broke up. But then they picked up Sonic Youth, and of course Nirvana exploded far beyond their expectations. They figured, "Migod, here's a whole new demographic bubble of young people with all this money to spend, being exposed in the suburbs to all this hardcore political rap music telling them what it's *really* like in Reagan-Bush America. We've got to *do* something about it! Migod, these kids really *don't* care what Bob Seger or Eric Clapton are doing these days. We're going to have to find them their own Bob Segers or Eric Claptons. We'll call it *grunge!*" Nothing against those bands, but very possibly they were signed to counter the effects of Public

Enemy, N.W.A., Ice-T, etc.

♦ *V: Back to the topic of fame one last time: what's the most negative aspect of being famous?*

♦**JB:** That people can look at you as a "thing" rather than a person. They do stuff with their friends, but you're not considered a friend—you're an "it." Little Richard put it this way: **"When your name is a household word, it's almost impossible to make friends."** I don't think it's that bad, but...

♦ *V: Where did you read this?*

♦**JB:** In an old *Playboy* interview which was done by John Waters. But these days, I'm sure Christy Hefner [*Playboy* publisher] has done the demographics and figured that people would rather see an interview with Michael Jordan or Schwarzenegger than anyone who actually has something interesting to say.

JOHN LENNON: *Dangerous?*

♦ *V: I still have a box of old* Playboys *from the sixties. They had great interviews with William Burroughs, Allen Ginsberg, Buckminster Fuller, Gore Vidal—*

♦**JB:** There was one with an interview with John Lennon that ran right after his death. That was pretty amazing. I was never a big Beatles fan and didn't know much about him, but he came across as really smart, really powerful and yet a dangerous person, too. I finally understood what people loved about him so much. Had he still been alive, I don't think Tipper Gore would have happened—let's put it that way. I mean, all the big names from Bob Dylan to Bruce Springsteen (or even Prince—Tipper's first big target) would not stand up against Tipper Gore when she was on her "censorship of rock music" rampage. But at least in that interview and a lot of the others that ran before he was killed, Lennon was very blunt. This was right before Reagan got

Alternative Tentacles compilation album of 17 punk bands.

in—we were deprived of "Lennon on Reagan"! The election had happened but Reagan wasn't officially in office, and the true looting, pillaging and corporate coup hadn't really begun yet.

Springsteen touched a little bit on this much later, after his appalling "Born in the USA" affair: "Well, if I let Reagan co-opt this for a little while, think of all the money I'll make." Later, he tried to distance himself from that—

♦ **V:** *Wait a minute—did he let Reagan use that song?*

♦ **JB:** I don't think so, but it was so seized upon by the worst elements of the Reagan era. He did admit he was told that if he put an American flag on the cover and make it into a patriotic package, it would sell better—and he did. Before punk even happened, when Springsteen hype was everywhere, he came across to *me* as "Bob Dylan for jocks." Think about it!

♦ **V:** *How have you managed to keep an edge for so long?*

♦ **JB:** It's partly the subject matter I'm interested in; I'm not a "love song" kind of guy. I'm not a "Woe is me, let's obsess over our personal self" kind of guy, either—you get too caught up in that and you run out of ideas, sooner or later. **The scary part is: some of the worst-case scenarios I put in my songs keep coming true.** I keep thinking, "Maybe I shouldn't write stuff like this anymore." For example, the Reagan legacy is actually *worse* than I thought it would be, in the long run.

♦ **V:** *I just read in the* New York Times *that for three decades every overseas long-distance phone call has been recorded and scanned by a computer programmed to look for words such as "drugs" or "marijuana"—*

♦ **JB:** "Anarchy" is in there, too. I'd heard years ago that the NSA [National Security Agency] was doing this, and that key trigger words start the tape recorder rolling. In the computer age, you don't even need a tape recorder anymore.

♦ **V:** *They had this technology (called "Echelon system") since the seventies, yet I never read about it.*

♦ **JB:** Winston Smith [Biafra's friend, and designer of Alternative Tentacles artwork] told me about it ages and ages ago. **In the late seventies he saw somebody (who had quit the phone company) give a lecture on this, telling which parts of everybody's phone are actually surveillance devices.** And even though the audience had come to hear something like that, it sounded so far-fetched that Winston said after a while they were hooting at him!

But this brings in a whole new area of thought: now that there's this glut of information storing what every single person said throughout their entire life, what the hell do you do with it? Who do you pay to listen to it all? How do you divide up and store this crap—which then prompts the question: how much of this do they really keep or pay attention to? I mean, the only way they could ever make it work would be to end unemployment once and for all and hire half the country to watch the other half, full-time! Everybody would have their guardian angel dressed in their McGruff the Crime Dog mask who follows them everywhere, even into the bedroom, and watches everything for them: "Just think of me as part of the furniture . . . and take a bite out of crime!" [laughs]

♦ *V: My paranoid theory on this is: "they" have such an incredible database capacity now, that they can store everything on "us."*

♦**JB:** Again, but then what do you do with it?

♦ *V: They only activate it if they've got enough evidence to put us in jail.*

♦**JB:** Who says you need to put somebody in jail? That costs far more money than, say, putting toxins in their homes so they have allergy attacks, or finding out what makes people unhealthy and then just make them ill. The Dead Kennedys' song "Government Flu" is about exactly that. And I originally got the idea from a *Hawaii Five-O* episode I saw as a teenager, where the evil Chinese agents, in order to get at somebody in Hawaii, put pollen in the person's air conditioner so that their seriously allergic child wound up in the hospital near death. I thought about it: "Wait a minute—it's not just villains on *Hawaii Five-O* that could do this; Uncle Scam, Inc. could be doing this to all of us at random or at will right now." And then I read in the *Chronicle,* "Stanford Labs admits testing germs on San Francisco," and they gave a date. I thought, "I was in town then, and I felt like s---!" Thus "Government Flu" was born.

There are more ways to neutralize a person than going through the trouble and expense of locking them up. You just screw up their lives.

♦ *V: Or assassinate them—*

♦**JB:** All you need for that is to find out if they're lonely, and send an undercover cop to fall in love with them and then stab 'em in the back and break their heart and out comes the noose. I'm sure there are people who would take that job just for kicks, just like there are lawyers who sue the s--- out of people just for the sadistic pleasure of tearing up other people's lives while making $200-$300 an hour doing it.

♦ **V:** *We're talking about something like "soft fascism"—*

♦**JB:** "Velvet Fascism"! Fascism with a Disney face. Your friend Annex [*Search & Destroy* writer] said years ago that the thing differentiating me from other punk people writing words is the way I would use Disney and cartoon influences, and put them in places where they didn't necessarily belong, to make a point. Another person who does that really well is Chuck D of Public Enemy. He turns all kinds of pop culture references inside out, into sharpened blades.

♦ **V:** *The control process has gotten so effective, it doesn't seem possible to have a global punk-rock-type movement ever again—*

♦**JB:** But there never was! I don't think there were ever a lot of hardcore thrash bands in India or Tibet—let alone most of Africa. It was and is a Western cultural thing. There are small scenes in Bangkok and whatnot, but it never became a world-wide movement. If it was a movement, as so many people claim it still is, well—movements generally *stand* for something.

Punk has inspired countless—maybe millions—of people to get off their asses and think for themselves, and become their own person, but that in itself is *not* a movement: it's an identity. Plus, punk has kinetic energy. Many people channel that energy and inspiration into genuine movements, while lesser forms of life channel it into drinking, fighting, and scamming.

Punk was and is *entertainment*. It has been used by a lot of people, including me, to get information out, and to try to inspire people to "Fight the Power," both in their daily lives and in other ways, but not all punk groups were like that. I mean, the Dickies weren't like that, neither were the Ramones or the Circle Jerks . . . almost none of the *blink-blink* punk bands that got big in the late nineties were like that at all. I mean, compared to them, the Clash seemed like hardcore revolutionaries! Obviously, I listened to and liked the Clash, but by the time I got to San Francisco [1977], at every party after a show—to play it safe and not offend anybody—you put on a Clash album. It got to where it felt like, "This is like the Beatles—it's everywhere! I don't ever want to hear this again!" Plus, I always had trouble with their political posturing on the one hand, and their playing the "corporate rock game" to the hilt, complete with drug problems and arena rock, on the other hand. I just never took the Clash that seriously.

♦ **V:** *You know, the Sex Pistols were on major labels like EMI and Virgin—well, wasn't Virgin small then?*

♦**JB:** Actually, they were huge; they had gone from being a tiny record store releasing Mike Oldfield's *Tubular Bells* to making all kinds of dough. They were a major, especially in Europe. **The seventies were such a rigid, entertainment-industry-run event: "You wanna go out and let off steam? There's a disco waiting for you."** There was so much to attack with punk that even people in high places got off on it—at least overseas. And England has much more of a flavor-of-the-month culture because of their weekly music magazines. If the Sex Pistols had happened in America, *Rolling Stone* might have written a little bit about them three years later. But England had the daily tabloid papers that Malcolm McLaren knew how to manipulate so well, and there were the music magazines that had to keep pushing new flavors or nobody would buy them anymore. So I got much more idealistic than maybe I should have been about those magazines, because they kept putting cool stuff on the cover, reviewing all the cool new singles, dismissing stuff I hated as passé . . . but then by '81, suddenly punk was passé, and Judas Priest was *back* on the cover! And I began to realize what the game really was.

♦ **V:** *Also, by 1981 a whole crop of young, idealistic journalists who had given almost messianic coverage to punk, had quit. And they were weirdos and outsiders, too, like Jon Savage—*

♦**JB:** The one person in each town who had a Stooges and/or Velvets and/or Beefheart album—found each other . . . .

♦ **V:** *But then it turned out that Jon Savage was gay, uncovering another layer of outsiderness.*

♦ **JB:** The early punk scene was not very accepting of gays—not even here.

♦ **V:** *I think it was accepting, but I also think "gayness" was not even mentioned. Don Vinil (Offs singer) and poster artist Rico were openly gay, and as far as I know nobody ever gave them trouble for that. And the trans-gender Bambi Lake and Ginger Coyote were obviously gay. Bambi has a book out, a memoir of her days in the punk scene [The Unsinkable Bambi Lake], and it's very good. The point is, there were so few of us back in those days that we welcomed anybody who seemed to be sincerely into punk, and not a poser—*

♦ **JB:** Plus, **the seventies were so horrible that almost anything that tried to blow a hole in the seventies was considered punk and therefore wonderful.** Thus, everybody from Mark Pauline to Bruce Conner to the Avengers were all punk, rather than all these other sub-sets. It wasn't all rigid and *genrefied* with a little uniform for everybody.

Seattle: No WTO!

♦ **V:** *Tell us more about your involvement in the Seattle protests against the WTO—*

♦ **JB:** I talked and performed several times in the middle of the protests. The Independent Media Center was Ground Zero for every non-corporate journalist covering the event. They were a clearinghouse, and occasionally a makeshift hospital for rubber bullet victims. Eventually the cops came right in and gassed *them* in their own building.

The "No WTO Combo" got started at one of the Spitfire shows [a package tour of musicians, actors and activists speaking out on global affairs]. Krist Novoselic [bass player from Nirvana] and I were talking to a guy who had been added to the Seattle

Biafra's *Become the Media:* a 3-CD set and
The No WTO Combo's *From the Battle in Seattle,*
both on the Alternative Tentacles label.

show to talk specifically about the WTO protest coming up, and what it meant. That was Dan Merkle, an activist lawyer who turned out to be one of the guys running the Independent Media Center. So after the Spitfire show, we all got together and started brainstorming. We tried to get some "name" acts to come out of their closet and play at this event, but not even Rage Against the Machine could be found, let alone Pearl Jam. So eventually Krist just called me up and said, "Okay, why don't *we* just be a band for the event? And we'll play with Spearhead," because Michael Franti was all up for it.

I've talked about new feudalism on my last album, by the way, and also on the album that was recorded live while surrounded by the police at the WTO protests in Seattle. I was finally in a band again—for four days: me, Krist, Kim Thayil [guitarist from Soundgarden] and Gina Mainwal on drums who they'd been working with. So we were the No WTO Combo. The whole opening is my ranting and raving about the WTO and corporate feudalism . . . and where to go from here (after Seattle). We played some old stuff and some new songs of mine.

Afterwards, Michael Franti came out to start the Spearhead set. He read a poem he had still been working on in the dressing room that practically brought me to tears—it was so powerful—summing up the events in terms of human feeling and emotions, and why we're here and where to go from here. It felt like Bob Marley was in the house for the rest of Spearhead's set—I mean, Michael keeps growing and growing.

♦ **V:** *The Spitfire spoken word tour seemed like a blast of fresh air, and one of the best events to happen—*

♦**JB:** It's nice to be able to get brain food from other people onstage! There's a rotating cast of characters and nobody is on all of the shows. Ironically, one of the people who conceived the whole thing—Zack de la Rocha, the singer from Rage Against the Machine—has yet to be on a single Spitfire show.

Anyway, Merkle and the promoters in Seattle found us a

place to play. I checked and checked with them as to what was going on, where I should go, and who I should talk to . . . **I was going to be one of the roving rabble-rousers. Abbie Hoffman ain't around anymore, so *somebody's* gotta do some of that!** It was weird to me, though, because at the Independent Media Center all of a sudden people sat down on the floor. And these people who were older, and veterans of far more protests than I, began asking me what to do because I was the "guru" figure. I kept thinking, "Why are you asking *me?*"

I basically wound up going into cheerleader mode, knowing that everybody has to keep everyone else *pumped* during an event like that. And in the end, it worked. My activities ranged from that, to talking at another punk show where Unwound was playing, and then at the last minute I got added on to the Anti-Gala Ball that was to be hosted by Michael Moore, right next to the *real* WTO Gala Ball. It was in a basketball arena where the Sonics play, so there were something like 7,000–10,000 people there. Someone said to me, "Well, Ken Kesey isn't showing—if you wanna talk, you're on!" It was organized by Mike Dolan of Public Citizen, who had been working on the protest for months. Moore's plane was late, so he never made it to emcee the event. Dolan ended up doing it himself on no notice, while having to coordinate this huge event at the same time—he was running around like a chicken with its head cut off. He handled it really well, though. They had the mayor of Seattle give a talk. One of the other speakers was Jose Bové, the farmer in France who had dismantled a McDonald's to protest the homogenization of food policies going on over there. It turns out he ain't no simple farmer; he was in Paris '68 and has always been a radical activist.

There have been a bunch of actions like that in France: farmers dumping truckloads of rotting produce at the front doorsteps of McDonald's. And part of it is because of the WTO trying to force Europe to skip strict labeling laws and accept American-made, genetically modified—or should I say, genetically

Biafra, the future thespian and entertainer, prefigured in this Kodak Brownie snapshot taken in Boulder, Colorado.

mutilated—Frankenfood. The Europeans and the Japanese are furious about this! Maybe if they keep at it, they'll be able to save America from itself . . . or from its own run-amok corporations!

The French in particular were getting all these tariffs put on their products coming into the United States, so that French wine and cheese cost triple the amount of money now, compared to before. And **what is the most hated symbol of American oppression and culture worldwide? McDonald's!** So the farmers are attacking McDonald's in France, big time.

♦ *V: I read that McDonald's sales are down. Finally people are boycotting their "McMad-Cowburgers" [that's a joke]. Apparently their "We Love to See You Smile" marketing campaign didn't improve the McDonald's "experience" for consumers. Imagine a world free from all marketing!*

♦**JB:** Right. Another speaker was the woman who runs The Body Shop, talking about "creative boycotting" as a way of sending a message to the big chains, the corporations who produce corporate products, etc. Then came Jim Hightower, the radio show host and former State Agriculture Commissioner in Texas, probably Number Two to Michael Moore as best-known rabble-rouser from that side of the fence. Then—I didn't even know he was in town but here he was—Tom Hayden appeared. All of a sudden I felt really emotional: "Ohmigod, this is who I wanted to be when I was in the sixth grade and he was sitting being tried in a courtroom [Chicago 8 Trial]—and here he is." Then it's my turn and I go, "Oh s..., *what* am I going to say? I have to follow Tom Hayden in front of 10,000 people!"

But first Senator Paul Wellstone talked—a great speaker. He was running briefly for the Democratic presidential nomination, but pulled out because he didn't think he could raise the money. Quite a shame. So people were basically going, "Yes, we're all here and we're fighting; isn't it great?" Then Hayden talked a little bit about the contrasting media coverage of protests in the sixties.

BECOME THE MEDIA!

Finally, I just did a "Well, *now* what do we do?" speech. "You can bet there's going to be a blackout on this, so…" A pet phrase of mine appeared that others have adopted: **"Don't hate the media: *become* the media!"** And this has gotta be one-on-one: everybody take what you learned in Seattle, tell your family, your relatives, people at work, people at school—people you normally don't talk to or agree with on anything—because it ain't gonna be on CNN. **We're "Behind the Corporate Curtain" now.**

♦ *V: Right. We used to feel sorry for people who were "Behind the Iron Curtain" [Russia] because allegedly they had no access to information and no voice to speak out about what was wrong in their country.*

♦**JB:** Yes, the Communists controlled their populace through lack of information, while corporate barons control us through too much information, most of it deliberately useless and meant to distract. "Survivor," celebrity divorces, weight loss freakouts to control and subordinate women *en masse*—you know: making it harder than ever to get the *right* information, and act on what's important.

But behind the Iron Curtain, word of mouth brought down the Communist bloc. And that's what we've got to do here: point out, especially to younger people, everything that's wrong, particularly behind the scenes . . . I was greatly relieved when I walked onstage to an audience of mostly steel workers and union people massing for the big march the next day, and discovered that a lot of people knew who I was after all. (Maybe it was more than just Rivethead [Ben Hamper, General Motors factory worker; author of *Rivethead: Tales from the Assembly Line*] who sang our "Forward to Death" song on the assembly line to make the job go by faster.) So it was nice to be cheered at that point, I must admit. Then I relaxed a little when I talked.

I was pointing out that this is a battle that's going to take at least as long as it took to stop the Vietnam War, and will be at least that hard—so be ready! I mean, **people are so used to changing what they don't like by channel-surfing** . . . and that's supposedly what creates the so-called "slackers" of Generation X: a sense of utter despair at not being able to change anything (because they're so used to change happening instantly, or not at all). But stopping the Vietnam war took damn near a decade and a half.

At the same time we have a kind of critical mass approaching: **so many people are so fed up with corporations, they hate corporate logos everywhere—having corporate logos stamped everywhere but their foreheads** (and they know *that's* coming soon). Finally, corporations are becoming a figure to rebel against among young people, instead of symbolizing something new to buy. They hate McDonald's, they hate Nike—the United Students Against Sweatshops movement is spreading on college campuses. And that's cool, not just because it's a great idea, but because the battle is *winnable*. And of all places, the first university to pull their merchandise contracts away from sweatshop companies making all the shirts and hats was a really conservative private Southern school: Duke University.

I like it when people realize something has international implications: "Yes, we do care if our Notre Dame sweatshirt was made by a slave in Suharto-land."

♦ **V:** *Tell us more about the Independent Media Center; it seems every city should have one!*

♦ **JB:** I think that's one of the most important things to come out of Seattle: the formation of an Independent Media Center. The police were so afraid of the real story getting out that they actually attacked the building! They did this in Los Angeles, too. Basically, it was a "Come one, come all" situation: you didn't have to go to modeling school in order to talk on camera, or have slithered up the casting couch ladder at the *Washington Post* to write an article. People just showed up with cameras and ideas and out they went. And what makes this important in getting the real story out is: for example, in Seattle, as the cops began going crazy, CNN claimed they were "remaining calm," and that "no rubber bullets had been fired." But within an hour, the IMC had posted on the Internet video footage of demonstrators being shot by rubber bullets. This instantly went all over the world, and CNN had to change their story!

More and more people are catching on to the fact that as our mass media gets more corporate, what they report is less and less accurate or reliable—*Pravda* by Disney, if you will. [*Pravda*, which means "truth" in Russian, was *the* state-censored Russian newspaper.] And so I think the independent media movement is going to grow by leaps and bounds, especially as the fascist corporate state bares its fangs a little more openly under the Shrub administration.

If I don't mention Gore again, at least change his name to Prince Albert once in this interview.

♦ *V: Right: comes in a can, not in Tipper—oh, awful pun.*

♦ **JB:** When I was in L.A., I got hold of a, shall we say, "borrowed" press pass and got into the Democratic Convention at Staples Center (arena named after an [office supply] corporation, yet again). **Imagine my nausea and horror when 5,000 Democrats broke out jubilantly in almost *Triumph of the Will*-style rabid obedience, waving signs that said "Tipper Rocks!"** What kind of brazen rewrite of history is that?! Just one more piece of evidence that the Democratic party are *not* our friends.

♦ *V: Everyone seems to have completely forgotten about her rock music censorship crusade.*

♦ **JB:** That's because she's been given quite a makeover. And even Hillary Clinton remarked, "Oh, she was right all along; she knew how bad things were going to get—"

♦ **V:** —*meaning, she saw how evil and wicked music and pop culture were going to get, way before anybody else.*

♦ **JB:** Plus, you don't need Tipper anymore when you've got people as rabid as Joseph Lieberman who, when it comes to music, free speech, and culture, is like Tipper Gore on crack! I've got a lot more remarks on Lieberman, including exact quotations from him, on my *Become the Media* spoken word album. [title of track: "If you like Tipper . . ."]

♦ **V:** *Apparently people will swallow almost anything now. Do you think Americans are becoming more conformist these days? So many people in my neighborhood have that Banana Republic/Gap clone look—*

♦**JB:** But how many of those people really live there? Maybe most of them just storm in at night or on weekends to wine, dine, wham-bam-thank-you-ma'am, and then go back to their luxury loft or their *Sillyclone Valley* kennel or whatever. And this newer generation is realizing that those people are The Enemy—especially in San Francisco. They're totally self-absorbed, totally money-hungry—they're just money-grubbing predators, and people are sick of that.

According to one veteran, the core shock-troops who stopped the Vietnam War numbered no more than 3,000–5,000 people, and everybody else just showed up for the ride. You remember in *Search & Destroy,* my first interview, I complained about people in the '60s and early '70s who showed up for the ride and then got off the bus and didn't finish the job: "The war is over, therefore we don't have to worry about human rights, or the environment, or corporate power anymore. Let's just go buy some hanging plants and a BMW and make babies." And guess whose babies are sick to death of that attitude now? [laughs]

Looking back, I think the Seattle WTO protests generated a lot of really good energy.

♦ **V:** *Do you think they could have happened without the Internet?*

♦**JB:** I don't know; it certainly helped. The cool thing about the

Net is that, now, the person who is the only weirdo in their town can find others in other parts of the country or the world—even if they are phantom weirdos or imaginary friends or whatever. It has let all kinds of different people know they're not alone.

♦ *V: Right, although to spend hours every day in front of a computer pecking away at a keyboard—*

♦ **JB:** That kind of life does not appeal to me—I still refuse to own a computer! Again, you talk about the price of fame: people have their pagers, their cell phones, their e-mail, their voice-mail—I'm the opposite. I try to make myself as hard to find as possible! No pager, no cell phone, no e-mail—well, I have an answering machine on my phone.

♦ *V: And you've never owned a brand-new car—although I have nothing against that, mind you—*

♦ **JB:** Well, I do—most brand-new cars suck! Why pay $20,000 or more for a piece of s---? Basically, I don't see any point in tying up money in stuff you don't need—and brand-new cars is one of them. People think I'm rolling in all this dough I don't have, but one of the reasons I'm able to keep buying records I like is that I hardly buy anything else. Music is my only vice.

I basically only buy what I need, and that's all. Some people have called me "cheap" on account of I don't want to spend money on this or on that. But part of me still lives in the time when I first came to San Francisco and had no money, and even an extra five bucks meant so much—it meant I could buy two or three more records at Aquarius Records [punk record store]. This helped keep me off drugs: I could buy speed, or I could buy records. So, sorry, Tipper; sorry, Senator Lieberman—music *saved* me from drugs!

The part of me that scavenges and finds ways to make something out of nothing is still very much there. **Why do I need a microwave oven if I'm never going to use one? You can find them often enough in dumpsters anyway.** All of the early furniture and even some of the computers at Alternative Tentacles were taken out of dumpsters.

♦ **V:** *I like the idea of buying four-year-old computers; they can usually be found for about a hundred dollars and do 99% of what most people need: word processing, database, spreadsheet, to-do lists—*

♦**JB:** The only reason I've ever thought of getting a computer is for porn on the Internet. I'm not sure one of the old ones would be sufficient.

♦ **V:** *Actually, the only porn that's interesting is pre-1982. Allegedly, the guitarist Michael Bloomfield used to make extra money playing on Mitchell Brothers porn soundtracks. Early or vintage pornography still has a kind of naïve quality—unlike modern porn in which all the actors were raised on TV, and every grimace and gesture looks like it was learned from a sitcom.*

♦**JB:** Even *Forum* magazine seems demographically *genre-fied* out. It's like they asked, "What is the most popular phone-f--- fantasy? Well, let's just print that over and over again." Every letter seems like every other one now, as if maybe one or two staff people write them all. Whereas when I was a teenager, you never knew what you would find in the *Forum* letters section, because all these different kinds of people and fetishes were all trying to come out of the closet, or at least let it be known that a particular fantasy exists—all at once! Now it's generic phone-f--- on the printed page, complete with glue-haired bimbos.

♦ **V:** *Tonight, at Tomata's event, you read a Kerouac piece about wanting to retreat to a cabin in Colorado. Were you reading that "ironically"?*

♦**JB:** I don't know whether I was or not; it's just that I had heard that fantasy before from Deanna Ashley in Frightwig in the middle of their heyday, and later from David Yow of Jesus Lizard. In the center of this wild, urban inferno of underground music and mayhem, they just wanted to get a house in the country and start a family! So part of the question I posed was: Did Kerouac *really* want to wind up that way? I kind of doubt it. I would think that after two or three days, he'd get a little bored with petting his dog, smoking his pipe, reading, and wandering around his mountain estate.

Personally, **I like having access to what's going on, or I would have moved back to the mountains a long time ago.** I tried it in Mendocino county at a place Winston Smith and I had near Lake Mendocino. But commuting was taking too long, so I figured, "I'll just stay in the city where things are happening."

♦ *V: It's important to have access to media. At Amoeba [huge Bay Area used record store], amazing records keep showing up, because people die. Almost any record you want will turn up there—*

♦**JB:** Not *all* of them. But even after *Incredibly Strange Music*, volumes One and Two, came out, and all the resurgence of looking for obscurities, **there are always going to be records in those stores that nobody has "discovered" yet. You just have to go for that, instead of looking for what everybody else already knows about.**

Napster and whatever replaces it can be handy, not just for old songs but tons of new unknowns who've never even released a single or CD. But again, watch out for becoming a cyber-potato. Music searching can cause it, too.

♦ *V: As an recording artist yourself, don't you have conflicted feelings about Napster?*

NAPSTER

♦**JB:** I guess they are conflicted. Remember when all the big movie barons wanted to *ban* video rentals? Now it's their bread and butter! Major music companies even tried to ban player pianos when they first came out [true].

When I first heard about Napster, I sided with Metallica. But the more I found out about it, the more I slid over to the other side—especially after I addressed that hacker convention last

July, where a lot of active Napster users told me that they *don't* use it to sneak songs away from artists who need the money, but use it as a "listen before you buy" service—which people find essential in the age of bad radio, EmptyV [MTV] and all. And so far statistics bear them out. Since Napster came in, CD sales have gone *up,* both for major labels and for small labels like Alternative Tentacles. So it's acting as a stimulant rather than the opposite.

♦ *V: I'm not surprised. There are a lot of people like me who want to own the full original artwork; we like to own "authentic" objects.*

♦**JB:** But I'll bet your daughter will stick to downloading! People at the convention said that if they like a song or two, they want to go out and buy the album, although they're less likely to want to buy an album chockful of lousy songs just because some corporate tastemaker *told* them to. But I like the way this technology is wrenching control of the music away from the major labels who play every single game in the book to pay their artists as little as possible. So downloading major label material from Napster is not really ripping off the artist, per se.

♦ *V: It's no different than recording songs off the radio onto a cassette, which I've done for decades.*

♦**JB:** Or taping something off TV or using a Xerox machine. On the other side of the coin, if there does come a day when everybody swaps music for free and there's no other way to get it heard, not only are many smaller niche artists like myself going to be in really deep trouble, but it also means that some people who work hard for years at a job they hate just to save up money and record an album of their music and present it to the world— they'll never be able to raise the money to make another one, and will quite likely give up and go back to breeding and sulking and making money at a straight job or something. I'd hate to see it cause a brain drain like that.

On the other hand, that hasn't happened yet. And Napster may be about to become irrelevant now that one of the majors,

BMG (part of the world's largest book-publishing/media conglomerate, Bertelsmann AG) controls it. That just means all the file-swapping will move over to Gnutella, Freenet, or whatever keeps coming after.

The Beauty and the Beast of computer technology is: no matter what kind of laws, rules and interference the Big Folks throw against the users—be it shutting down Napster or implementing tollbooths along the Information Highway—some bored teenager (of any age) out there somewhere is going to find a way to f---the whole thing up! So far, it has happened every time.

Plus, if the three ex-Kennedys succeed in swiping the Dead Kennedys catalog and dumbing it down to the level of The Exploited or worse, and people don't want to give their money to someone who files dirty lawsuits and plays games like that, well, Napster may turn out to be my best friend!

♦ *V: I read that Courtney Love was in favor of Napster—*

♦**JB:** She wrote a long and interesting piece on it that's floating around on the Net and is probably posted on any number of Courtney-Hole sites. There's a lot in there echoing what I'm saying, although some of what she says clearly emanates from someone who's grazed in Spoiled Showbiz, Inc. too long. For example, it does not take $1.5 million dollars to make an album—unless you're as wasteful as a B-1 Bomber factory!

♦ *V: About eight years ago there appeared an essay by Steve Albini showing how you could get a huge advance from a major record label, yet easily end up owing the company a lot of money—*

♦**JB:** The figures in Albini's *Baffler* #5 article are good; he's basing his figures on the $300,000-type deals that are a little more common.

♦ *V: Napster proves there are still a lot of unknowns making music and putting it up on the Net. Hopefully, some of it is great. Making musical discoveries—that's one of our few hopes for the future—*

♦**JB:** Yes, fun things can still be found—especially regional recordings. Paul Major was the one who clued me in on the virtues of D.I.Y. homemade records from nowhere, before there was a punk distribution system to get them around. Who saw these bands play? Did anybody buy these records? Did they ever even try to sell them anywhere? There's one that turned up by a band called Raven titled "Back to Ohio Blues," where the whole thing is so negative and so antisocial in the lyrics department—it's as if the Dwarves had happened in the middle of Ohio in 1972 . . . and had nobody but each other to express how much they hated the rest of the world! And Paul tracked down a former member of the band, but the guy picked up the phone and said, "Don't call me again or I'll kill you!" That was the end of that. People like that . . . *they're out there!*

♦ *V: What happened to your book project,* Burning Down the Magic Kingdom *(with Winston Smith illustrations)?*

♦**JB:** The publication date was set for late 1998, but then the lawsuit happened. It was supposed to be a print version of the early spoken word albums, but I fixed a lot of sections, added new material, and wrote a lot of additions trying to make sense of it all. It will eventually come out. AK Press originally talked me into it, saying that there's a whole different audience for a book than for a spoken-word recording.

LAWSUIT

♦ *V: That's true. So what's happening with your lawsuit?*

♦**JB:** The other guys just announced they're reissuing all the old albums, plus a mediocre live album they didn't tell me about. They have not let me see the cover, although they've billed me for the cost of the artwork they commissioned. Also, I don't think it occurred to them that the judge's decision didn't give them the right to *anybody's* art from the original albums, should the re-issues get made. John Yates, Charles Gatewood and I all want our artwork pulled from the albums. We've talked about corporate branding in this interview, but **with this lawsuit, globalization über alles and corporate branding have come to my house!**

♦ **V:** *Can you sum up the trial? I attended only part of it.*

♦ **JB:** The trial verdict ended up awarding the other ex-Dead Kennedys full control over much of the DK catalog, and awarded huge damages against Alternative Tentacles and me personally for failure to promote the Dead Kennedys' back catalog, if you can believe that! This whole thing started when I refused to license "Holiday in Cambodia" for a Levi's commercial. As it stands now, they are finally set up to pimp our message to corporate labels, TV commercials, etc. I also got word they have a booking agency pitching a bogus Dead Kennedys reunion tour! Apparently they're not exactly advertising the fact that I'm not included.

♦ **V:** *Your Web site press statement said,*

"I was shocked they would even consider the idea, let alone pressure me to do it. Talk about being on the wrong side of an issue. So many people are upset with growing corporate branding and intrusion into our daily lives, from the WTO to the Buzzcocks' song in an SUV commercial. I could think of no worse way to stab Dead Kennedys fans in the back than to turn around and trash everything we ever stood for and allow one of our best (and my favorite) song to be used to sell products by a global corporation with controversial labor practices. Dead Kennedys always stood against things like that."

♦ **JB:** And as for their charge that I withheld monies due them, I admitted there was an honest accounting mistake in the royalties accounting, and paid them before their lawsuit was even filed.

♦ **V:** *Nobody I've talked with believes you deliberately and knowingly defrauded your band members out of money due them. As label owner, didn't you delegate work? You didn't do the bookkeeping and writing of checks, right?*

♦ **JB:** Not usually. There was no court order or cover-up. But on the witness stand Klaus, Ray and Darren lied. They claimed they wrote the music to all of my songs because allegedly I'm not a musician, don't play a musical instrument, and don't read sheet music. I said in my press release, **"How many artists do you know who teach their songs to the band by humming the parts? I still do. Charlie Chaplin did it with a full orchestra."** They also claimed that I somehow sneaked the writing credits by them (giving myself too much)—they had just never noticed the credits on the albums or their BMI statements for the past twenty years!

They also demanded damages because their own solo projects did not sell as well as Dead Kennedys albums! In the trial they brought in an expert witness, a CPA who had worked with Grateful Dead Records—

♦ *V: Right, Timothy Jorstad. I saw him testify; he obviously didn't know anything about punk rock or underground punk labels. It was outrageous to hear him say that you owed hundreds of thousands of dollars because you didn't take out endless cheesy ads for the band's albums, which are 15-20 years old, in expensive media like* Rolling Stone, Billboard *and* VH1.

It seemed especially lunatic when he testified that if "x" more dollars had been spent on advertising, then "x" more albums automatically would have been sold. Come on—the DKs have a niche audience, not a mass one. This was under the umbrella charge of "Failure to Promote Back Catalog." Yet the jury seemed to swallow this deluded speculation. This seems a terrible precedent for ALL businesses, big and small. For someone to be able to sue somebody else claiming that more ads would automatically have sold more product, is a really dangerous, b.s. precedent.

♦**JB:** And then they filed a motion to expel me from the ex-band member partnership, so they could throw a small lump sum at me and never pay me again. But their motion was denied.

♦ *V: I felt a fundamental point that was overlooked in the trial was that, historically, the band had made decisions not by majority vote but by* consensus. *Huge difference!*

♦JB: Yes, but now they're operating their so-called "democracy" and since it's always the three of them against me, in effect I have no say as to how any decision is made. Take this live album they want to release—I only got a cassette of it last week. And this live recording is full of guitar mistakes, vocal drop-outs—and worse yet, lack of fire and energy. I definitely don't recommend it.

And get this: Ray admitted in court that he had been skimming "commissions" for himself, even though he had assured me he wouldn't do that. He also has yet to grant me a full and proper accounting of the partnership's books—there are no invoices, statements; just vague deductions for unspecified "expenses." When I asked for proof, Ray sent only four invoices, and it looked like the names had been newly blacked out. They looked like John Lennon's FBI file or something—totally dishonest.

♦ V: *The jury didn't seem to understand or respect punk rock culture, or the fact that your high profile is mainly what kept those old DKs albums selling to this day, not to mention paying to keep the DKs in print. Those guys haven't done f---all in 20 years! Very few bands in the early punk days had written partnership agreements or contracts of any kind, and in my opinion your ex-bandmates pulled the wool over the jury's eyes, especially with regard to the so-called partnership agreement, how decisions were really made, and who really wrote the songs. Now, it seems the only way you can save the Alternative Tentacles label and the integrity of the band's recorded legacy is to appeal for a new trial. And that must be disgustingly expensive…*

♦JB: I'd much rather be doing other things, believe me.

San Francisco's brain drain

♦ V: *Speaking of "expensive"—can you talk about the impact of the dot-com gold rush on San Francisco?*

♦JB: Let's put it this way: as long as I've been here, I have never seen the price of real estate go down in San Francisco. I've seen some spikes in prices, but neither the home prices nor the rents ever seem to go down. For every failed dot-com entrepreneur who has gone back home with their tail between their legs, their expensive yuppie loft just gets taken over by another employee of Intel, Oracle, or whatever tech behemoth swallowed up their enterprise or put it out of business.

Even the independent entrepreneurs aren't quite as threatening as the hardcore drones of The Borg that is Sillyclone Valley. **I hate to use such a tired radical cliché, but right now in San Francisco it's full-on *class warfare*: the upper class waging relentless war on the lower class.** Our flamboyantly corrupt Mayor Willie Brown's planning commission rubber-stamps every single gentrification and dot-com office mega-project without even giving it a hearing. They don't care where it is, and they don't care what happens to all the artists—or in many cases, families—who have been there for decades. Even my veterinarian got evicted! They closed the wing of a nursing home on South Van Ness Boulevard, because nobody could afford to work there. The *S.F. Bay Guardian* interviewed a Latina woman who was booted out of her Mission district apartment along with her three kids. She's now living in Sacramento where the rents are cheaper, but she can't find a job there, so she's commuting to San Francisco every day!

As local people know, musicians, writers, visual artists, dance companies—practically everybody creative—is either getting evicted or just getting the hell out of town. They're not just going to Oakland; they're going to Portland, Seattle, and even L.A.! This is a long-term brain drain that has many of us worried that San Francisco is never going to feel like San Francisco again. All of that volatile cutting-edge culture that has given the city such a rich history clear back before the Gold Rush days: will it be allowed to happen now?

When I moved to San Francisco, I was 19 years old with no money—I just had a dream. If I were 19 years old now and had that same dream, I sure as hell wouldn't move to San Francisco. I moved here to get away from Boulder, Colorado and now San Francisco has turned into a giant Boulder—no, worse yet: *a dot-com Monte Carlo!* **It can't just be me who fantasizes about chasing dot-com yuppies down Valencia Street waving a chainsaw, or printing up giant waterproof stickers saying "Yuppie Parasite" on them, with a skull and crossed cell phones, and pasting them on SUVs and those BMW convertibles, until they all leave town!**

The same gentrification is going on in other places. It's not as insane as it is in San Francisco, but I see the disease spreading. After 30 years of battles to preserve green-belt land and open space, now, thanks to the dot-com boom, the Denver-Boulder corridor along US Highway 36 is considered one of the worst examples of urban/suburban sprawl in the country. I mean, the megamalls sprang up so fast they forgot to look out the back door and see whether the same chain outlets were a quarter mile away!

The newest and most hyped one in Broomfield is right downwind of Rocky Flats, the old plutonium trigger plant that's considered one of the most polluted places in the world. I don't know if there's still radioactive tritium in Broomfield's water supply, but I don't remember anyone doing a thing to get rid of it after it was first discovered. Broomfield is between Denver and Boulder, and was one of the very first crackerbox, tract-home suburbs. They called it a bedroom community, but there never really was a community. Imagine my laughter when I saw a notice posted by someone saying they were trying to preserve "Historic Downtown Broomfield"—Broomfield never *had* a downtown! It had one seedy shopping center and a bunch of look-alike tract homes. The developers put the town there only because that was where the toll gate was, when U.S. 36 was still the Denver-Boulder turnpike and hadn't been paid for yet.

♦ **V:** *Do you have any thoughts about how San Francisco's Presidio district is being developed? [Until recently it was a military base with an extensive forest.]*

♦**JB:** This is just one more example of how corrupt both of our ruling political parties are. There's not really that much disagreement between the Democratic and Republican parties anymore; now they're both "the corporate party." Keep in mind it was a Democratic congress-creature (hey, it's non-sexist!) with a relatively liberal record by today's standards, Nancy Pelosi, who rammed through the Presidio giveaway. Now George Lucas, the family that owns the Gap, and others get to run rampant inside a national park!

♦ **V:** *Let's talk about the topic of privatization—*

PRIVATIZATION

♦**JB:** Privatization drives me up the wall! It's a typical scam where you keep de-funding important programs and then point the finger, saying, "Oh, look. The government can't run the bus system anymore. We should hand it over to some money-grubbing corporation for free." King George the Second [George W. Bush] even tried to turn the Texas welfare apparatus over to Lockheed Corporation, but at least public outcry put a stop to that, for now. Why would Lockheed want to get into the welfare "business" at all? Well, it was simple: you just cut off as many benefits as possible. Instead of going to a government-bureaucrat hearing about your benefits, you have to grovel before an executive of Lockheed.

It's the same with privately-owned prisons: how do you make money with a jail? You make the food even worse, get rid of the mental health professionals, the career counselors, the library, and in some cases even the weight-lifting

room. There have been far more prison riots going on in this country than have been reported in the corporate media— and a lot of them have been in private prisons. Some also appear to be easier to escape from!

It also really galls me that these same people who want government services handed over to them—whenever they have to pay for something, they expect the public to pay for it instead! Take, for example, sports stadiums. In Denver, these developers hornswaggled the voters into passing a bill to publicly fund a big new monument—excuse me, *stadium*—for their beloved Broncos football team. The Calgary oil baron in a fur coat who owns the team threatened to move the Broncos to L.A.—as if L.A. would ever root for the Denver Broncos. Now the stadium is publicly funded, but they're going to sell off the name to a corporation, and the oil baron, *dba* [doing business as] the Denver Broncos football company, is going to get all the money. In other words, the taxpayers don't get reimbursed!

Another example would be when they rigged another ballot initiative here [Colorado] against the wishes of people in four rustic old mining towns to turn them into gambling zones. Now the narrow road up a canyon to Blackhawk and Central City, Colorado, is constantly clogged with buses, tourists, and drunk gamblers. A train would be a really good idea, but the public "can't afford it." So why shouldn't the *casinos* be made to pay for the damn train—they're making money hand over fist.

Worse example: remember when our previous mayor, Frank Jordan, handed over the San Francisco Zoo to a private consortium, who then voted huge salaries for themselves (as if they needed the money) and began laying off service workers? In only two years they ran the zoo $4 million dollars into debt. Guess what they did? They put up a public ballot initiative to "Save the Zoo!" with cute little watercolor animal posters plastered all over telephone poles. Sure enough, people fell for it and reimbursed the private racketeers for looting the zoo . . . and they're letting them do it again now!

During part of the Spitfire tour, they had a token right-winger, Kennedy, a former MTV veejay who is a radio show host in Seattle now. She's kinda being courted by right-wing interests. **Whenever you get somebody young and "hip" starting to spout right-wing opinions, it's amazing how quickly they can slide up the ladder—senators love them!** Her talk on the Spitfire tour concerned the urgent need to privatize social security, which is actually just a giveaway of our tax money to Wall Street to the tune of $600 billion dollars! Clinton pushed it first, then he backed down; King George II says he'll try again.

I had some great examples to throw at Kennedy as to why privatization is a corporate scam and a nightmare for everybody else. For example, how many people out there know that **for the first half of the 20th century, the greater Los Angeles area had a kick-ass light rail mass transit system, with street cars and trains going everywhere, well outside the city limits of L.A.?**

♦ *V: I read there were 200,000 miles of light rails there—*

♦**JB:** Then somebody got the bright idea to privatize the service, and handed it over to a consortium made up of guess who: General Motors, Phillips Petroleum, and Firestone Tires! Within a few years the L.A. Interurban rail system was bankrupt (deliberately, I suspect) and the tracks were ripped up and destroyed before anyone realized what was going on! Those companies' gift to the world is the smog and gridlock known as L.A. today. That's what privatization does.

A more recent example was in Ontario, Canada, where a rabid privatization fiend named Mike Harris is their premier right now. He thought it would be a really good idea to privatize water inspections. Of course, the people he hired started "forgetting" to do it—but taking the money anyway. There was an outbreak of *E. coli* bacteria in the city water supply of Walkerton, Ontario—seven people *died* and dozens more wound up in the hospital. It was *murder by privatization.*

I think people who still think things would have been vastly better under Gore should keep an eye on how many Democratic senators and congress-creatures vote exactly the same way the Bushniks do. I'll bet you the first turds that bob to the surface are going to be names like Feinstein, Lieberman, Robert Byrd (West Virginia), John Breaux (Louisiana) plus that electric-chair fetishist from Florida who went to the Senate, Bob Graham—another right-wing corporate Democrat. I'm worried that because Bush is so bad, people will get desperate enough to go running to the next Bush-in-liberal-clothing corporate Democrat and we'll get stuck with another Clinton and it'll be Business As Usual. As Michael Moore pointed out at the Ralph Nader super-rally in Chicago, "We are now in the 20th year of the Reagan administration—"

♦ **V:** —*i.e., kowtowing to corporate interests—*

♦**JB:** Yeah! **Some of the biggest pet projects of Reagan and King George the First were: dynamiting the welfare system, NAFTA, WTO, more death penalty crimes, drug wars, more people in jail—and look who got it all through!** The wolf in fuzzy-wuzzy yuppie liberal clothing: Clinton, and his Clintonoids. People are so upset that Bush got in that even my own family were pointing the finger at me, saying how "Nader cost Gore the election"—*growl growl snarl*—"those goddamn Greens!" That's going to make it all the more intimidating for people to run for smaller offices as Greens in 2002; the people pointing the finger say, "If it weren't for you, Gore would be in there, and everything would be wonderful." Well, *wrong.*

I have to remind them that **the reason I got into the Green party was: I long ago went through "Democrats Anonymous" to wean myself from this addiction to the Evil of Two Lessers.** And as far as I'm concerned, anybody who supports the drug war, the prison boom, the death penalty, the WTO, gutting the welfare system, putting nuclear weapons in outer space, privatization, etc.—those are non-negotiable issues to me—f--- 'em! If people like the Greens and other independents wind up costing spineless corporate Democrats some elections, maybe that's a good thing. I'd love to see enough of a Green Wedge in legislatures and city governments, that neither side can get all their corrupt bills through unless they talk turkey with the handful of people who actually give a s---.

Granted, Germany has a parliamentary system, but the Greens have had a great effect in that country. After Helmut Kohl finally got voted out (or should I say, rolled out in a wheelbarrow), all of a sudden **Germany's doing things like shutting down all their nuclear power plants. There's a law that by 2003 (or so) all cars manufactured in Germany have to be returnable to the factory a few years later so every single part can be recycled!** I didn't know that was technologically possible, but now in Germany it's the law. I can't imagine that kind of change coming from the Social Democrats. They had to form a coalition with the Greens, and I'll bet it's the *Greens* who got that through. Of course, the WTO can rip all of that to pieces with the stroke of a pen. But on the other hand, it seems like Europeans are a lot angrier and are taking to the streets far more often than Americans are. "Seattle" seems to happen fairly regularly across the European continent.

Europeans are far more on top of the *Frankenfood* problem than we are; for example—ah ha, another reason Gore should be in jail instead of almost being in the White House—it was Clinton and Gore who went to the WTO to try and wipe out European laws requiring clear labeling of genetically modified Frankenfood, and banned milk and beef tainted with Bovine Growth Hormone. Overseas, Frankenfood is a *huge* issue, and that's precisely why it's kept out of corporate media here. What if American consumers became like Europeans and quit buying Kellogg's and Total corn flakes and Fritos because real corn wasn't in them anymore? I'm not sure how long it's been since there *was* real corn, but I think you know what I mean.

Howard Lyman was on some Spitfire shows. He's a cattle rancher turned hardcore vegan who wrote a book on Mad Cow Disease [*Mad Rancher: Plain Truth from the Cattle Rancher Who Won't Eat Meat*]. After he talked about the book and his findings on the Oprah Winfrey show, Texas cattlemen sued the s--- out of both him and Oprah for "slandering cattle." It got laughed out of court, but the cattlemen keep appealing.

It seems there's a real purpose behind all these product slander laws that states keep passing, where it's a punishable crime to make fun of cauliflower or peaches or whatever. If those peaches start being genetically mutilated and you point out something's wrong, a company like Monsanto could theoretically file a SLAPP suit [that's what "product disparagement" lawsuits are called] against you, and rip your life to pieces and throw you out on the street. Lyman pointed out that **the reason Mad Cow Disease spread in England was that the Thatcherites got the bright idea to privatize meat inspection.** And guess who did it over here: Clinton and Gore. Now the slaughterhouses inspect themselves!

♦ *V: At this date, over 80 people in England have died from Mad Cow Disease. It takes a long time to incubate, too—that's really scary. And even after England discovered that ground-up meat and bones (euphemistically titled "meat meal") was the cause, it knowingly continued to export this meat meal overseas to countries. So it's a much bigger deal in the news in the U.K. than here.*

♦ **JB:** Oh, yes. **The worst form of censorship going on today is corporate-controlled media deliberately omitting important stories from the news.** We're conditioned to think it's more important to worry about "Survivor" than *surviving* . . . corporate-sponsored global warming, Mad Cow Disease, and whatever Frankenbugs break out and spread, after all these antibiotics in the cows and chickens make us immune to anything that would have killed them off.

♦ *V: Back to the topic of of genetic mutilation, Japan has banned*

StarLink (genetically modified corn manufactured by Aventis) and many other U.S.-made genetically modified foods. Several times they've discovered Starlink in samples that the U.S. declared negative, proving their suspicions that testing procedures in the U.S. are inadequate or incompetent. They're angry!

♦**JB:** Aventis claim they've taken Starlink off the market, by the way.

♦ *V: The* New York Times *said this Starlink product might cause allergies, but I suspect it might cause worse reactions than that—*

♦**JB:** I'd rather not go to Taco Bell to find out! **Whenever a label says "Not fit for human consumption; suitable only for agricultural use" and doesn't tell you *why*, I fear the worst!** Maybe it was designed to grow giant *Frankenpigs* and get them fatter, quicker. That could happen to humans, too—in fact, it already is. Little girls are developing breasts at younger and younger ages, clear down to six and seven. A prime suspect is milk containing Bovine Growth Hormone [BGH]—another ingredient that the Europeans banned and then got hit with sanctions by the WTO, thanks to our lovely liberal environmentalist Democrats, Clinton and Gore.

♦ *V: And Al Gore brought us the Information Superhighway.*

♦**JB:** Right—remember his proposal to privatize the Internet, putting up all these corporate tollbooths up along the way? It was intended to *price* people out of sharing information that corporate McNews doesn't want you to know!

♦ *V: In the elections, Gore got almost 600,000 more popular votes than Bush did, and Nader got 2.7 million votes. Obviously, that's 3.3 million more voters who didn't want Bush in the presidential office—*

♦**JB:** Let's look at the big picture. Florida was hilarious; it was like the cast of the movie *2,000 Maniacs* was suddenly in charge of stealing the election! It was a typical Florida election, only this time they got caught. Here were these two pampered children of old money families bitching over who got a slightly higher number than 24% of the eligible vote. People forget that only slightly more than half of the eligible voters in America actually voted. Gore and Bush got 24% apiece, and Nader got the difference, and then a little bit for Buchanan. **What about the other 50% who are so fed up they won't even vote at all?! That is the *real* majority in this country.** The challenge, of course, is how to get them off their asses. It's not that they don't care; it's that they care so much that they've given up! They've thrown up their hands.

On a lighter note, when I was watching the election results on November 7th, I stayed up 'til 3 A.M. in Maine waiting for Gore to concede, just so I could see Tipper cry on camera! To kill time, the camera panned the crowd both in Austin and Nashville. At Gore Victory Central in Nashville, they held on a forlorn-looking young girl holding up a "Tipper Rocks!" sign—"Well, Tipper, you still rock for *ME!*" *sniff sniff.*

♦ *V: Of course, it's so suspicious that this vote scandal happened in a state where a Bush relative rules the roost—*

♦ **JB:** I know; it cracks me up. The exit polls showed Gore way ahead, so the networks called the state for Gore early. But then right on camera, Jeb Bush [Florida governor] said to King George, "Don't worry; *it's in the bag*"—an exact quote. And sure enough, it was. Think how much fun it will be if all these lawsuits and recounts show that Gore really did win Florida, and monkeying with elections goes clear on up to the governor's office and Jeb winds up in one of his own brand-new prisons.

♦ *V: I can see why you campaigned for Nader. You spoke at three Nader rallies: in Chicago, Long Beach, and—*

♦ **JB:** I also spoke at a Nader rally in Oakland, talking to 10,000 people. On the bill was Cornel West, who wrote *Race Matters.* He is way more animated than his public reputation would have you believe—Harvard professor and all. He gave an amazing '60s-style, fire-and-brimstone sermon in the "black church" tradition.

Medea Benjamin, the Green candidate for the Senate, also spoke—she's pretty kick-ass! She's part of Global Exchange, which nailed Nike on their sweatshops and got concessions. They're the ones spearheading the anti-sweatshop movement on college campuses—important, because all the campuses have rah-rah mascot merchandise. Global Exchange has an outlet store in San Francisco selling all kinds of imported goods, guaranteed *Fair Trade;* the people who made 'em got treated fairly and *paid* fairly.

♦ *V: College is the last place where most people actively campaign for social ethics and reforms—*

♦**JB:** Not true at all! Remember Vietnam, anti-apartheid . . . Well, students have their parents paying their tuition, so they can go out and agitate and not worry about losing their jobs . . . or having to pay rent in San Francisco!

Global Exchange is also deeply involved in anti-World Bank activity. They publish books, plus a quarterly newsletter that's available with membership. One issue early on gave a detailed exposé on what's really going on in Columbia, where we're sinking billions. This is like El Salvador, only worse. Of course, we're really there to run indigenous tribes off their land and take the oil. This time it's a triangular fight between government, different guerrilla groups, and narco traffickers—who get whatever guerrilla group is handy, or death squads, to protect them.

♦ *V: Do you have any comment on the PG&E scandal? Recently they declared a $1.5 billion profit for their shareholders; then almost immediately they had to purchase $3 billion worth of power, so they're ending up declaring bankruptcy—*

♦**JB:** Thanks to deregulation, PG&E and SoCal Edison got caught with their pants down. Again, this is an example of deregulation and privatization and the wonders they wreak. And why is it that there's not one word in the corporate press about solar energy, windmill farms, and all the other ways to not just "reduce our dependence on foreign oil" but also our dependence on Piggy&E?!

A great way to revitalize the farm belt would be to give grants for people to put up thousands of windmills or solar panels on their farms, then sell all the extra electricity. And let's not forget that some cities in Southern California haven't had blackouts at all because they own their utilities! The *S.F. Bay Guardian* has made this their pet issue for decades, but every time the S.F. Board of Supervisors even orders a study of public power, City Hall blocks it. After all, PG&E is one of Willie Brown's law clients.

Basically, corporate media and the twenty years of the Reagan administration have brainwashed people into thinking that "community" no longer matters, and that the community is somehow against you, so you'd better get what's yours, and f... everyone else. Therefore, it's not a community responsibility—social essentials like a clean environment, child care, health care, and homes for people sleeping in the street are not a community responsibility. **Privatization is the exact opposite of community and responsibility. It's every cutthroat for themselves!**

It was bad enough in the Reagan era when this mantra was repeated everywhere: "Greed is good." Now, what you have is the children of these Reagan parents turning into these venomous dot-com yuppies—that's where they came from.

♦ **V:** *Well, the dot-commies are disappearing now—*

♦ **JB:** Dude, they're *NOT* disappearing: they're multiplying. Even if they're not independent anymore, it's still a case of yet another money-grubbing drone trying to slime up the ladder at Intel or Oracle or Hewlett-Packard, cell phone in mouth instead of a pirate sword.

How do you find information?

♦ **V:** *Right. A feature in a recent* New York Times *quoted some tech workers as basically saying, "Well, we had our dot-com fling and it* *tanked, so now we're returning to work at Microsoft." Apparently, many of Microsoft's newest recruits are former employees . . . How do you get your information?*

♦**JB:** A lot of what I know comes from articles or anecdotes people send me or tell me to my face. At this point, I don't really have to hunt for information; it finds me! There are always far more piles of it at my house than I have time to deal with. I read commercial mags and daily papers, too—it's important to analyze *what they want you to think.* And you never know what you may find buried there. **Noam Chomsky reads the *Wall Street Journal* and a lot of the business magazines, because they're much more open with each other about what their dirty plans and visions are.**

Get this—*Business Week* has gotten interesting. After the Seattle No WTO protest, they took a poll and over 50% of *their readers* thought the protestors had a point. An even higher percentage felt that U.S. corporations should be held to the same workplace and wage standards overseas as they are here. And this is *Business Week?!* Then, last September they had a cover story saying, "Too much corporate power?" Ralph Nader had great fun with that as a prop! He opened up the magazine and pointed out that ***"Business Week* said Yes, there *is* too much corporate power—quote: 'Corporations should get out of politics,' thus putting *Business Week* to the left of the Democratic party!"**

♦ *V: What other media have you found?*

♦**JB:** Today at a thrift store I found a record with an amazing cover, titled *Lose Weight Through Hypnosis.* Weight paranoia is the major control tactic in the war against women's self-esteem, in order to sell them obscenely profitable, overpriced products—

♦ *V: That reminds me: there was a great (and creepy) article in the* Wall Street Journal *last week based upon a 150-page sales training manual for Estée Lauder. Their techniques of presentation and manipulation were ingenious—talk about the Control Process! It gave the example of a mother and daughter coming to the counter for just a lipstick, and walking away carrying two shopping bags full of makeup.*

♦JB: [laughs] I just found a record of commercials for Preparation H! The one I'd really like to find is the American Standards sales convention album from 1968. They hired a musical troupe to come in and sing songs about the corporation and its products, which was common in those days, but this time the songs were all about how much they love toilets and bathroom fixtures! Steve Young, the guy who supplies David Letterman with the weird records for his show, collects these sales convention records, but I have yet to hear about one anywhere near as demented as this one! A bootleg CD titled *Product Music,* featuring songs from sales convention albums, was released on an allegedly Japanese label, but somebody we both know actually put it out.

♦ V: *In the past you told me that you don't read books, like David Shenk's* Data Smog, *Kalle Lasn's* Culture Jam, *or Naomi Klein's* No Logo; *books I find inspiring—*

♦JB: Shocking, isn't it? **I told Allen Ginsberg that almost all of my literary influences were from song lyrics and comic books. He said, "Oh, that's fine."**

♦ V: *Which comic books?*

♦JB: Jack T. Chick publications containing fanatical religious cartoons. You know, those little religious tracts with the gnarly drawing style and vengeful messages? Chick and Daniel Clowes are by far my favorite comic artists. And let's not forget Tom Tomorrow's cartoons [syndicated in the *S.F. Bay Guardian* and many other weeklies]. I really love the way he can boil down some pretty important media distortion on issues into four frames in a comic, and get it across—he can take a whole issue of *Z* magazine and fold it into four frames and make it clear!

I also read *Extra* magazine—you should subscribe to that. It's published by FAIR (Fairness & Accuracy in Reporting) which picks out and analyzes every single corporate media distortion they can get their hands on. They include all of this in their monthly magazine *Extra,* and in their *Extra* bulletins as well. It was started by Martin A. Lee, who has written a couple of books: *Acid Dreams,* and *The Beast Reawakens: Fascism's Resurgence from Hitler's Spymasters to Today's Neo-Nazi Groups and Right-Wing Extremists.*

Some of *Extra's* stories are just appalling. They've completely debunked the *New York Times* as any kind of paper of record—let alone one of any true liberal leanings. They're the ones who counted how many times a certain person appeared on Nightline or MacNeil-Lehrer [now the Jim Lehrer Newshour], which debunks that as a relatively unbiased source, too. They pointed out that in the Reagan era, the most common guests on those shows were people like Henry Kissinger and Elliot Abrams, that death squad cheerleader in the State Department. They just adore William Bennett, too!

Marty Lee was in San Francisco during the early punk years. I met him on a bus when I was running for mayor [1979] and he told me he had worked on a congressional committee that had looked into something called Operation Artichoke in the late fifties. The goal was to see if they could literally program or hypnotize a human being to go out and commit a crime and then not remember it afterwards. And according to the documents he later mailed to me, the project failed and was abandoned. Yet a few years later, Lee Harvey Oswald happened. *Go figure!* ◆ ◆ ◆

RECOMMENDATIONS

WEB SITES:

www.alternativetentacles.com (AT Legal Defense, too!)
www.indymedia.org
www.globalexchange.org, tel 415-255-7296
    (books available)
www.worldbankboycott.org
www.50years.com
www.greenparty.org
www.citizen.org
www.asm.wisc.edu/usas (United Students Against Sweatshops)
www.adbusters.org, www.thebaffler.com

BOOKS:

Jello recommends *Job Jumper* by the Whiskey Rebel, aka Phil Irwin, on Steel Cage Books. *Rivethead: Tales from the Assembly Line. Mad Rancher: Plain Truth from the Cattle Rancher Who Won't Eat Meat.*(Vale recommends: *Days of War, Nights of Love* by Crimethinc. *Hollow City. Culture Jam. No Logo.*)

MOVIES:

5,000 Fingers of Dr. T

Putney Swope

Hotrods to Hell

Sin City U.S.A. aka the *Phenix City Story*

Boat People (really powerful movie made in the mid-eighties by a woman in Hong Kong, about Vietnam after the end of the war. Somebody tries to escape a communist dictatorship, and this is what they go through, the message being: "You call these people 'boat people'?"

Guns, Girls and Gangsters—a really wild noir movie. Mamie Van Doren and Lee Van Cleef in the same movie; not a single unseedy character. It's exactly as the title implies.

Incredibly Strange Creatures Who Stopped Living and Became Mixed-Up Zombies

Humanoids from the Deep

Blood of Jesus

The Sadist

MAGAZINES:

Z Magazine

Adbusters

The Nation

The Progressive

The Baffler

Multinational Monitor: concentrates on corporate wickedness. Nader started it years ago.

San Francisco Bay Guardian—every town should have one; most weeklies are just trendy fluff, by comparison.

The Evening Whirl—from St. Louis. It has gone way downhill. The old man retired and a daughter took it over and decided to go mainstream, with color pictures and all, but it still is the *Evening Whirl!*

Murder Can Be Fun—how dare he quit doing this?! This is one of my favorite publications. Back issues available from John Marr, POB 640111, SF CA 94164. Sample issue $3 cash.

RECOMMENDED BAND:

16 Horsepower from Denver, Colorado. Indescribable; like 19th-century Goth music!

LAWRENCE FERLINGHETTI

Lawrence in Italy, Roma, 1995; the poet visiting the land of his ancestors.
Photo: Massimo Sestini, courtesy Lawrence Ferlinghetti

L awrence Ferlinghetti was the first San Francisco Poet Laureate. Besides poetry and prose, he has produced hundreds of paintings, drawings and other works.

In 1953 he and Peter D. Martin co-founded City Lights Bookstore, which published Allen Ginsberg's seminal poem, *Howl*. His own *Pictures of the Gone World* and *A Coney Island of the Mind* became poetry best-sellers. Ferlinghetti has spoken out against HUAC, the Vietnam war, and numerous other political and social violations.

He continues to write, give readings, paint, and write a monthly column for the San Francisco *Chronicle,* "Poetry As News," archived on *www.citylights.com*. His numerous books are listed at the back of this interview.

Currently there are five biographies in English of Lawrence Ferlinghetti: Neeli Cherkovski's *Ferlinghetti: A Biography* (1979; personable, not a critical biography); Barry Silesky's *Ferlinghetti: The Artist in His Time* (1990; a more scholarly account); Larry R. Smith's *Poet-At-Large,* (1983; not a full-scale biography); Michael Skau's *Constantly Risking Absurdity* (1989, Whitson Publishing Co.) and Christopher Felver's *Ferlinghetti Portrait,* an art-photography hardback. Numerous books containing Ferlinghetti biographical data and interviews exist in other languages. He has also been documented on videos such as *Lawrence Ferlinghetti: Rivers of Light* and *An Evening with Lawrence Ferlinghetti)* as well as on various audio recordings, including some poetry-and-jazz sessions..

Lawrence Ferlinghetti has two children, several grandchildren, and lives in San Francisco.

Overpopulation & Socialism

♦ **VALE:** *What do you think are the most pressing problems of today?*

♦ **LAWRENCE FERLINGHETTI:** Today, there are two words that absolutely won't be discussed—or even mentioned—by government functionaries, politicians, or commentators on "straight" radio or commercial television. One is "overpopulation," and the other is "socialism."

Probably the one problem behind all the other crises on earth right now is overpopulation. You could take any daily newspaper and probably 60% of the stories could be traced back to some overpopulation cause. For instance, why do loggers want to cut down rain forests? Because people need more houses. Why do they need more houses? Because there's a huge increase in population worldwide.

In the Bay Area, why does the traffic commissioner say we need to build another Bay Bridge? Because there's more cars. Why is there more demand for more cars? Because there's more population. You can cut right across the newspaper, and in one problem story after another you can come up with temporary solutions, like "Build another Bay Bridge," but that'll only be good for ten years. Probably by the time it's built, it will already be insufficient—

♦ *V: Right, and we'll need a third Bay Bridge, and a fourth. You haven't talked about "Autogeddon" yet—*

♦ **LF:** Autogeddon was a term invented by a British poet, Heathecote Williams, which is what's happening as soon as you go out on the freeway. Every morning I listen to the radio and am pretty happy that I don't have to commute, because it sounds awful out there.

♦ *V: In a better world, you wouldn't own a car, would you? But how else would you get down to Bixby Canyon in Big Sur? And you have to haul your paintings around—*

♦**LF:** I have a truck. I need it. But I would go for a horse and a carriage if they'd let me keep it in the garage. We may get to that. The automobile is just a passing thing; the horse is here to stay!

From a different point of view, in the ecological battles, every victory is temporary and every defeat is permanent. For instance, when they cut down redwoods, it's a permanent defeat. It's shocking that unknown people have cut halfway through the tree that Julia Butterfly was up in for over a year. This huge, ancient redwood—I don't know how old it is; maybe a thousand years— was cut halfway through. I don't think anyone knows if it can be saved or not. But this is the kind of thing I'm talking about.

So you have overpopulation, which no politician will dare mention. For instance, two years ago at the Watershed Conference in Berkeley, which has a supposedly very hip audience—a Green audience—I read a long poem called "Overpopulation." But before I read it, I said that the United States tax code should be revised so that people weren't rewarded for having babies—right now you get a tax reduction for every child you have. I think the tax code should be revised to say that the first child is free; after that, you pay the government for each child you have—except for low-income families. But even this audience didn't accept this. Afterwards, people came up and said, "You can't tell me how many children I can have!" Etc., etc.

Of course, that's good for the United States, but when you get to Third World countries where the worst overpopulation exists, here you have a really stupid policy of the Bush administration, which is to cancel family counseling that includes birth control information, in other countries. This is really a "cutting its own throat" policy, because—well, of course, they want more people so they'll have more consumers so they'll sell more American goods. But that's a very short-term view.

One of the most effective programs that was tried out used

Nancy Peters, V. Vale, Lawrence Ferlinghetti, Anarchist Book Fair, 2000
Photo: Charles Gatewood

commercial television soap-opera techniques to create a soap opera series to be broadcasted in Third World countries. These had a typical dramatic soap opera plot, but always had it hinge on some kind of birth-control or overpopulation-control message. A pilot program that was tried out was a huge success—in one year the birth rate very decidedly went down in the countries this was tried in.

For instance, in a country such as the Philippines, where my son's wife comes from, the women would like to have some alternative to having lots of babies and being enslaved for the rest of their life. But they really don't have any other alternative offered to them. The prevailing social mores from ancient times say that if they can't have children, then they're a failure as women. This is the kind of thing that a popular soap opera program can attack and change.

Also, in a Third World country like the Philippines, if the men can't have children, well, they're not considered *men.*

Something's wrong with them; they're not macho; they're not really male. So they have to have children or else they're nowhere. This is a big problem that can be overcome by nothing other than pure education. And even in the poorest huts you'll quite often find a TV aerial sticking out of the roofs. The people who need to be instructed *can* be reached very easily; all you have to do is finance the right program. This is much cheaper than a new missile defense system—by far. The powers that be could probably finance a soap opera program of this kind in a Third World country for the cost of a couple of big bombers.

♦ *V: Or less, now that we have cheap mini-DV camcorders and Final Cut Pro software. This could be done on a shoestring budget if necessary.*

♦ **LF:** The next forbidden word is "socialism." That word is anathema; you never see it *anywhere* these days. It's strictly taboo, even in Leftist circles. But the actual fact is that, ecologically speaking, **the world is in such a dire state that a form of universal socialism is needed**. A form of universal social, ecological and economic planning on a worldwide basis—I mean, Paine Weber had a motto for fifteen or twenty years: "Go global." Well, it's too bad they don't mean "Go global with the government." And I don't mean *American* government. It would have to be multi-ethnic.

It sounds like I'm wanting to have a huge super-state government which would be worse than Orwell's *1984,* but that's not necessarily so, because you could have a form of socialism which is humanitarian socialism, or civil libertarian socialism, which has nothing to do with mind control or thought control, but controls by *education* such problems as birth control. Universal education on the subject of birth control could be done on a *worldwide* basis, not just piecemeal.

In Edward Bellamy's *Looking Backward,* he's looking back to around 1887 when the book was first published. But he's looking backward from what turns out to be today, and they have developed this ideal society I'm talking about. They're looking backward at the civilization we still have today and are considering it really barbaric and undeveloped, because we're so consumed with greed and blind stupidity on matters such as ecology.

We haven't even mentioned global warming, which is a perfect example of willful blindness—

♦ **V:** *Right—literally. Various species of fish and animals at the Arctic are going blind because of the hole in the ozone layer—*

♦ **LF:** They won't even believe the scientific evidence. There *is* global warming and there is a huge hole in the ozone layer that's growing larger, and this is a total ecological crisis which, just out of greed and stupidity, we are choosing to ignore.

Anarchism & Capitalism Today

The thing is, you could say, "I thought you were an anarchist." The trouble is, we can't *afford* anarchism today—which sounds like a cop-out. But it's not—we can't afford capitalism, either. We can't afford unrestrained capitalism, just like we can't afford unrestrained anarchism. In fact, unrestrained capitalism is the ideal of the Free Trade movement and the whole Republican policy in this country. **Democracy is increasingly defined as successful capitalism . . . which is not necessarily so. Thinking the unthinkable, you could say that unrestrained capitalism is a form of anarchism!** [laughs] Or, you could say that it's anarchism carried to greedy extremes.

As far as George the Second goes—George W. Bush—it's like the Old Boy Network, the Texas Know-nothing Yahoos have taken over (I'm speaking as of February, 2001). When Henry Miller came back to the United States after many years of living in Europe, he wrote a book called *The Air-Conditioned Nightmare.* He was shocked with what he found: a total consumer culture had taken over America (and that was only the *beginning* compared with today). He said, "Another breed of men have taken over."

Two days ago I was at Gasser's Photographic Supply, and Mr. Gasser himself was there. He's about ninety years old now, and he comes in on Saturday morning to check on his workers to see how things are going. I just happened to meet him, and I asked, "When did you start Gasser's?" He said, "1950." I said, "That makes you three years older than we are; we started City Lights Bookstore in 1953." He said, "Well, you know, it was a different age then, and it was a different mentality"—which is just what Henry Miller was saying. In fact, I quoted that Henry Miller quote, and he said that when he opened up in the fifties, his neighbor was Brooks Camera, in the same block on Kearny Street. He said he had very good relations with Mr. Brooks, and since they've both retired, they've become friends. He said that when they were competing, they competed not as friends, but as gentlemen competitors. They didn't have that mentality of "I'll do anything to run you out of business, short of cutting your throat"—

♦ **V:** *Right, the Microsoft mentality of today, where I think they* would *cut your throat.*

♦ **LF:** In those days there was a certain overarching civility which seems to have evaporated today.

So we have the new George the Second, who usurped our democracy for his plutocracy. Plutocracy means rule for the rich and by the rich. What's getting him by is his charm, a certain Southern civility. It's on an illiterate level, but nevertheless, there's a certain Southern charm and civility which he has emphasized in dealing with members of the government and Congress. In fact, there's always been a tradition of "civility" in Congress—presumably, they treat each other with great politeness. But at the same time they're knifing each other in the back, so it's a bit of a hypocrisy.

Public Ownership of Resources

♦ **V:** *On the topic of socialism and making power public, do you recall that Vladimir Lenin defined socialism as the soviets (i.e., workers' councils, by which workers owned and ran the factories) plus electricity—*

♦ **LF:** Well, it's obvious that the state of unrenewable resources in the world cries out for a form of planned economy. Capitalism is the most wasteful ecological system in the world! *It's so obvious that these days what is needed is a form of planned economy on a worldwide scale, with public ownership of natural unrenewable resources.* It's so obvious right now with the present electrical and energy crisis in California, that it's a perfect opportunity for San Francisco to take over the electrical and gas supplies and the whole Hetch-Hetchy water system and everything that's been privately farmed out and making lots of private money for people. This is a perfect opportunity for this city to finally reclaim all this for the people. I mean, the people are supposed to own these resources.

I think that under the present Board of Supervisors, it's quite possible to do this. During the recent elections, across the nation the only bright spot in the whole country was the results of the San Francisco Board of Supervisors race. Finally, there's a board that's not beholden to large business interests, that can really be on the side of the people, and that has some really independent thinkers on it.

It seems obvious that the utilities have to be socialized, rather than privatized, across the country, everywhere.

♦ **V:** *Right. It's not so necessary in San Francisco, but in wintertime in Chicago and New York, if you don't have heat, you die.*

♦ **LF:** I guess you could burn wood—if you could find any.

♦ **V:** *The whole PG&E debacle is too complicated to discuss now, but*

I read that $1.5 billion dollars of "profit" got dispersed to owners and stockholders just before PG&E declared it had a $3 billion dollar deficit, and then that escalated to $12 billion. I think this information was from The San Francisco Bay Guardian, which for years has been advocating public ownership of utilities.

♦ **LF:** A lot of money was siphoned off to the parent company.

♦ *V: Continuing the dialogue about socialism and its implications and applications, the last time I was in France, the person I was with became very ill. She went to a doctor, and even though she wasn't a French citizen, all she paid was $12.*

♦ **LF:** Around 1967 I had pneumonia in Russia, under the Soviet regime. I took the Trans-Siberian railway and got pneumonia in Siberia and was treated in a Soviet hospital for ten days, and this didn't cost me anything. But of course, if you went out of the hospital, it was another scene—it wasn't so happy. This was the 50th anniversary of the Communist Revolution, 1967, and in this forlorn seaport I found myself in, there were these huge banners everywhere stretched across streets.

♦ *V: Where was this?*

♦ **LF:** This was near the Sea of Japan, in Nahodka, near Vladivostok. The town was all cement buildings. It was February, deep winter, 20 degrees below zero, mammoth snowdrifts everywhere, and there were large black masses of people outside. This could have been a hundred years ago in the time of Leo Tolstoy: these black masses crawling along the streets under these huge, monumental buildings. Above them were these enormous banners proclaiming the glorious 50th anniversary of the Soviet Revolution. But the people themselves were so depressed.

After I got out of the hospital, I stayed in a hotel where they had ballroom dancing. And the ballroom dancing was being done to 1940s straight ballroom orchestra music. Small men in blocky suits were dancing with these huge *Katrinkas,* waltzing around the room very stiffly with no expression on their faces, while this ancient orchestra sawed away under the potted palms.

And everybody looked so unhappy. In the dining room, no one raised their voice; they were all whispering.

No one spoke anything except Russian. Once you got outside of Moscow, nothing else worked. Italian didn't work, French didn't work, English didn't work—nothing but Russian. Finally I found a woman who spoke a little bit of French—she was the hostess in the hotel dining room. She was telling me how awful things were there—she was telling me this in whispers while she was looking all around, even though she was speaking in French. She made a date to take me to a Sunday afternoon movie, which evidently was the high point of the week in this dreary workers' town.

We went to this movie, which turned out to be a Soviet propaganda film. It showed Soviet armies marching through the streets. There was all this martial music and applause on the screen, but the audience just sat there completely silent. When it was over, the lights came on, and 300 people just *slunk* out of the room looking all mournful and dejected. The whole country was very depressing to be in; I couldn't wait to get out.

This was not what *I* had in mind for socialism. Stalinism and Soviet Communism was a perversion of socialism—a perversion of Leninism, actually. It was a perversion of Marxism. Real humanitarian socialism has never been given an actual chance. In France under Mitterand it was possible, but then the capitalist nations and bankers ganged up on the French socialist party and they had to retract a lot of their programs, and their whole socialist experiment was sabotaged, you might say.

Of course, socialism works in the smaller Scandinavian countries. You can say, "Well that's okay for a country that's only the size of Rhode Island." But besides there, it really hasn't been tried anywhere. Salvador Allende's Chile showed a promising beginning, but it was sabotaged by the U.S. government—especially by Henry Kissinger.

There was an article in the February-March [2001] issues of *Harper's* magazine by Christopher Hitchens laying out the case against Dr. Henry Kissinger as a war criminal. This is an article written from a legal, factual standpoint that makes it imperative for the U.S. Government, if it's going to live up to the protocols that it signed at the Nuremberg trials, to prosecute Dr. Kissinger. It's a really devastating two-part series. [titled "The Case Against Henry Kissinger"]

♦ *V: Let's change the topic. Tell us about your concern for the possible demise of KPFA, the radical Berkeley radio station—*

♦**LF:** I'm actually writing my next column for the *San Francisco Chronicle* on the KPFA situation.

♦ *V: Is the Pacifica Foundation the owner of KPFA?*

♦**LF:** The original station was KPFA, founded by Lewis Hill around 1948 or 1949. Then they added more stations: WBAI in New York, KPFK in Los Angeles, and a few others. That became the Pacifica Network, and the Pacifica Foundation is the legal owner of the frequencies from the F.C.C., which allows them to broadcast.

What the present struggle boils down to is: the national board is taking control away from the local stations—completely taking local control of the programming away from KPFA and the other stations, centralizing it all in Washington, D.C., so it becomes more and more like NPR (National Public Radio) or more like commercial radio. What's ignored in all these debates is—well, no one mentions that the *reason* the national board wants to take away local control is because they want to broaden the listener base of the station so that it will reach a larger audience. And this is what all the commercial radio stations do: they reach for a lower common denominator.

That's just what's behind this whole Pacifica board's philosophy: they want to increase the listener base, increase the number of listeners, and make the station more valuable so that under the new bylaws they've just promulgated, they can even *sell* the stations to a commercial bidder . . . even though the Pacifica Foundation is a non-profit foundation. So they're trying to increase the listener base as much as possible . . . which has become the yardstick measuring the success of a radio or television station: its listener ratings. When listener ratings go up, then the station is a "success." So that's what they're doing: making the station become a part of The Dumbing Down of America. Because they're lowering the common denominator of the intelligence of the people they want to listen to the station.

♦ *V: Well, it's also taking away the autonomy and independence of the local station, whose character is formed by its neighborhood. KPFA sprang out of Berkeley, and Berkeley is a radical hotbed—*

♦**LF:** It *WAS.*

Travel

♦ *V: You've traveled a lot; tell us about something that struck your fancy—*

♦**LF:** In Santiago, Chile, I saw a publisher's Bookmobile. Whenever they published a new book, they took out the Bookmobile and spread it out in a public park, with awnings, outside displays and everything. They sold out a whole edition in one weekend, just by putting on this big show.

♦ *V: Was this a radical publisher?*

♦**LF:** It was a leftist press. When our bookstore had to be closed on account of the seismic retrofit, I thought we might get a Bookmobile or a big cart to shuttle from here to Washington Square Park. But in the end the logistics were too much; the city defeated it. You have to have too many damn permits. You can't do anything now without permits for this and that—it's not the way it was once upon a time, where you got an idea and just went out and did it.

♦ *V: Right; permits and insurance prevent anything spontaneous from happening. What else have you seen in your travels?*

◆**LF:** A tiny bookstore, City Lights Italia, opened up in Florence, Italy. It features City Lights Books in Italian and their own publications—it's a Theme Bookstore. They also stock Beat, surrealism, anarchism books, and that's about it. There's no financial connection with us, but it's run by Italian friends of mine. They're so idealistic.

◆**NANCY PETERS:** And they have a wonderful system; when they publish books, people subscribe and are patrons. I wish we could do that here.

◆**LF:** We didn't want to get into that because you have to meet deadlines. We do publish a few books that can *only* be bought at City Lights Bookstore.

Nonprofits & Fund-raising

We recently created a separate City Lights Foundation and are now an authorized nonprofit foundation.

◆**NP:** We're going to start our nonprofit activities with readings, discussion groups and symposiums, and publish non-commercial books.

◆**LF:** But we have to get some donors first.

◆ *V: City Lights is so connected; couldn't you get philanthropical grants?*

◆**NP:** Anything is possible. When you look at arts funding, you see enormous sums donated to the opera, theater, music, fine arts, visual arts, but very little to literary arts. **Somebody will give fifty million dollars to the visual arts and only a thousand dollars to the literary arts. We're always at the bottom of the donations barrel.**

I was really astonished to learn that the Bay Area Book Council, which sponsors the annual S.F. Book Festival, gets a bit of hotel tax money, a little dribble of money here and there, but almost no corporate funding. You'd think Bay Area tech-stock companies making millions would want to support something like the S.F. Bay Area Book Festival—it's so important for the community! But many corporations do not want to contribute to the spread of radical new ideas that might be contrary to their particular mission and aim.

♦**LF:** I think it's a *systemic* problem, and the whole [book publishing] system is undergoing a revolution. We're in the middle of this revolution—an electronic revolution, basically. Amazon.com wasn't here ten years ago. Amazon couldn't be in business without the Internet.

♦ *V: That's for sure. There are people who peruse books in bookstores, then go home and order from Amazon to get a discount. Don't you think the Internet is adversely affecting the book trade?*

♦**NP:** I think it's affecting, in the long run, people's book-reading habits and book-buying habits. You hear more about "The Post-Book Era." People are sitting at their screens, downloading bits of information, and viewing the book as obsolete.

♦**LF:** You can't read a whole book on a screen. Can you imagine reading a Dickens novel, or *Remembrance of Things Past* . . . on a SCREEN?! [laughs]

♦**NP:** I think books will survive. But it's going to become very difficult for important facets of the book world. Not only are the independent publishers being wiped out, but the independent bookstores as well.

Small publishers always depended on the independents because they would try out things that were new and different. Book buyers knew the importance of selling something that might be exciting and revolutionary, but not necessarily sell a million copies. **It's critical to personally promote ideas that are really revolutionary—that initially only reach a small audience.** Some books will be read by a small percentage of the population: people who *think*—whose influence might be great in other ways. Creative people. **Independent publishing and**

bookselling keep books that are original, creative and unpopular *out there*, so people can be influenced by them— and that stimulates other creativity and other new ideas.

♦ *V: How is City Lights' business doing?*

♦**NP:** This year has been very difficult for us because of the changes going on with distributors, corporate mergers and on-line bookselling.

♦ *V: Right. All I know is that a lot of small stores and small distributors have gone under recently. At least City Lights got a loan to buy their building. Now you can't arbitrarily be kicked out—*

♦**LF:** No, no! **All this time—for 47 years—we were on a three-year lease; we never knew how long we were going to last.** This building was built by a French family the year after the 1906 earthquake, and their heirs finally agreed to sell it to us.

"God" & the "Afterlife"?

♦ *V: That almost makes one believe in divine providence. You don't believe in "God," do you?*

♦**LF:** "God"—how do you spell that?

♦ *V: G-a-w-d.*

♦**LF:** Yeah, I thought there was a "w" in there. It's an unusual concept—a very fantastic idea that there's somebody up in the sky. He'd have to keep moving further and further away as they get more and more astronomical probes and rockets going higher and higher up. Gawd has to keep moving further out of sight, so people can still believe he's there.

♦ *V: What is your philosophy? Buddhism?*

♦**LF:** Well, I believe Buddhism is a lot more attractive than Christianity. Gary Snyder always makes a point of pronouncing it *"Bud*-ism" [as in flower buds]. It doesn't lay any guilt trip on you—**Buddha didn't die for my sins! Whereas in**

Christianity, Christ died for my sins—even though I hadn't even been born yet.

♦ *V: Do you believe in an afterlife?*

♦ **LF:** I saw a photograph of Gregory Corso sitting next to Allen Ginsberg's body, just after Allen died in his loft in New York City. This was taken twelve hours after his heart had stopped beating, and yet he looked totally at peace—I'd never seen such a peaceful-looking man—more peaceful than he ever was in "real life"! It looked like he wasn't dead at all—he was just *continuing.*

Regarding death, I think the best you can hope for is a rearrangement of your atoms in some kind of a conscious form. *That's* possible. It may be a *lower* form of consciousness. You know games like "What would you like to come back as? . . . What's your totem animal?" So I think maybe I'd be lucky if I came back as a horse, or a unicorn, or a dog—

♦ *V: Or a cat—*

♦ **LF:** Well, cats are of a higher order than dogs. Cats look down on dogs, like they're some lower species they have to tolerate. It wouldn't be bad being a cat, but I wouldn't want to be a bug, for instance, or a rock—it would be so limited if you were a rock!

♦ *V: Personally, I think about death every day—*

♦ **LF:** I always say, "Well, I'm not ready to think about it—I'll put it off. I'll think about it tomorrow." I'm *only* eighty; I'll put it off for another few years!

♦ *V: My Italian landlord died when he was 100; he had a shoeshine stand for most of the twentieth century.*

♦ **LF:** One of those old shoeshine stands that used to exist on Columbus Avenue here?

♦ *V: Right. He was here when the 1906 San Francisco earthquake happened, and he swore they laid out bodies in Washington Square Park . . . Do you think you got more into your Italian roots as you got older?*

♦ **LF: Yeah, I've been to Italy every year for the past ten years. I've been studying Italian extensively,** and so has

Nancy—she's really fluent. I performed in a theater in Florence, Teatro Studio Scandicci, about ten years ago and got to be friends with the director, Antonio Bertoli. I visit him and stay in his farmhouse, in the hills above Florence, with his family.

He and Marco Cassini founded the City Lights Italia I mentioned earlier. They have cultural events and a big festival every year and bring over poets from America. In the last two or three years, besides myself they've had Anne Waldman from Naropa, Ed Sanders, John Giorno, and others.

When I went, we toured around Italy, did a big show in Sardinia, then Florence . . . it was a traveling show with poets from Spain and France, with the filmmaker Alejandro Jodorowsky and the playwright Fernando Arrabal. I was supposed to go this year and take part in Arrabal's new play, but I was too tied up here.

♦ **V:** *You've met a lot of artists, playwrights and writers over the years. I remember when you had a small apartment at Grant and Filbert. Charles Bukowski broke out a door when he stayed there!*

♦**LF:** Bukowski gave a big poetry reading at the Telegraph Hill Center. We had a refrigerator onstage filled with beer. He sat at a table with a red-and-white checkered tablecloth, and got drunker and drunker as he read. And the more he drank, the more hostile he got toward the audience and the more hostile the audience got toward him—he was throwing beer bottles at them and they were throwing beer bottles back at him.

Bukowski didn't associate with the Beats. He didn't consider himself one or want to be one—but he seemed a little jealous. He had no use for the "literary scene"; he never went around to universities—you could never get him to teach a class or anything like that. He just went to the races and bet on the ponies.

♦ **V:** *Well, there are people who applaud that—*

♦**LF:** He was . . . *rough.* I think writers like Raymond Carver learned a lot from him . . . another alcoholic!

♦ **V:** *Well, Carver's much softer than Bukowski—*

♦**LF:** You mean his drinks were softer! [laughs] I've just been re-reading Carver—great stuff. But Bukowski's much wilder and rougher. Some feminists have attacked Bukowski, but actually he *loved* women—he wrote mostly about women. He was hard on them but they were hard on him—it was 50/50; it wasn't something feminists should attack.

Fame & Creativity

♦ **V:** *You've traveled a lot, doing readings for the past half-century; how have you dealt with the problem of "fame"?*

♦**LF:** **Fame is a *disaster* for any creative person.** Look what it did to Kerouac, for instance. Look what it did to Ginsberg—or rather, in Ginsberg's case it was the *pursuit* of fame that (you might say) ruined his poetry in the end. In the last ten years of Allen's life there's a shocking decline in the quality of his poetry on the printed page. The thing is, he was more and more successful as a performer—he was a genius performer. **Allen could read the phone book and make it sound like a great epic. But then on the printed page the phone book is just the phone book!**

Allen did some beautiful things with music—like when he sang William Blake's "Songs of Innocence and Experience" with his harmonium—that was really beautiful; I can hear it now. Allen's voice was wonderful: "Ah, Sunflower, weary of time" . . . and he would have the whole audience singing: "When the voices of children are heard in the land, and the laughter is heard on the hill," and at the end the last line is "and all the hills echo-ed." He'd go on for ten, fifteen, twenty minutes with the audience singing back to him the same line . . .

Then he got into using reggae beats and doing reggae songs.

They were great songs when he *performed* them—but the trouble was: on the printed page, if you juxtaposed them with his earlier poetry, they couldn't compare.

I also felt that Buddhist practice—at least, *some* Buddhist practices like meditation, sitting—tends to turn you inward so you're facing a blank wall, and this affects one's poetry. **If you spend an enormous amount of time every day sitting, you're not observing the outside world anymore. That can be very limiting for a poet—it cuts down on your input.**

Of course, in the case of Allen Ginsberg I can see why Buddhism would appeal to him. He was so gregarious. Sometimes he would go on a retreat for two weeks and write a thousand postcards! [laughs]

♦ **V:** *So you've dealt with the problem of fame—you've consciously given it some thought—*

♦ **LF:** Fame really is a disaster for a creative person because it eats up all your time. As San Francisco Poet Laureate, the time I would have spent painting I had to spend answering correspondence. And it affects your personal life. You start going out with a woman, but she doesn't see you for yourself—she sees this image of you that's been created exterior to you. It's really hard to get past this with someone. You have to keep saying "That's not me. Where did you get that idea?"

Someone like Kerouac couldn't handle fame; he cut out early on. Right after he started getting famous for *On the Road,* he was already trying to escape.

Early City Lights' History

♦ **V:** *Can you summarize the early City Lights history?*

♦ **LF:** Pete Martin had *City Lights Magazine* before there was the City Lights Bookstore. **Paperback books weren't consid-**

ered real books by the book trade (this was 1953), so his idea was to start an all-paperback bookshop to pay the rent for the magazine, which was sort of one step up from mimeograph. I think there were a total of five issues. It was really an early— maybe the *first*—pop culture magazine. Those early *City Lights* magazines were the first to publish Pauline Kael's film criticism and jazz critic Grover Sales's columns. I remember one article on the sociological significance of the *Moon Mullins* comic strip.

The magazine went out of existence in about a year. Pete got divorced, moved to New York, and started the New Yorker Bookstore there, leaving me with City Lights. Then I started publishing books. But it was Pete's idea—it was a brilliant idea— because there were no paperback bookstores in this country. **The only place you could buy paperbacks was at a drugstore or newsstand where people didn't care what they were selling.**

The only paperbacks back then were imported Penguins and cheap Signet or Avon books. So when we opened up, that was about all we had. Paperbacks were distributed and merchandised like magazines by magazine distributors then. The local Golden Gate Distributors had a stranglehold; you couldn't get a direct account with a New York publisher—you had to go through them. It took years to break that down.

Then the "paperback revolution" happened; the first quality paperbacks appeared—Jason Epstein's Doubleday Anchor books were the first. That was around 1953 when we were just getting started.

After World War II, I had come to San Francisco from France where my friend George Whitman had started a used bookstore called Le Librarie Mistral. So my first idea was to have a used bookstore where I could sit in the back and read all day and growl at the customers. But after the paperback revolution I never got back to the used bookstore I originally wanted to have.

Pete—Peter D. Martin—was a brilliant guy. From the beginning of the store, we had an anarchist bias. I got my anarchism

In 1967, Ferlinghetti did a *zine: Interim Pad No. 1,* printed (mimeographed?) on goldenrod card stock and typeset on an old manual typewrter. Page 1 proclaims: "Interim Pad? A misreading of Hermann Hesse's Unterm Rad? A launching pad (into inner space)? A writing pad? A temporary home? A staging-area between two revolutions? Life itself an Interim Pad, a place a poet might be found turned-on." Editorial policy: "F... for peace, Legalize Marijuana, Rock Folk, Demystify Human Violence, Super-impose Images of Ecstasy: 'What is here is Elsewhere, what is not here is Nowhere.' " Editor: Lawrence Ferlinghetti. Production: Jan Herman & Gail Dusenbery. Contributors include Carl Solomon, Allen Ginsberg, Janine Pommy-Vega, Bob Kaufman, Claude Pelieu & Mary Beach, and Jean-Jacques Lebel.

from Kenneth Rexroth and from Herbert Read in England. Read wrote a marvelous book called *Poetry and Anarchism*. It was published by The Freedom Press in England, an anarchist press. Anyway, Pete was the son of Carlo Tresca, a famous Italian anarchist who was assassinated on the streets of New York, probably by Italian fascists.

So **our store had an anarchist background from the beginning.** We sold the Italian anarchist newspapers, and I remember one of the people who bought those papers was the garbageman. He would jump off the back of the garbage truck and come in and buy an Italian anarchist newspaper, then jump back on—this was in the 1950's.

Busted for publishing "Howl"

♦ **V:** *Your early radical publishing wasn't without peril; you got busted for publishing* Howl—

♦ **LF:** Well, Shigeyoshi Murao was the one who actually got busted for selling *Howl* to an officer of the juvenile department. The first printing was done in England, and then customs seized it—they thought it was "obscene." When the U.S. District Attorney refused to prosecute, customs released the book, and then the local police got into the act and busted *us* for selling it. There was a court trial before Judge Clayton Horn—it's all written up in books like *Howl of the Censor.* I wrote an essay in the *San Francisco Chronicle* titled "Horn on Howl" which contains a history of the *Howl* trial. [reprinted in *A Casebook on the Beat.*]

♦ **V:** *From the beginning of your publishing, you've had to deal with police censorship*—

♦ **LF: The fascist mentality persists throughout the world; it keeps coming back so you have to keep beating it down. It's a continuing battle.** In the sixties we were busted for selling

Lenore Kandel's *Love Book,* as well as *Zap* comics.

There have been lots of other cases where we weren't the defendants, such as the trial of *Lady Chatterley's Lover.* Grove Press had to go through a big trial over William S. Burroughs' *Naked Lunch.*

♦ **V:** *Did you have to pay lots of money to defend yourself?*

♦ **LF:** We would have been out of business if we hadn't had the American Civil Liberties Union (A.C.L.U.) defending us. We didn't have a cent—we were just a little one-room bookstore. **The government—the F.B.I. particularly—knew they could drive a lot of counterculture organizations out of business just by indicting them, because then you have to get lawyers.** So thank gawd for the A.C.L.U.; they saved our neck. Al Bendich was the young attorney who carried the case and made the constitutional points upon which the case was won. He was fresh out of law school and this was his first court trial. He's now vice president of Fantasy Records, and is still active in the A.C.L.U.

The famous criminal trial lawyer Jake Ehrlich associated himself with our case, but he spent most of our defense time reading from Defoe's *Moll Flanders* and other ancient works, and left Al Bendich about fifteen minutes on the last day to make the constitutional points. Ehrlich got his photo in *Life* magazine for defending us in court, but it was Al Bendich who won the case.

So **we would have been out of business if we'd had to hire lawyers. I was prepared to spend a few months in jail; I could have gotten a lot of reading done—I wouldn't have minded too much!**

♦ **V:** *Do you remember many people of color in the early Beat days?*

♦ **LF:** Shigeyoshi "Shig" Murao, who managed City Lights Bookstore [died Feb. 23, 1998]. There were a few we hung out with, like Victor Wong (before he got famous as an actor). He was around here a lot. Victor Wong was from one of the most powerful families in Chinatown, I think, but he was sort of on the outside, a rebel.

♦ **V:** *What about Ted Joans?*

♦**LF:** He wasn't here, he was in New York. In the fifties he used to rent himself out as a beatnik for parties. He made enough money to get to Europe and didn't come back for forty years; he lived in Paris, Timbuktu, and elsewhere. He returned to Seattle and now lives in Vancouver. Coffee House Books published a large book of his poems, *Teducation*.

♦ **V:** *Right; he also has another book out with Hart Leroy Bibbs titled* Double Trouble. *You know, Bob Kaufman was another person of color who was around.*

♦**LF:** Bob Kaufman was *the* black poet in San Francisco—who else was there?

♦ **V:** *I don't think Ishmael Reed was around then.*

♦**LF:** No, he was more of a novelist and was over on the other side of the Bay. Janice Mirikitani, who is now married to Cecil Williams, recently became San Francisco's second Poet Laureate. As of now San Francisco is the *only* city in America with a Poet Laureate, I think—

♦ **V:** *Lawrence, what have you been reading lately?*

♦**LF: I've been reading a lot of history, because I'm writing a long poem that's going to go on for the rest of my life. It's called *Americus.*** So I'm re-reading Dos Passos' *USA*, a lot of the Chicago School like James T. Farrell's *Studs Lonigan,* and Dostoyevsky's *Notes from the Underground*. I'm also reading William Carlos Williams' *Paterson,* Ed Sanders' *America: A History in Verse*—he calls this "documentary poetry" in the lineage of Ezra Pound's *Cantos,* Charles Olson's *Maximus Poems,* and *Paterson*. This is the tradition I'm working in.

♦ **V:** *What does "Americus" mean? I've never seen that word.*

♦**LF:** I made it up. There's a town in Georgia called Americus, but that has nothing to do with anything. Do you know who Amerigo Vespucci was?

♦ **V:** *Wasn't he the one who really discovered America?*

♦**LF:** Well, that's erroneous. He was a Florentine navigator who worked with the Medicis on their foreign expeditions, and discovered South America in 1499. Like Columbus, he worked for the King of Spain and made many voyages. He discovered how to determine longitude three centuries before the British; in 1499 he determined the circumference of the earth within fifty kilometers. So he was the ancestor of "Americus"—that's what I'm claiming! [laughs]

The "Process"

♦ *V: Let's talk about the creative process—*
♦**LF:** Oh, I *hate* to talk about "process." That emphasis on process is big in schools and in the art world now. Painting, sculpting, conceptual art—it's all about process . . . and it's a total bore, as far as I'm concerned. The same thing's going on in poetry.

If I give a poetry reading at a university, I now avoid the question-and-answer period after the reading, because the questions are always about process: "Well, what time do you get up? Do you start writing right away? What time of day do you write? What's your routine? How do you go about conceiving a poem? *Blah blah blah.*" So my answer always is, "It's a trade secret."

So, I never have a question-and-answer session, because the idea of the poetry is to get people high, and if you have a question-and-answer session, it's a complete bringdown—it brings everything down to the level of *prose.*

That's why I'm not a professor. I had plenty of chances to teach in universities, but that's what you *have* to do: you have to do "the process" instead of the poem itself.
♦ *V: You know, Lawrence, when I first met you, what impressed me most was your keen sense of sarcasm—*
♦**LF:** Everyone who worked at City Lights in those days was

pretty sarcastic: Pete Martin, to begin with, and Shig. Shig had one of those egg-beaters you buy in Chinatown—it's like a wooden spindle. He used to fiddle with one at the bookstore counter. Some tourist would ask, "Would you mind telling me what that is?" and he'd say [deadpan], "It's a Tibetan prayer wheel." Shig loved to put on the tourists!

♦ *V: The "put-on" was a signature creative social prank of the Beat Generation—*

♦**LF: William Burroughs—being an ex-junkie, he was always putting you on.** His whole writing; the whole entourage of Burroughs characters, like Doctor Benway, was inspired by the junkie mentality—the mind-set of a hustler—you know: do anything to score! He had this total deadpan humor; he was his own straight man. You could be in a room with him and you felt he wasn't really there; he really *was* "El Hombre Invisible" (the Invisible Man). He looked totally straight; always wore a suit and tie and felt hat. A master of the put-on. But he wasn't around the bookstore in the early days. He never lived here . . .

♦ *V: Where did you first meet Burroughs?*

♦**LF:** It must have been in Tangier; I went there in 1963 to see Paul Bowles and edit *A Hundred Camels in the Courtyard* [first City Lights book by Bowles]. The beat poets were living in the Hotel Villa Muniria. Burroughs was there at the time, but I didn't get to know him—I don't think I ever had a whole conversation with Burroughs.[laughs]

♦ *V: Did you ever try heroin?*

♦**LF:** No, I never took any hard drugs, just acid and marijuana. I took LSD a couple of times in Big Sur; I wouldn't think of going to a rock dance on acid like a lot of people did. I took it one time in Big Sur with Michael McClure and Shig and a couple of other people; this must have been around 1959. I wrote a long poem on acid ["After the Cries of the Birds Have Stopped"] on the beach at Bixby Canyon.

♦ *V: Had you read* The Tibetan Book of the Dead?

♦ **LF:** I read *at* it; I never really *read* it. I'd open it up here and there and I'd stare at the pages. **I think it's pretty absurd to base your life's decisions on a chance opening of the *I Ching*, for instance, or throwing yarrow sticks—you might as well go to Las Vegas!** Also, to think you're going to find guidance by chanting various mantras? Someone asked Krishnamurti about chanting "Hare Krishna," and I heard him say, [imitates high-pitched, Indian-accented voice] "Might as well chant 'Coca-Cola'!"

♦ *V: So you actually saw Krishnamurti speak?*

♦ **LF:** Yeah, I heard him in Berkeley and then I went to the reception afterwards at a big house up in the Berkeley hills. There was this huge dining room with an elaborate banquet spread. There were a lot of rooms, and all the people were in the other rooms when I happened to find myself alone at the banquet table with Krishnamurti. I said to him, "I haven't touched meat in three months"—I was just starting to be a vegetarian. Do you know what he said? [high voice] "My lips have never touched meat!" I felt about two inches tall. [laughs]

♦ *V: Did you know Richard Brautigan well?*

♦ **LF:** I had very little conversation with him over the years, and usually it was a one-sentence interchange. The last time he was in San Francisco before he returned to Bolinas and shot himself, he was in Vesuvio's drinking a lot. He came out pretty tanked up. In the little window by the entrance to City Lights I had placed some blades of grass from Walt Whitman's grave I had plucked. It was just ordinary grass. So I had this in the window with a sign, "Leaves of Grass from Whitman's grave." Brautigan stared at it for a minute and said, "Good argument for cremation!" Then he staggered up the street, and that was the last time I ever saw him.

♦ *V: Alan Watts was on the scene early on, wasn't he?*

♦ **LF:** One time I saw Alan Watts at a memorial concert at the Opera House when Ravi Shankar played with Ali Akbar Khan—I think it was Ravi Shankar's 60th birthday. About a year before, I had visited him at his houseboat in Sausalito. I was looking for a houseboat to live on, so I thought he would know if there were any others available, but he didn't know of anything. Then at this concert, at the intermission, I saw him coming toward me wearing Buddhist robes. The press of people sort of pushed us together, and as I passed him I said, "I'm still looking." I meant that I was still looking for a houseboat to rent, but he gave me this look like I had said something very profound and spiritual, clasped both hands together and bowed his head. He'd thought I was looking for a great spiritual nirvana, but I was just looking for an apartment.

♦ **V:** *You've lived through most of the 20th century. What annoys you about life now?*

500 Years of Decadence!

♦**LF:** Five hundred years of decadence! In the graduate department at Columbia University I took classes from Jacques Barzun. In his latest book he says that our civilization has been in decline most of the twentieth century, and I agree with him. We're talking about European civilization—that's what our American culture still is, mainly. But probably for not much longer!

I laid this notion on my son-in-law, who is an advanced computer engineer in charge of a huge computer network for a large insurance company, and he said: "Civilization is in decline? Look what we're doing on the Internet!" But from the European point of view, it's all over. The quality of life is declining, and the proof is in the details. For example, right outside you may come across an old-fashioned manhole cover which has a beautiful art deco design on it. But when you see a new one, there's nothing but straight lines—there's been a huge decline in the design. If you look at the old Italian houses in North Beach (say, along

Stockton Street), they all have beautiful marble steps. But when one of those steps breaks today, quite often it's replaced by a cement slab! That's what I'm talking about.

The use of plastic utensils and dishware instead of real silverware or tableware—that's another sign. You now have a throwaway culture. And throwaway culture leads to throwaway children. (I have a poem about this.) The falling apart of the family is another case in point for this argument.

Look what happened to the beautiful old Bank of America building across from City Lights. It was one of the first Bank of Americas in the whole city, and now it's a Carl's Jr! They put up a garish neon sign on this classic Roman façade. [laughs]

♦ *V: The world's population has at least tripled in the 20th Century. You'd think that with all these extra people around, we'd have a lot more beautiful hand-carved furniture and artifacts, but instead we have far less.*

♦ **LF:** Yeah. I remember **when I first used to go to Mexico, the outdoor public markets were absolutely full of all kinds of handmade local products. Now you go to those same** *mercados* **and it's all plastic**—well, not *all;* you can still go to Oaxaca and find hand-woven serapes made locally, but about two-thirds of the market will be plastic *junk,* a lot of it imported from other parts of the world.

♦ *V: I remember when I first heard the term "planned obsolescence" and was horrified by the idea that corporations would deliberately, knowingly, make products shoddier so people would have to replace them sooner—like those $3 umbrellas that break after one rainstorm.*

♦ **LF:** I remember when throwaway ballpoint pens first appeared—that was really shocking! Up until then, everyone took pride in having a pen that was really a beautiful object, like a Parker pen you refilled from an inkwell or a bottle of ink. I think the first throwaway ballpoints showed up in the fifties.

It's even getting hard to find a lead pencil, unless you go to an art supply store. But around 1970, I discovered the first Pentel pens from Japan—they still make them and I still use them. They have a felt tip and the ink is water-soluble, meaning you can make a drawing and then add a drop of water and get these wonderful shaded gray effects. I did a lot of drawing in the studio with these. I also wrote many poems with the Pentel.

♦ **V:** *That's one of the few "improvements" of the past thirty years. Also—medical technology advances; you're still alive—*

♦ **LF:** How can you tell?! [laughs]

♦ **V:** *Today, do you think we have more freedom?*

♦ **LF:** Oh, much more. When I grew up you had to get married if you wanted to live with someone—that was true up through the fifties. Oh, there were always Bohemian enclaves where they ignored all that—even in the twenties. In 1910 the Bloomsbury group in England completely ignored the idea of marriage and believed in free love, but they were a very small percentage of the population. I mean, you couldn't go to a hotel and register together unless you were man and wife. People born since the sixties are way ahead of us—from the moment they're born they're way ahead of us! They don't have to fight all of that.

But it would be interesting to know what percentage of the population under 25 or 30 voted for Bush instead of Gore. I've found that the people who grew up using computers, and are making this into a computer world, don't read the daily newspapers. There's a café near me, the Francisco Café, which is inhabited largely by people new to North Beach who live in the condos around me. They all look like they work at some computer firm. Every time I go there in the morning wanting to read a paper, there are no daily newspapers anywhere.

♦ **V:** *They're all sitting there getting the news on their laptops, along with a slew of banner ads—*

♦ **LF:** But how much are they reading on the Internet? They're only reading soundbites, or just enough to see whether it's a good time to invest using E-Trade or not.

George W. Bush—George the Second—will have the "atomic

suitcase" under his bed; it's scary to think that. This know-nothing President has the little dispatch case with the [Doomsday] activator in it.

I thought Nixon was scary, but Nixon had brains, even though he was a ghoul. But Bush hasn't got any brains; he probably *is* dyslexic. He's a "good ole boy"; that's why he got elected. There are millions and millions of Middle Americans who identify with that good ole boy lingo. They see him talking up there, "Well, I wanna tell you: I'm for the people." During the debates they asked him, "Isn't it true that your tax plan benefits the rich and penalizes the poor?" and all he would say was, "Well, I'll tell you. I'm for the people."

♦ *V: G.W.'s father was head of the CIA and gained a lot of experience "fixing" elections around the world; his CIA toppled Allende's socialist regime in Chile. So the Bush dynasty probably planned this coup years ago. They planted Jeb in Florida well in advance, knowing it would be the turnkey state. It's obvious the American people didn't want Bush. And the Supreme Court disgraced itself.*

♦**LF:** It's probably best that Bush became President because the way Congress is constituted, the Republicans won't be able to get through any of their programs, and the American people will be so fed up there'll be a Democratic landslide four years from now. The same thing would have happened in reverse if the Democrats had won the Presidency; they wouldn't be able to get any of their programs through, and in four years there would be a Republican landslide.

Gore won't be the Democratic nominee in four years because he's completely charmless. He was born in Tennessee but had not a bit of Southern charm, and had absolutely no wit whatsoever. He and Clinton were so close to the Republican party anyway; "the American government is a bird with two right wings." **If Gore had been smart, he would have persuaded Nader to be on his ticket.** But he was so far right, that Nader was too far left for him.

Gore was just giving lip service to environmental issues. He was for the death penalty, the Iraq war, building up the military budget—he was practically like a Republican. **Actually, he should have chosen Clinton for Vice President**—why not? Clinton needs a job! That way he would have saved the American government a huge amount of money, because retired Presidents get an enormous pension for the rest of their lives. Also, the campaign would have gotten some wind behind it, because Clinton is a great campaigner—he would have given the campaign just what Gore couldn't give.

♦ *V: I heard people say that if Bush got elected, they would move to Canada—*

♦**LF:** That's what people said when Reagan got elected, when the first George Bush got elected—people were saying that when *Eisenhower* got elected!

♦ *V: I guess some things never change . . .* ♦♦♦

"Love in the Days of Rage," assemblage by Lawrence Ferlinghetti. George Krevsky Gallery, San Francisco.

Recommendations

I'm not much on furnishing reading lists. But—here are a few titles from my shelves.—Lawrence Ferlinghetti

Jacques Barzun: *From Dawn to Decadence: 500 Years of Western Cultural Life, 1500 to the Present*
Gray Brechin: *Imperial San Francisco*
Howard Zinn: *A People's History of the United States*
Arts plastiques Paris/Paris Paris 1937–Paris 1957
Charles Dreyfus: *Happenings & Fluxus*
Blaise Cendrars: *Complete Poems. Selected Writings.*
Thomas Albright: *Art in the San Francisco Bay Area*
Ferlinghetti & Peters: *Literary San Francisco*
Odilon Redon (monograph)
Sotheby's catalog #7351, Allen Ginsberg & Friends
Gavin Arthur: *The Circle of Sex*
Charles Perry: *The Haight-Ashbury, A History*
Jaroslav Hasek (tr. C. Parrott): *The Good Soldier Svejk*
1929: Peret - Aragon - Man Ray
Charles Plymell: *The Last of the Moccasins*
Richard Aldington: *A Dream in the Luxembourg*
Giacomo Leopardi/Di Piero: *Pensieri*
Malcolm Barker: *More San Francisco Memoirs 1852-99*
Joseph Heller: *Catch-22*
James Laughlin: *Stolen & Contaminated Poems*
William Everson: Remembrances and Tributes
James Broughton: *Making Light of It*
J. Gil de Biedma: *Las personas del verbo*
Pier Paolo Pasolini: *The Divine Mimesis. Roman Poems*
Ulrike Heider: *Anarchism: Left, Right, and Green*
Hermann Broch: *The Death of Virgil*
Sawyer-Lauçanno: *Destruction of the Jaguar* **(continued next page)**

The Viking Portable Library: Cervantes
Georg Buchner: *Lenz*
William Carlos Williams: *Spring and All*
Walt Whitman: *Leaves of Grass*
Jeremy Reed: *Red-haired Android*
James Salter: *Burning the Days*
Twenty Poems of Neruda
Edward Fitzgerald: *The Rubaiyat of Omar Khayam*
Rumi: Poet of the Heart
Alberto Moravia: *The Comformist*
Bertolt Brecht: *Selected Poems*
The Complete Works of Oscar Wilde
Herbert Marcuse: *The Aesthetic Dimension*
Benjamin Pêret: *Remove Your Hat*
William Least Heat Moon: *Blue Highways*
Breyten Breytenbach: *Mouroir*
Kimon Nicolaides: *The Natural Way to Draw*
Betty Edwards: *Drawing on the Right Side of the Brain*
Leo Tolstoy: *The Death of Ivan Ilyich & Other Stories*
Allen Ginsberg *Planet News*
Jack Kerouac & Joyce Johnson: *Door Wide Open*
Gilles Deleuze: *Spinoza: Practical Philosophy*
Angelo Maria Ripellino: *Magic Prague*
Cola Franzen: *Poems of Arab Andalusia*
Hiroaki Sato: *One Hundred Frogs*
Dino Campana: *Orphic Songs*
Jacques Prévert: *To Paint the Portrait of a Bird. Paroles*
Eric Bentley: *Before Brecht*
Dennis McNally: *Desolate Angel*
Guillaume Apollinaire: *Poems*
Hayden Carruth: *The Voice That is Great Within Us*
Philip Lamantia: *Becoming Visible. Selected Poems.*
The Columbia Encyclopedia, 3rd Edition

Some books by Lawrence Ferlinghetti:

How to Paint Sunlight (Spring, 2001)
A Far Rockaway of the Heart
These Are My Rivers
Wild Dreams of a New Beginning
European Poems and Transitions
Over All the Obscene Boundaries
The Mexican Night (travel journal)
Life as a Real Dream
The Secret Meaning of Things
Landscapes of Living & Dying
A Trip to Italy and France
The Populist Manifestos
When I Look at Pictures
(included in) Penguin Modern Poets 5
The Illustrated Wilfred Funk
Seven Days in Nicaragua Libre (travel journal)
Her, a novel
The Anarchist Banker (a novel; Fall 2001)

Some Beat Web sites:

www.citylights.com—has an archive of Lawrence Ferlinghetti's "Poetry As News" columns, other articles, and reviews of recommended books.

www.boppin.com/poets/ferlinghetti.htm
www.levity.com/corduroy/ferling.htm
www.charm.net/~brooklyn/
www.beatbooks.com
www.greatmodernpictures.com/newpage26.htm
ils.unc.edu/~andra/beat.html
www.connectotel.com/marcus/beatchr1.html
www.connectotel.com/marcus/beatfaq.html
www.hotelboheme.com/beat/
www.rooknet.com/beatpage

A FEW QUOTATIONS

"Working in an office for a great many years can be one of the most crucifying experiences. You are forced to repress your biological need to kill everyone around you."
—J.G. Ballard

"A mere half-dozen corporations provide the content for most of the nation's media! And these are corporate conglomerates."—Jim Warren

"Today's average American consumes twice as many goods and services as in 1950 . . . A decade ago, most grocery stores stocked about 9,000 items; today's stores carry some 24,000."—Richard and Joyce Wolkommir, "You Are What You Buy," *Smithsonian*

"You are what you buy"—James Twitchell, ad guru

"You are what you eat"—genetic engineering protest

"The right laws of dress are dictated by science, and not by fashion."—Oscar Wilde

"Our challenge is to find the common within the dissimilar, the pearl of truth within the contradictions."
—Katrina Hopkins

"I have a passion for landscape, and I have never seen one improved by a billboard . . . When I retire, I am going to start a secret society of masked vigilantes who will travel around the world on silent motor bicycles, chopping down posters at the dark of the moon. How many juries will convict us when we are caught in these acts of beneficent citizenship?"
—David Ogilvy, *Confessions of an Advertising Man,* 1963

"Do what you will, but harm none."—Anonymous

RE/SEARCH CATALOG

PUNK '77: an inside look at the San Francisco rock n' roll scene, 1977 by James Stark

Covers the beginnings of the S.F. Punk Rock scene through the Sex Pistols' concert at Winterland in Jan., 1978, in interviews and photographs by James Stark. James was among the many artists involved in early punk. His photos were published in *New York Rocker, Search & Destroy* and *Slash*, among others. His posters for Crime are classics and highly prized collectors' items. Over 100 photos, including many behind-the-scenes looks at the bands who made things happen: Nuns, Avengers, Crime, Screamers, Negative Trend, Dils, Germs, UXA, etc. Interviews with the bands and people early on the scene give intimate, often darkly humorous glimpses of events in a *Please Kill Me* (Legs McNeil) style.

"The photos themselves, a generous 115 of them, are richly satisfying. They're the kind of photos one wants to see..."—Puncture. "I would recommend this book not only for old-timers looking for nostalgia, but especially to young Punks who have no idea how this all got off the ground, who take today's Punk for granted, to see how precarious it was at birth, what a fluke it was, and to perhaps be able to get a fresh perspective on today's scene needs..."—MAXIMUMROCKNROLL

7½x10¼", 98 pp, 100+ photos, on archival art paper. PB, **$13.99.**

SEARCH & DESTROY: The Complete Reprint

(in 2 big 10x15" volumes)
"The best punk publication ever"—Jello Biafra

Facsimile editions (at 90% size) include all the interviews, articles, ads, illustrations and photos. Captures the enduring revolutionary spirit of punk rock, 1977-1978. Vol. I contains an abrasive intro-interview with Jello Biafra on the history and future of punk rock. Published by V. Vale before his RE/Search series, *Search &*

Destroy is a definitive, first-hand documentation of the punk rock cultural revolution, printed as it happened! Patti Smith, Iggy Pop, Ramones, Sex Pistols, Clash, DEVO, Avengers, Mutants, Dead Kennedys, William S. Burroughs, J.G. Ballard, John Waters, Russ Meyer, and David Lynch (to name a few) discussing philosophy, creativity, their own work, & still-contemporary social issues.

10x15", 148pp, **$19.95 each, $35 for both**

PUNK & D.I.Y.

LOUDER FASTER SHORTER punk video by Mindaugis Bagdon

San Francisco, March 21, 1978. In the intense, original punk rock scene at the Mabuhay Gardens (the only club in town which would allow it), the AVENGERS, DILS, MUTANTS, SLEEPERS and UXA played a benefit for striking Kentucky coal miners ("Punks Against Oppression!"). One of the only surviving 16mm color documents of this short-lived era, *LOUDER FASTER SHORTER* captured the spirit and excitement of "punk rock" before revolt became style. Filmmaker Mindaugis Bagdon was a member of *Search & Destroy*, the publication which chronicled and catalyzed the punk rock "youth culture" rebellion of the late '70s. "Exceptionally fine color photography, graphic design and editing."—S.F. International Film Festival review, 1980. 20 minute video in US NTSC VHS only. **$15.**

ZINES! Vol. One & *ZINES! Vol. 2: Incendiary Interviews with Independent Publishers*

In the Punk Tradition of Do-It-Yourself, these (2) books present interviews with zine creators telling why and how they publish. Some of the strangest obsessions and most gnarly personal revelations and fetishes haunt the pages of zines. Following the imperative: "Destroy the society that seeks to destroy you!", *ZINES!* #1 & 2 show how easy it is to express yourself, and thus change your world. Vol.1: *Beer Frame, Crap Hound, Fat Girl, Thrift SCORE, Bunny Hop, Housewife Turned Assassin, Meat Hook, X-Ray* & more! Vol. 2: *Murder Can Be Fun, 8-Track Mind, McJob, Dishwasher, Temp Slave,* Bruno Richard. EACH: 8½x11″, quotations, excerpts, zine directory, historical essay, index. Vol.1: 184 pp. PB, **$18.99;** Vol.2: 148 pp. PB, **$14.99. 2001 SPECIAL: Both for $20!**

RE/SEARCH #1, #2, #3—the shocking tabloid issues. Deep into the heart of the Control Process; Creativity & Survival, past, present & future. ◆ #1: J.G. Ballard, Cabaret Voltaire, Julio Cortazar, Octavio Paz, Sun Ra, The Slits, Conspiracy Theory Guide. #2: DNA, James Blood Ulmer, Z'ev, Aboriginal Music, Surveillance Technology, Monte Cazazza, Diane Di Prima, German Electronic Music Chart. #3: Fela, New Brain Research, The Rattlesnake Man, Sordide Sentimental, New Guinea, Kathy Acker, Pat Califia, Joe Dante, Johanna Went, SPK, Flipper, Physical Modification of Women. 11x17″, Heavily illus. **$8 ea, all for $20** (Rare, fragile, and red-hot. Not at stores, direct order only)

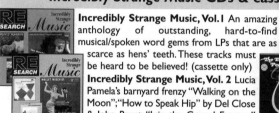

MUSIC: Read & Listen!

SWING! The New Retro Renaissance Rockabilly, swing, lounge and Vegas Show Acts figure in this celebration of "born again" retro artists who feel the past is more nutrifying than the crass corporate present. America used to be an amazingly lively cultural force, before monolithic mega-entertainment conglomerates turned its popular music into kitty-porn drool for the slobbering TV-worshipping masses. Fads can come and go, but the music of Lavay Smith, Big Sandy, and Sam Butera will remain with us! Learn about *the life:* vintage clothes, hairdos, shoes, cars, books, movies. Photos of bands, aerial dancers, classic cars, hairstyles, clothes, shoes, ties, accessories, and interiors of homes.

8½x11", 224 pp, with hundreds of photographs; lists of recommended books, records and films; informative essays; movie reviews; index. PB. **$17.99.**

Listen to 3 of the bands you read about in SWING!

From the lovely Lavay Smith & her Red Hot Skillet Lickers to the "swing-from-hell" of Lee Press-On & the Nails to The New Morty Show's modern take on a '50s Vegas, Louie Prima-Keely Smith Show. These are sexy, exciting and danceable CDs—all on independent labels, impossible to find outside of San Francisco! Own a rarity! **$16 each, all 3 for $36.**

ME AND BIG JOE by Michael Bloomfield

BLUES—A classic coming-of-age tale, illuminating black American culture before its dilution by encroaching white American television. Bloomfield's amazing guitar artistry emblazened Bob Dylan, Paul Butterfield Blues Band, and the Electric Flag. In this narrative, Michael befriends great blues legend Joe Lee Williams (*aka* Big Joe) and together they embark on an odyssey through the dark, smoky blues clubs of the Midwest. *Me and Big Joe* is a classic American adventure story, a must read for any blues lover or musician. "I can't recommend *Me and Big Joe* highly enough. It is a beautifully realized American miniature—nearly as scary as Melville's white whale, fully as grotesque and funny as a Fellini dreamscape and as exhilarating as Bloomfield's best solo."—*American Journal.* 5x7", 60 pp, illus., PB, **$5.99.** Impossible to find; order direct!

BODY MODIFICATION and S&M

RE/Search 12: MODERN PRIMITIVES [part of our S&M Library]The *New York Times* called this "the Bible of the underground tattooing and body piercing movement." *Modern Primitives* launched an entire '90s subculture. Crammed with illustrations & information, it's now considered a classic. The best texts on ancient human decoration practices such as tattooing, piercing, scarification and more. 279 eye-opening photos and graphics; 22 in-depth interviews with some of the most colorful people on the planet. "Dispassionate ethnography that lets peo-

ple put their behavior in its own context."—*Voice Literary Supplement* "The photographs and illustrations are both explicit and astounding . . . provides fascinating food for thought." —*Iron Horse* 8½x11", 212 pp, 279 photos and illus, PB. Great gift! **$17.99**

SPECIAL OFFER: Modern Primitives book & T-shirt gift-pack—only $25.00

T-shirt!

Modern Primitives T-shirt!
Multi-color on black 100% cotton T-shirt
Illustrations of 12 erotic piercings and implants. **Xtra Large only. Dare to Wear It! $16.**

BOB FLANAGAN: SUPERMASOCHIST [part of our S&M Library]
Bob Flanagan (1952-1996), born in NYC, grew up with Cystic Fibrosis (a genetically inherited, nearly-always fatal disease) and lived longer than any other person with CF. The physical pain of his childhood suffering was principally alleviated by masturbation, wherein pain and pleasure became linked, resulting in his lifelong practice of extreme masochism. Through his insider's perspective on the Sado-Masochistic community, we learn about branding, piercing, whipping, bondage and endurance trials. Includes photos by L.A. artist Sheree Rose. "...an eloquent tour through the psychic terrain of SM, discussing the most severe sexual diversions with the humorous detachment of a shy, clean living nerd. I came away from the book wanting to know this man."—*Details Magazine.* 8½x11", 128 pp, 125 photos & illustrations. PB. **$14.99.**

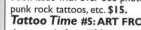

***Tattoo Time* #3: MUSIC & SEA TATTOOS** Deluxe double book issue with over 300 photos. Mermaids, pirates, fish, punk rock tattoos, etc. **$15.**
***Tattoo Time* #5: ART FROM THE HEART** Bigger than ever before (128 pp) with hundreds of color photographs. Featuring in-depth articles on tattooers, contemporary tattooing in Samoa, a survey of the new weirdo monster tattoos, and much more! *(These are out of print; only a few left.)* **$20**

The Torture Garden by Octave Mirbeau This book was once described as the "most sickening work of art of the nineteenth century!" Long out of print, Octave Mirbeau's macabre classic (1899) features a corrupt Frenchman and an insatiably cruel English-woman who meet and then frequent a fantastic 19th century Chinese garden where torture is practiced as an art form. The fascinating, horrific narrative slithers deep into the human spirit, uncovering murderous proclivities and demented desires. "Hot with the fever of ecstatic, prohibited joys, as cruel as a thumbscrew and as luxuriant as an Oriental tapestry. Exotic, perverse . . . hailed by the critics."—Charles Hanson *Towne* 8½x11", 120 pp, 21 mesmerizing photos. **PB: $15.95. Rare Hardcover (edition of only 100; treat yourself!): $29**

MASOCHISM, FEMINISM

Confessions of Wanda von Sacher-Masoch Married for 10 years to Leopold von Sacher-Masoch (author: *Venus in Furs* & many other novels) whose whip-and-fur bedroom games spawned the term "masochism," Wanda's story is a feminist classic from 100 years ago. She was forced to play "sadistic" roles in Leopold's fantasies to ensure the survival of herself & their 3 children—games which called into question who was the Master and who the Slave. Besides being a compelling story of a woman's search for her own identity, strength and, ultimately, complete independence, this is a

true-life adventure story—an odyssey through many lands peopled by amazing characters. Here is a woman's consistent unblinking investigation of the limits of morality and the deepest meanings of love. "Extravagantly designed in an illustrated, oversized edition that is a pleasure to hold. It is also exquisitely written, engaging and literary and turns our preconceptions upside down."—*L.A. Reader* 8½x11", 136 pp, illustrated, PB. **$13.99**

RE/Search 13: Angry Women 16 cutting-edge performance artists discuss critical questions such as: How can revolutionary feminism encompass wild sex, humor, beauty, spirituality *plus* radical politics? How can a powerful movement for social change be *inclusionary?* Wide range of topics discussed *passionately*. **Included:** Karen Finley, Annie Sprinkle, bell hooks, Diamanda Galas, Kathy Acker, Susie Bright, Sapphire. Armed with contempt for dogma, stereotype & cliché, these visionaries probe into our social foundation of taboos, beliefs & totalitarian linguistic contradictions from whence spring (as well as thwart) theories, imaginings, behavior & dreams. "The view here is largely pro-sex, pro-porn, and pro-choice."—*Village Voice* "This book is a Bible—it hails the dawn of a new era—the era of an inclusive, fun, sexy feminism. Every interview contains brilliant moments of wisdom." *Am. Bk Review* 8½x11", 240 pp, 135 illus. PB. **$18.99**

TWO BY DAN MANNIX

MEMOIRS OF A SWORD SWALLOWER Not for the faint-of-heart, this book will GROSS SOME PEOPLE OUT and delight others. "I probably never would have become America's leading fire-eater if Flamo the Great hadn't happened to explode that night ..." So begins this true story of life with a traveling carnival, peopled by amazing characters—the Human Ostrich, the Human Salamander, Jolly Daisy, etc.—who commit outrageous feats of wizardry. This is one of the only *authentic* narratives revealing the "tricks" (or rather, painful skills) involved in a sideshow, .and is invaluable to those aspiring to this profession. OVER 50 RARE PHOTOS taken by Mannix in the 1930s and never before seen! Sideshow aficionados will delight in finally being able to see some of their favorite "stars" captured in candid moments.

8½x11", 128 pp, 50+ photos, index, PB, **$15.99**
Signed copies available for only $30

FREAKS: We Who Are Not As Others

Amazing Photos! This book engages the reader in a struggle of wits: Who is the freak? What is normal? What are the limits of the human body? A fascinating, classic book, based on Mannix's personal acquaintance with sideshow stars such as the Alligator Man and the Monkey Woman. Read all about the notorious love affairs of midgets; the amazing story of the Elephant Boy; the unusual amours of Jolly Daisy, the fat woman; hermaphrodite love; the bulb-eating Human Ostrich, etc. **Put this on your coffee table and watch the fun!** 8½x11", 124 pp, 88 photos. PB. **$15.95**
Author died in 1997. **Signed, hardbound copies available for $50**

TWO BY CHARLES WILLEFORD

Wild Wives A classic of hard-boiled fiction, Willeford's *Wild Wives* is amoral, sexy, and brutal. Written in a sleazy San Francisco hotel in the early '50s while on leave from the Army, Willeford creates a tale of deception featuring the crooked detective Jacob C. Blake and his nemesis—a beautiful, insane young woman.

5x7", 108 pp. PB. **$10.99, o.p.**
High Priest of California Russell Haxby is a ruthless used car salesman obsessed with manipulating and cavorting with a married woman. A classic of hard-boiled fiction, hypocrisy, intrigue and red-hot lust. Every sentence masks innuendo, every detail hides a clue, and every used car sale is an outrageous con job.
"A tempo so relentless, words practically fly off the page."
—*Village Voice*
5x7", 148 pp. PB. **$10.99 o.p.**

J.G. BALLARD

RE/Search 8/9: J.G. Ballard J.G. Ballard predicted the future better than anyone else! His classic, *CRASH* (made into a movie by David Cronenberg) was the first book to investigate the psychopathological implications of the car crash, uncovering our darkest sexual crevices. He accurately predicted our media-saturated, information-overloaded environment where our most intimate fantasies and dreams involve pop stars and other public figures. Also contains a wide selection of quotations. "Highly recommended as both an introduction and a tribute to this remarkable writer."—*Washington Post* "The most detailed, probing and comprehensive study of Ballard on the market."—*Boston Phoenix.* 8½x11", 176 pp, illus. PB. **$17.99**

Atrocity Exhibition A dangerous imaginary work; as William Burroughs put it, "This book stirs sexual depths untouched by the hardest-core illustrated porn." Amazingly perverse medical illustrations by Phoebe Gloeckner, and haunting "Ruins of the Space Age" photos by Ana Barrado. Our most beautiful book, now used in many "Futurology" college classes. 8½x11", 136 pp, illus. PB **$13.99. LIMITED EDITION OF SIGNED HARDBACKS $50**

HUMOR

RE/Search GUIDE TO BODILY FLUIDS by Paul Spinrad. Everything you ever wanted to know about: Mucus, Menstruation, Saliva, Sweat, Vomit, Urine, Flatus, Feces, Earwax & more. Topics include: constipation (such as its relationship to cornflakes and graham crackers!); history and evolution of toilet paper; farting; smegma and more! Ideal bathroom reading! A perfect gift for that difficult-to-shop-for person! Our funniest scientific text. Educational, yet fun. 8½x11", 148 pp., PB only. **$15.99**

RE/Search 11: PRANKS! (A favorite of Napster-lovers & Geeks!) A prank is a "trick, a mischievous act, a ludicrous act." Although not regarded as poetic or artistic acts, pranks constitute an art form and genre in themselves. Here pranksters such as Timothy Leary, Abbie Hoffman, Monte Cazazza, Jello Biafra, Earth First!, Joe Coleman, Karen Finley, John Waters, Henry Rollins and more challenge the sovereign authority of words, images and behavioral convention. This iconoclastic compendium will dazzle and

delight all lovers of humor, satire and irony. *Pranks!* is a classic of the *rebel literature canon.* The definitive treatment of the subject, offering extensive interviews with 36 contemporary tricksters . . . from the Underground's answer to Studs Terkel."—*Washington Post* "Pranks comes off as a statement of avant-garde philosophy–as a kind of wake-up call from an extended underground of surrealist artists."—*San Francisco Chronicle* Our heftiest book. 8½x11", 240 pp, 164 photos & illustrations, PB, **$19.99**

W.S.Burroughs, I.S.Films

R/S 4/5: WS Burroughs, Brion Gysin, Throbbing Gristle

A great, unknown Burroughs-Gysin treasure trove of radical ideas! Compilation of interviews, scarce fiction, essays: this is a manual of incendiary insights. Strikingly designed; bulging with radical references. **Topics discussed**: biological warfare, utopias, con men, lost inventions, the JFK killing, Hassan I Sabbah, cloning, the cut-up theory, Moroccan trance music, the Dream Machine, Manson, the media control process, prostitution, and more.
8½x11", 100 pp, 58 photos & illus. PB, **$15.99** Order Direct!

William S. Burroughs T-shirt! Black & red on white, 100% cotton T-shirt.
"We intend to destroy all dogmatic verbal systems."—WSB. Original design hand-screened on 100% heavyweight cotton T-Shirt. **$16** XL only.

RE/Search 6/7: Industrial Culture Handbook

This book is a secret weapon—it provided an educational upbringing for many of the most radical artists practicing today! The rich ideas of the *Industrial Culture* movement's performance artists and musicians are nakedly exposed: *Survival Research Laboratories, Throbbing Gristle, Cabaret Voltaire, SPK, Non, Monte Cazazza, Johanna Went, Sordide Sentimental, R&N, & Z'ev.* **Topics include:** brain research, forbidden medical texts & films, creative crime & *interesting* criminals, modern warfare & weaponry, neglected gore films & their directors, psychotic lyrics in past pop songs, and *art brut*. This culture influenced you—without your knowledge!
8½x11", 140 pp, 179 photos & illust. PB, **$15.99** Join the cult!

RE/Search 10: INCREDIBLY STRANGE FILMS

First to champion Herschell Gordon Lewis, Russ Meyer, Larry Cohen, Ray Dennis Steckler, Ted V. Mikels, Doris Wishman & others who had been critically consigned to the ghettos of gore & sexploitation films, this book allowed artists to rationally explain how they made gripping dramas with zero budgets and overflowing imaginations. 13 interviews, A-Z of film personalities, "Favorite Films" list, quotations, bibliography, filmography, film synopses, & index. "Flicks like these are subversive alternatives to the mind control propagated by the mainstream media."—*Iron Horse* "The interviews are intelligent, enthusiastic and articulate."—*Small Press.* Has been used as a textbook.
8½x11", 224 pp, 157 photos & illus. PB, **$17.99**

LIBRARIES & PACKAGES

Just The RE/Search Library: All RE/Search serials #1-16 (complete set; save $25!)

Offer includes *RE/Search #1, 2 & 3* tabloids, *#4/5: Burroughs/Gysin/ Throbbing Gristle, #6/7: Industrial Culture Handbook, #8/9: J.G. Ballard, #10: Incredibly Strange Films, #11: Pranks!, #12: Modern Primitives, #13: Angry Women, #14: Incredibly Strange Music, Vol. 1, #15: Incredibly Strange Music, Vol. 2,* and *#16: RE/Search Guide to Bodily Fluids.* **$175.** Will autograph upon request.

The Classic RE/Search Library: All RE/Search classic reprints (Save $15!)

Offer includes *Freaks: We Who Are Not As Others, The Torture Garden, The Atrocity Exhibition, The Confessions of Wanda von Sacher-Masoch, High Priest of California* and *Wild Wives.* **$75.** Note: some of these books are in extremely short supply.

The S&M Library (Our Best-Seller!)

Includes The Torture Garden, Confessions of Wanda von Sacher-Masoch, Bob Flanagan, and Modern Primitives. **$55.** *Please call for updates and additional books available.*

Incredibly Strange Music Packages

1) Incredibly Strange Music Vol. One and Two (BOOKS) & their companion cassette & CD; a set which satisfies the soul. **$54.**
2) RE/Search Incredibly Strange Music Library (no books): *ISM Vol.1* cass., and *ISM Vol.2, Perrey & Kingsley,* and *Ken Nordine* CDs: **$54.** *Note: this is our 2nd best-seller. Many people have ordered the Incredibly Strange Music Packages and been thrilled—their lives and lusts changed forever!*

RE/SEARCH PUBLICATIONS
20 ROMOLO #B
SAN FRANCISCO, CA 94133
tel (415) 362-1465 fax (415) 362-0742
EMAIL: *info@researchpubs.com*

Order from our secure server:
www.researchpubs.com
Phone, fax, mail or email orders

SHIPPING USA: $4 for first item, $1 per additional item. (Add $2/item for Priority Mail USA.)
Overseas Global Air: $9 per item. For seamail (allow 2 months): $6 for first item, $2 per additional item.
Contact us to request a complete catalog!

INDEX

I think any biography is bound to be a work of fiction, just like most interviews have to be. In an interview you're creating yourself, and in a biography somebody else is creating you—they're painting their picture of you.—Lawrence Ferlinghetti